COMPLEXITY THEORY AND THE SOCIAL SCIENCES

An introduction

David Byrne

London and New York

First published 1998
by Routledge
2 Park Square, Milton Park, Abingdon, Oxon, OX14 4RN

Transferred to Digital Printing 2005

Simultaneously published in the USA and Canada
by Routledge
270 Madison Ave, New York NY 10016

©1998 David Byrne

Typeset in Baskerville by Routledge

British Library Cataloguing in Publication Data
A catalogue record for this book is available from the British Library

Library of Congress Cataloging in Publication Data
Byrne, D. S. (David S.), 1947–
Complexity theory and the social sciences : an introduction / David Byrne.
Includes bibliographical references and index.
1. Social sciences – Mathematical models. 2. Chaotic behaviour in
systems. 3. Social sciences – Research. I. Title.
H61.25.B95 1999
300′.1′5118 – dc21   98 – 23769

ISBN 0–415–16295–5 (hbk)
ISBN 0–415–16296–3 (pbk)

CONTENTS

CONTENTS

ACKNOWLEDGEMENTS

A lot of people have helped me play with the ideas which are the foundation of this book. T. R. Young sent me a lot of interesting material down
the internet and whilst I remain in radical disagreement with him about
the postmodern status of complexity, this helped a great deal. Will Medd
has commented on some draft chapters and provided many references. I
have been grateful for the opportunity to discuss these ideas in seminars
with Will Medd, Dan Shapiro and colleagues at the University of
Lancaster and with Malcom Williams and colleagues at the University of
Plymouth. The members of the Durham University Complexity Group
whom I will not name individually (but they know who they are!) have
provided a stimulating context for discussion and thought. Tim
Blackman made me think about the application of these ideas to actual
governance.

I have presented papers at the 1997 European Sociological
Association Conference and the 1997 Annual Conference of the Polish
Sociological Association and am grateful for the comments of those
participating in the relevant sessions. The anonymous referees of articles
submitted to *Critical Social Policy* and *Environment and Planning A* were also
constructive and helpful.

My personal acknowledgements are to Sally and Alissa for being
supportive about everything, especially given the arrival of Clare and the
extent to which this book distracted me from concentrating on them and
her, and to my mother Kathleen, to whom this book is dedicated. Her
help has taken various and essential forms over the years from teaching
me to read in the first place to providing me with a roof whilst I was
completing this text in a period between houses.

I am grateful for the following permissions to reproduce quotations
cited in this book: to the University of Michigan Press for permission to
quote from Kiel and Elliott (eds) *Chaos Theory in the Social Sciences*, to
Addison Wesley Longman Australia for permission to quote from

Brotchie *et al.* (eds) *Cities in Competition*, to W. H. Freeman and Co. for permission to quote from Peak and Frame *Chaos Under Control: The Art and Science of Complexity*, to University College London Press for permission to quote from Williams and May *Introduction to the Philosophy of Social Research* and Gilbert *Analysing Tabular Data*, to Heinemann Education for permission to quote from Everitt and Dunn *Advanced Methods of Data Exploration and Modelling*, to Harvard University Press for permission to quote from Massey and Denton *American Apartheid*, to Routledge for permission to quote from Davies and Kelly (eds) *Healthy Cities*, Blaxter *Health and Lifestyles*, Blane *et al.* (eds) *Health and Social Organization*, Mouzelis *Sociological Theory: What Went Wrong?*, Khalil and Boulding *Evolution, Complexity and Order*, Blackman *Urban Policy and Practice*, and Marsh *The Survey Method*, to Ottar Hellevik for permission to quote from his *Introduction to Causal Analysis*, to Cambridge University Press for permission to quote from Nicolis *Introduction to Nonlinear Science*, to Verso for permission to quote from Williams *Politics and Letters* and Fitch *The Assassination of New York*, to Blackwell for permission to quote from Adam *Timewatch*, to Little Brown for permission to quote from Gell-Mann *The Quark and the Jaguar*, to Macmillan Press Ltd for permission to quote from Outhwaite *New Philosophies of Social Science*, to Sage Ltd for permission to quote from Bagguley *et al.* *Restructuring: Place, Class and Gender*, Crooke *et al.* *Postmodernization*, Dale and Davies *Analyzing Social and Political Change*, Brown *Chaos and Catastrophe Theories – Sage Quantitative Applications in the Social Sciences 107*, and Eve *et al.* (eds) *Chaos, Complexity and Sociology*, to Kogan Page for permission to quote from Blowers *Planning for a Sustainable Environment*, to Stanford University Press for permission to quote from Wallerstein (Chair) *Open the Social Sciences*, to the University of Chicago Press for permission to quote from Hayles *Chaos and Order*, and to the University of Cornell Press for permission to quote from Hayles *Chaos Bound*. Full bibliographical details are given in the bibliography.

INTRODUCTION

The pattern of contingent events which led to the writing of this book began when I picked Mitchell Waldrop's *Complexity* (1992) off the popular science shelves in a large Newcastle bookshop. I've always read popular science since I was a sixth former, and *New Scientist* remains my Friday teatime indulgence read, so I had had some hints about the ideas Waldrop was dealing with in his account of the work of the members of the Santa Fe Institute and others who had gone beyond chaos theory, but it was the subtitle of the book which caught my imagination – complexity was defined as the domain between linearly determined order and indeterminate chaos. That rang so many bells and seemed to offer a solution to so many problems. After all it is a commonplace to say that the social world has been tricky territory for scientific investigation, precisely because it is complex, whereas the methods and forms of understanding generally employed in 'science' are absolutely dependent on things being sorted out in simple terms. What this new field of 'complexity theory' seemed to be doing was to take the idea of complexity seriously and say something about what complexity is and how it might be investigated. That got me started.

Over the years I've taught research methods, statistics, urban theory and the sociology of health and medicine to both undergraduate and postgraduate students. At the same time I've worked as a social researcher on issues of social division and social exclusion in relation to urban, educational and health policies. The same questions have kept recurring. The most basic of these has been: in what way can the things you are dealing with be understood? Like many people with a generally Marxist viewpoint and an interest in the quantitative investigation of the social world, I was greatly relieved by the formal emergence of scientific realism (see Bhaskar 1986; Sayer 1992) as a metatheoretical account which was neither phenomenological nor positivist and reductionist. To a considerable extent realism's own foundations were in

1

empirically based accounts of scientific practice, and one of its substantial attractions to researchers was that it enabled so many of us to realise that we had been realists in our practice all along. The name made the thing respectable.

Yet there were some remarkable absences in realist thinking. Realist work on urban and regional issues, for instance (see for example Bagguley *et al.* 1990), whilst accepting the general realist account of complex and contingent causation, made no attempt to use quantitative models of such processes. Data served, usefully, as description of trends, but there was no substantive quantitative programme in realist social science in these areas. Only Catherine Marsh's *The Survey Method* (1982) seemed to take up realist ideas in relation to the actual analytical strategies which were appropriate for the handling of quantitative accounts of complex and contingent causal processes in the social world. When researchers did get quantitative they often employed factor analysis of all things without regard either for that procedure's implicit causal model or its origins in the eugenic programme. In the mid-1980s, stimulated by Marsh's approach, I had attempted an explicitly realist analysis of survey data (Byrne *et al.* 1985). The substantive research attracted considerable interest but the methodological programme was ignored. I have to say that I left it there, assuming more or less that the points made were so obvious that they had been taken for granted. I think I was wrong.

The best way to show why I have found this a problem is by reference to the important statistical concept of interaction. Interaction is what happens in applications of the general linear model when the effects of multiple variables are not additive. In the simplest three variable case, the relationship between two variables is modified by the value of a third. As Marsh put it, interactions are 'something that is a headache from a technical point of view but most exciting from the standpoint of substantive sociology' (1982: 91–2).

In general, in building causal models either interaction terms are inserted into linear equations, or separate models are drawn up for each of the values of the variable that is causing the interaction. Essentially the use of interaction terms is a kind of grudging recognition paid by statisticians to the actual complexity of the world with which they are dealing. It is a recognition generally required in work using survey data where measurements are taken on an extensive range of variables as they co-vary in the real world, as opposed to in experiments where simple abstractions from the world serve as the basis for the production of 'laws'. Well, in the sort of work I was doing and am still doing, you can't move for interactions but the general practice has been (in the relatively few instances in which the analysis of survey data gets this sophisticated) to write interaction terms into the general linear model and ignore the complexity that they indicate. This always made me worry. Linearity and order seemed to be being forced on a world which isn't really like that, but I didn't have a vocabulary for doing more than worry.

There were flashes of light on the way to the sunrise of complexity theory. A lot of my own research has always been as much historical as quantitative, and in that it has used historical data, it has frequently been both. Through my popular science reading I became acquainted with the work of Stephen Jay Gould and was enormously excited by *Wonderful Life* (1991) and its account of the contingency of the evolutionary process as a model for the general process of historical change. However, there were problems with accepting Gould's commitment to complete contingency in that account. This approach explicitly abandoned any notion of science as providing a basis for prediction. The abandonment of law specified complete determination I could live with, but the abandonment of any way of viewing the future, even in terms of distinctive possibilities, was too much.

Another important strand came from working as a teacher on topics in the sociology of health and medicine. One of the key themes in the historical account of the development of the 'biomedical model' was that medicine, which is considerably older as an organised intellectual activity than post-Newtonian science, had, at least formally if not necessarily in clinical practice, abandoned its old holistic approach and made a commitment to the reductionist biomechanical, 'scientific' programme. Whilst this had led to very considerable gains in curative power in the individual case, its overall impact on human mortality had been trivial (see McKeown 1979). In fact the most substantive contribution of medical 'science' to the improvement of the health of human populations had been through a public health programme based on a complex (and originally wrong in detail but right in effect!) understanding of the ecological relationships among people, disease and ways of living (see McNeill 1979).

So, a key word in the critical response to the reductionist programme is holism – in summary the view that the whole is greater than the sum of its parts. In discussions of the philosophy of social science, the term 'holism' is not generally used. It is more usual to write of 'emergent properties'. Whatever the expression, this contradicts Dirac's claim, made when he had developed a quantum model of the electron, that by so doing he had solved in principle all problems in chemistry, which claim has been generalised to the assertion that this reductionist

3

programme could, in principle, solve all problems in biochemistry, and hence in biology, and hence in health and illness. On the contrary, illnesses of the mind in particular but by no means exclusively (the word 'stress' is the general connector of the social and the physical here) can only be understood in a non-reductionist way which rejects the theory of levels, the proposition that the simpler can explain the more complex but not vice versa. Contemporary theories of the genesis of schizophrenia, an illness so reactive that it has no natural history (Wing 1978), assert a complex causation in which there are certainly genetic liabilities but in which those liabilities are only expressed under specific stress conditions. Such aetiological explanations involve complex causes and emergent properties.

Moreover, for many 'health problems', notably but by no means exclusively in relation to mental health and illness, this reductionist programme seemed to have limited effect. Even in its core locale, i.e. in the development of magic bullets which killed infectious diseases without killing the patient, the emergence of AIDS showed the limits of the reductionist monocausal approach. That word 'limits' will be very important in this book – particularly in the conclusion when an effort will be made to indicate possible directions for future work. The extent to which this relationship between the social and natural worlds matters, and the link in terms of resource limits in general and of the limitations of biomechanical medicine in particular, are both clearly asserted in Benton's interesting think piece of 1991. Ecology keeps coming into the debate.

The final element in my concerns in this period derived from my studies of urban changes consequent on the deindustrialisation of industrial cities. The key word here is polarisation – there is a general account of cities which emphasises the extent to which cities have become systems in which there are two very different sorts of social spaces and quite distinctive ways of living available to those who live in those different spaces. Polarisation is not just a description of state but is also an account of the processes by which a state of acute social division has emerged. Cities which – whilst never equal – were nonetheless, in the Fordist era of the post-war years, unequal in a gradual and graded way, seem to have become divided into spaces occupied by people whose lives and life chances are radically different (see Byrne 1997a, and subsequently in this book for a more developed account). This has occurred when there have been extremely important changes in the organisation of systems of production and of the work relations which depend on those systems of production. Changes in key determinant variables have generated social changes which take the form of bifurcation – a key word which describes in an exact way the process of polarisation.

What the above amounts to is a shopping list. I was looking for some sort of general account which combined non-linear relations, multiple and contingent causation, non-linear but not unbounded determination and emergent properties/holism. I needed a new vocabulary and an overall view based on that vocabulary which could serve as a framework for understanding. In Waldrop's (1992) work, and later in Lewin (1995), I found both the vocabulary and the framework.

Chaos theory, from which accounts of complexity have developed, deals exactly with non-linear relations, with changes which cannot be fitted into a simple linear law taking the form of statement of single cause and consequent effect. It is true that chaos theory taken alone resonates (a word which has more than metaphorical connotations here) with the general postmodernist account (and there is such a general account, despite postmodernism's strident denunciation of all meta-narratives – it is a meta-narrative itself) in which no determination is possible. As Williams and May put it in their cogent account of the 'post-critiques': 'Chance and chaos, not the discovery of "truth" and "progress", now enter research endeavours' (1996: 160).

But the usage of chaos here is not the scientific one in which chaos is absolutely not to be equated with randomness (see Littell (1993) *The Visiting Professor* for an entertaining account of the differences). The central point is that in this scientific usage chaos is the precursor of order, not its antithesis.

The order that emerges from chaos is generally described in terms of 'strange attractors', existing in the first instance as products of the experimental mathematics made possible by the development of computing power, and visually (and elegantly) expressed in images derived from the graphical representation of such functions. These abstract conceptions are now attached to 'real entities', particularly in the actual body forms of organisms. One of the most interesting things about reading complexity is the evocations of past experience. I was almost expecting the name D'Arcy Thompson, whose *On Growth and Form* (1942) I first read as a teenager, to crop up in Kauffman's book on *The Origins of Order* (1993) about three pages before it actually did! Anyhow, it is important to point out here that complex order, if it is thought of as describing the realm between simple order and chaos, can emerge not only from chaos but also from order and that a central and useful idea is the notion of movement from simple attractors to strange attractors through a process of bifurcation, dependent on key changes in the magnitude of underlying causal variables.

The nature of changes is described by the set of Feigenbaum numbers, and a crucial transformation occurs from the simplest form of strange attractor, the self-replicating and delimited torus, into the dual form of the 'butterfly attractor' when key variables change by magnitude of three. This process of bifurcation implies neither simple linear determination – if A happens then B happens, nor random process where anything can happen, but rather complex change. In the first bifurcation if A happens then B *or* C happens, but which occurs will depend on small initial variations in the form of A. This fitted very well with what I was trying to deal with in changes in urban forms. Strange attractors offered a description of outcomes which was neither linear nor indeterminate, but different. Moreover, without abandoning a notion of structures, this account allows for agency, and does so explicitly (see Nicolis and Prigogine 1989). People certainly can make history because reflexive agency can influence crucial information changes in systems where the modulating role of information over energy is absolutely significant, but they do so from a given starting point, i.e. not in circumstances of their own choosing.

The complex combination of multiple and contingent causation and emergent properties/holism was to be found in that important part of complexity theory which derived from the work of biologists writing about evolutionary processes, especially Kauffman (1993, 1995). There seems to me to be a very important distinction between two approaches to complexity which can be associated separately with each of the Santa Fe Institute's professorial fellows. Gell-Mann (1994) asserts that whereas in principle the complex can be reduced to the simple, principle is not practice and that it is essentially pointless to attempt reductionist explanations when they are not needed. In contrast Kauffman does believe in *The Emergence of Order*, and thereby explicitly accepts the holistic premise that the complex is not inherently analysable into its simple components. Although ideas of complex and contingent causation are implicit rather than explicit in Kauffman's account, the resonance between his discussions of the three level evolutionary process in terms of the evolution of species, co-evolution of species in environments, and the co-evolution of co-evolution itself through the transformation of environments/genetic potential/ morphological expressions, and the realist account of complex and contingent causation, is extraordinarily strong. Note that Kauffman's account can be summed up as dependent on either or both contingency and the transformation of quantity into quality.

I have introduced a lot of terms so far without necessarily defining them, other than by the context in which they are used. Definitions will follow, but I thought it was important to get over the idea that for me, and I hope for other social scientists, the point about complexity is that it is useful – it helps us to understand the things we are trying to understand. This is a claim for its usefulness in substantive areas of social inquiry, and much of this book will take the form of efforts to demonstrate that utility. This is its appeal. However, complexity, inductively founded though it is, is not innocent in metatheoretical terms. It does have ontological and epistemological implications, implications which make it essentially part of the realist programme of scientific understanding and inquiry. Moreover, the account it offers challenges in the most fundamental way the postmodernist view of the nature of social science and the potentials of its application. It is necessary to say something about these things here, although I am adamantly committed to not writing a book about the philosophy of social science, nor even one about the philosophy of social research.

Likewise it will be necessary to say something about how the tools used in complexity-based research can be adapted to social scientific purposes, and perhaps even more about how the existing tools of social scientific research can be used as part of a complex programme. It is worth noting that in a handbook written for doctoral students in physics and chemistry, Nicolis remarks on the impossibility of a full quantitative understanding of complex phenomena and the consequent requirement to turn to qualitative approaches (1995: 49), so any accusations of physics envy remaining even after the previous noting of complexity's necessary rejection of reductionism ought to be junked forthwith. The tools of understanding suggested here will be both quantitative and qualitative, and quantitative usages will be primarily exploratory (see Tukey 1977).

So having said why I wanted to write this book, let me say how it is organised. There are two sorts of chapters here. Chapters 1 to 4 are expository in the abstract. They are concerned with laying out the ideas of complexity/chaos in relation to the general programme of social science and of sociology in particular. Chapters 5 to 8 are expository in application. They deal with a set of themes, themes chosen because they interest me and I know something about them, and apply a 'complexity' fix or gloss to them. All the chapters except Chapter 1 are really constructed around doing just that, around thinking about issues in the social sciences with the ideas of complexity/chaos theory brought into play.

Chapter 1 introduces the broad framework of the dynamic ideas of chaos/complexity and explains the key terms employed in the programme. It centres on the difference between linear and reductionist science as it has been done and non-linear and emergent science as it will be done. The sources referenced in the discussion here are not usually social scientists, although Reed and Harvey, and Hayles will make a preliminary appearance. Instead they are physical and biological scientists and mathematicians. The point of the chapter is to explain what they have been saying, to introduce the language they have used for saying it, and to begin the argument that these things matter very much for the social sciences as well. I have continued this exposition with special reference to the mathematical language and its implications in the glossary at the end of the book.

Chapter 2 is where the social science begins in earnest. Here I draw on a range of sources, but particularly Reed and Harvey (1992, 1996), Harvey and Reed (1994) and Hayles (1990, 1991). These writers have used the complexity/chaos programme in relation to debates in social science and literary/cultural theory. One of the themes around which the chapter is structured is a confrontation between the implications of a realist account of the social world, reinforced by the complexity and chaos programme, and the general postmodernist account. The other is a more general consideration of the implications of the complexity and chaos programme for the set of key issues for sociological theory identified by Mouzelis in his recent consideration of what has gone wrong with sociological theory (1995).

The first point being made here is an absolute endorsement of Reed and Harvey's linking of critical realism as a philosophical ontology with chaos/complexity as a scientific ontology. The second is that this combination should be fatal for postmodernism as an intellectual project. The third is that if we use this approach, then we can resolve the major issues for sociological theory of the relationship between macro and micro, and structure and agency. Finally, the chapter takes up the issue of metaphor and analogy, drawing on the clear exposition of Khalil (1996) in order to illustrate the very important implications of the use of these terms. The whole chapter is unashamedly systemic. We urgently need to revive systems approaches to the social sciences, and the complexity/chaos programme provides us with a way of doing this which overcomes the very real difficulties encountered when the models of systems available to us were equilibric or at best close to equilibric. Far from equilibric systems are very different indeed.

Chapter 3 is where the mathematics comes in, although there are no calculations and virtually no formulae in the whole of it. The chapter is about mathematics as analogy, as analogy for the world as it is. To quite a substantial degree it is based on reading in popular mathematics, in those books which seek to explain to a lay audience just what has been happening to mathematics in the twentieth century. I make no apology for that. These developments have the most profound importance for the way we think about the world and the way we use mathematics as a description of it, and if they are presented in clear and accessible terms by writers like Stewart, Barrow and Ruelle, then it is only sensible (and, moreover, a real pleasure) to access them through books written to make that possible.

The chapter is an argument for social statistics as it was originally conceived, as exploratory descriptions of a social world so complex that it can only be known adequately through measurement of indicators of the character of the social system as a whole, and against social statistics as it has become, a reductionist, positivist, linear and individualised programme which is not isomorphic with the world and is now very largely disconnected from the central issues in social science as account and social policy as practice. Where linear approaches are connected, in areas of health and education, there is a serious risk of them getting very important things absolutely wrong. In terms of formal debates about quantity and quality in social science, Chapter 3 is intended as a theoretically grounded reinforcement for the pragmatic dismissal of the significance of these very arguments. As such it well accords with the views and practices of most practising sociologists and geographers (the two disciplines which give most thought to these issues) and the implication of the arguments presented is that the disagreements between positivists and adherents of the strong interpretative programme of qualitative social science are really profoundly irrelevant and pointless.

Chapter 4 is about the actual use of quantitative methods in a complex way. I had originally intended to devote much of this chapter to an exposition of the quantitative methods used in complexity/chaos in the physical sciences, and to consider how these might be applied to the kind of quantitative descriptions of the social world social scientists have available to them. However, whilst I make some reference to those approaches, I now argue that I do not think they are particularly useful to us. There are two aspects to this dismissal, although I think they are really intimately connected. The first aspect is that we do not have the sort of data used by physicists and physical chemists in looking for chaos. As Lewis-Beck (1995) remarks, our data is typically for many units but with only a few observations on each, whereas the physical sciences generally have many observations for single units over a long time period. The second is that it isn't really chaos which is of interest, but rather complex transformation of state. Here we are following Prigogine rather than the US school (see Chapter 1 for a development of this important theme).

So, instead of presenting what I regard as non-applicable approaches (although references are given to examples where their use has been attempted), I have instead looked at the methods actually used by quantitative social scientists, with a particular emphasis on the use of numerical taxonomic procedures across time. Consideration is also given to the analysis of contingency tables when we can order the data through time. The purpose is to reinterpret what we actually have been doing, by seeing how our actual procedures look from a complexity/chaos viewpoint. The argument is explicitly for exploration and against reductionist explanation.

In this vein the chapter does take up the very important use of visual methods in understanding the evolutionary development of complex systems. It does this in two ways. One is by reference to the use of computer simulations as part of the complexity programme. The other is by a reinterpretation of the very interesting technique of correspondence analysis as a method of seeing how complex social systems change. The implications of this iconic turn are very profound.

An argument constantly reiterated in this chapter is that we must understand hierarchical data as reflecting the character of the social world as consisting of complex nested systems with a two-way system of determinant inter-relationships among the levels. We absolutely must relate containing systems to contained systems.[1] In other words we must have measures of individuals, of households, of neighbourhoods, of localities and so on, and we must recognise that we need to be able to relate all these levels to each other.

Chapters 5 to 8 all take the form of looking at important issues in substantive areas from a chaos/complexity-informed perspective. In these chapters the argument frequently proceeds in large part by a critique of a recent important contribution, which critique is sometimes confrontational and sometimes based on a very strong resonance of the arguments with the chaos/complexity perspective. A good deal of the argument in this book as a whole is founded around this idea of resonance, of hearing echoes of the chaos/complexity account in accounts of social reality which were written without explicit reference to it. I hear resonances everywhere, and I don't think this is a matter of faulty hearing.

Chapter 5 deals with recent debates about the spatial, and in particular about the idea of emergent properties at spatial levels. The most important level here is that of 'locality' and the argument in this chapter is against Warf's (1993) postmodernist version of this concept, but the chapter is also very much concerned with spatial levels as the nested systems of the social world. Examples drawn from the recent revival of real social ecology in US studies are used to develop the general argument.

Chapter 6 is about health and is tied closely to the important contemporary debate about the origins of ill health in general social inequality (see Wilkinson 1996). Here the critique is related particularly to Tarlov's (1996) fascinating account of health as the property of a series of nested systems with the individual at the core. The chapter also includes a confrontation with one of the best and clearest applied postmodernist pieces (Kelly *et al.* 1993). Tuberculosis, the iconic disease of industrialism, is considered in relation to its modern re-emergence as a way of illustrating the absolute necessity for a complexity-founded approach to social epidemiology and to public health practice.

Chapter 7 is focused on educational differentiation and is founded around a confrontation with one of the most interesting and significant studies to derive from the current Economic and Social Research Council's programme dealing with the 'Analysis of Large and Complex Data Sets' – Goldstein and Spiegelhalter's critique of the use of league tables as measures of institutional performance. The argument is with the linearity of the approach and the way in which the use of linear models decontextualises and disconnects schools from the social world of which they are a part. Again, the arguments are advanced by reference to recent interesting US studies, here examining the impact of the ethnic character of schools on the educational attainment of the children attending them.

Chapter 8 is about urban governance with special reference to the role of planning in the creation of urban forms and possibilities. Here the argument was helped enormously by the re-emergence of systems approaches in planning, systems approaches which are now explicitly informed by the general chaos/complexity programme and by the possibility of complex computer simulation processes. However, these abstract approaches are now being connected to the real data flows of contemporary urban governance. This chapter is where the determination of robust chaotic processes begins to seem a real possibility.

For a book about chaos and complexity the actual presentation of this text is rather straightforward and linear. I propose to depart from this in the Conclusion. Here I want not so much to conclude the arguments of the book thus far, indeed hardly to conclude the arguments of the book thus far at all, but instead to start hares running and unravel a lot of loose ends. The loose ends will take the form of suggestions about actual research informed by the account presented in the book. The hares are two in number and will run in tandem. One will be a consideration of the implications of the very important report of the

Gulbenkian Commission on the Restructuring of the Social Sciences (1996), which report was explicitly informed by the chaos/complexity perspective (not surprisingly since Prigogine was a Commission member). The other will be a preliminary discussion of the implications of the chaos/complexity perspective for the nature of applied social science as a social practice. I think the nature of the relationship between social science as academic practice and the application of social science really needs some close attention and will attempt to be provocative on this topic.

Let me (almost) conclude with a confession about and justification of omissions. This book's title indicates that it is about the implications of complexity theory for the social sciences in general. The disciplines of sociology and geography and the applied areas of health, education and urban governance are given serious attention here (which means that two areas of social policy are dealt with) and the processes of history are central to the whole account, but economics, anthropology, political science, and psychology don't get a look in. Neither, on the applied side, are the important fields of criminology and business explicitly addressed. Of course, no book can do everything and the exclusion of anthropology, criminology and business is really a matter of manageability, coupled with a belief that they have so much in common with sociology and geography that the lessons are easily carried over. The other exclusions I would justify in two ways.

The first is that this book is founded around a consideration of the nature of the quantitative programme in social science, which quantitative programme is fundamental to all inductive social science. By the quantitative programme in social science I mean exactly and assertively the actual inductive processes of measurement and the direct analyses of measurements, and do not mean, and reject, the abstract formalising of models which are not isomorphic with the real world. So much for economics and much of quantitative political science.

Psychology is much more complicated. It isn't dealt with here precisely because it has a very strong and interesting complexity programme of its own, which for the moment centres around the inter-relationships between the psychological and the biological. I am aware of this, but I think it needs consideration in a different way from that which is appropriate for a generally focused social science text, although there is a real need for a complexity fix on the intersection of the social and the psychological.

And (finally) to conclude – as a teenager I read and enjoyed John Brunner's award-winning science fiction novel *Stand on Zanzibar* in which one of the protagonists had the interesting job of 'synthesist'.[2] I have been looking for that post advertised ever since, but have never seen it. To a considerable extent this book is my effort at self-employment in the field.

1

UNDERSTANDING THE COMPLEX

> Nonlinear Science('s) . . . aim is to provide the concepts and the
> techniques necessary for a unified description of the particular,
> yet quite large, class of phenomena whereby simple determin-
> istic systems give rise to complex behaviours with the
> appearance of unexpected spatial structures or evolutionary
> events.
>
> (Nicolis 1995: xiii)

Introduction

The language of chaos/complexity[1] is relatively new in science in
general, and in the social sciences in particular. It is, therefore, necessary
to begin this book with this chapter, to which I had considered giving the
title 'naming of parts'. However, one of the most important things about
the approach is precisely its rejection of the validity of analytical strategies in which things are reducible to the sum of their parts. We are
dealing with 'emergent properties' and must begin with a holistic statement.[2]

The quotation from Nicolis provides us with much of that statement.
It tells us that we are dealing with aspects of reality in which changes do
not occur in a linear fashion. In reality, as opposed to mathematical
models, the crucial dimension along which changes occur is time. In non-
linear systems small changes in causal elements over time do not
necessarily produce small changes in other particular aspects of the
system, or in the characteristics of the system as a whole. Either or both
may change very much indeed, and, moreover, they may change in ways
which do not involve just one possible outcome. Nicolis says that there is a
large set of systems which have this character. I would suggest that this set
includes most of the social and natural aspects of the world, particularly
inter-relationships between the social and the natural.

There is a third component of 'chaos/complexity' in addition to non-linearity as mathematical description, and realism as an ontological principle, which can be found in Nicolis' statement. He uses the term 'evolutionary'. This means that we are dealing with processes which are fundamentally historical. They are not time reversible. As Adams (1994b, 1995) has pointed out these approaches involve an explicit rejection of the Newtonian concept of time as reversible in macroscopic systems of significance to us in general. The work of Prigogine (see Prigogine and Stengers 1984) replaces the clock as the iconic symbol of the modern with the heat engine. Mechanics gives way to thermodynamics. That notion appeals to me very much indeed, as a native of one of the world's oldest locales of carboniferous capitalism and as a descendant of pitmen and collier seamen and their wives, whose labour provided precisely the thermal energy input which underpinned the transformations which led to modernity.

The principle of holism[3] is implicit in Nicolis' description but Hayles provides us with a succinct explicit assertion of it, which completes the preliminary specification of subject matter:

> From the system's point of view, there is only the totality that is its environment. So strong is our belief in analysis, however, that we take the environment to be the artificial and the collection of factors to be the reality.
>
> (Hayles 1991: 16–17)

The two themes of evolutionary development and holistic character have to be taken together. This is what is meant by the title of Kauffman's influential book *The Origins of Order* (1993). At the points of evolutionary development through history, the new systems which appear (a better word than 'emerge' because it is not gradualist in implication) have new properties which are not to be accounted for either by the elements into which they can be analysed (i.e. they are holistic), or by the content of their precursors. The approaches we are dealing with are necessarily and absolutely anti-reductionist, although this point is not always appreciated even by those who propose them. Gell-Mann's remark (in an interesting book on these themes) that:

> In general, scientists are accustomed to developing theories that describe observational results in a particular field without deriving them from the theories of a more fundamental field. Such a derivation, *though possible in principle when the additional*

> *special information is supplied* [my emphasis], is at any given time
> difficult or impossible in practice for most cases.
>
> (Gell-Mann 1995: 111)

is simply wrong so far as the emphasised phrase is concerned. Quite the
contrary. Not only can the complex not always be derived, even in principle, from the less complex, but, as we shall see, we can often only
understand the simpler in terms of its origins in the more complex.[4]

Before going any further it is necessary to say something about the
words 'chaos' and 'complexity'. The best and clearest commentary on
'chaos' is provided by Hayles (1990, 1991) and what follows derives from
her account. The word has its origins in the Greek for void and Hayles
suggests that the contrast between chaos as disorder, and order, is a
continuing dichotomy in the Western mind-set. She contrasts this binary
logic with the four-valued logic of Taoism in which not-order is not
equivalent to anti-order. This is persuasive and the point being made is
that whilst 'chaos' in its popular usage is to be understood as a description
of anti-order, to all intents and purposes as a synonym for randomness,[5]
the scientific usage is far more equivalent to not-order, and indeed sees
chaos as containing and/or preceding order. The and/or is necessary
because there are at least two approaches, which as Hayles indicates seem
determined to ignore each other (1991: 12). One is concerned with the
order that lies hidden within chaos and is essentially US-based. The
other, European and represented particularly by Prigogine, focuses on the
order that emerges from chaos.[6]

Actually I think that another synthesising account is implicit in both
schools. Waldrop subtitled his popular text on *Complexity* (1992): 'The
emerging science at the edge of order and chaos', and the account of
bifurcation in complex systems certainly suggests that there is a domain
between deterministic order and randomness which is complex. This is
important in relation to the notion of 'robust chaos'. For the moment the
popularly oxymoronic but scientifically accurate expression of 'deterministic chaos'·can be used to convey the difference in quality in the two
usages.

Hayles leads us into this nicely when she remarks that: 'In both literature and science, chaos has been conceptualised as extremely complex
information, rather than as an absence of order' (1991: 1). The point is
that chaos remains deterministic – we are not, necessarily, dealing with a
scientific pessimism equivalent to the abandonment of rationalism by
postmodernists. This means that we may have the basis of a technology
in which we can use the understanding derived from chaos/complexity as
a way of guiding purposeful action towards desired outcomes, although

to do so we have to know a lot and be able to manage what we know in rather different ways. That is extremely important.

The rest of this chapter will be concerned with an exposition of the concepts and models which constitute the 'chaos/complexity' approach. It will not attempt to reproduce the more detailed accounts of the mathematical models associated with chaos/complexity, for which see Peak and Frame (1994), Casti (1994) and Nicolis (1995). Neither will it attempt to replicate the good scientific journalism of Waldrop (1992), Lewin (1993) or Johnson (1996), all of which in varying ways give an account of the US-based development and context of these ideas. Rather, it will contain a general account of the character of complex systems and of the way in which they develop over time, in order to provide an overview and a working vocabulary for the rest of the book.

We will begin with a consideration of chaos and discontinuity, continue with an examination of development through bifurcation, examine the character of strange attractors, and consider the nature of what Prigogine calls 'far from equilibric systems'. Along the way, related ideas, and in particular that of fitness landscapes, will also be introduced and there will be a review of the importance of a complexity-based understanding of time and space for the social world. There is one important point which needs to be made here before we start, even though its development will form the conclusion to this chapter as a whole. In no sense whatsoever is the project of applying the ideas of complexity theory to the social driven by any sort of physics envy. That ought to be obvious from the explicitly anti-reductionist character of the form of the complexity programme which has already been endorsed in this book. However, I want to go further than 'mere' anti-reductionism. It is true that chaos/complexity emerges from experimental mathematics (think about the revolutionary implications of that expression) and thermodynamics, and has been particularly developed in physical chemistry and evolutionary biology. The social sciences have a good deal to learn from these fields. But, and it is a big but, once the social sciences get going, then other fields of inquiry will have a lot to learn from them. Indeed, this project is already well under way in relation to the development of fundamental metatheoretical ideas (see Reed and Harvey 1992, and Harvey and Reed 1994). There is no hierarchy here, no more or less fundamental field of science and/or disciplinary perspectives. We are in this together on equal terms.

Of course, one of the great attractions of the approach is that in fact we have been in it together for quite some time. Once we have the name we can recognise that we have been doing the thing – we have been talking prose for a long time without knowing it. For sociologists the work of Talcott Parsons provides an interesting illustration. Crooke *et al.* (1992) sum this up in terms which resonate very strongly with the complexity account:

> Parsons makes a distinction between what might be called developmental processes and what might be called phase-shift processes. The former consist in a continuous and incremental elaboration and separation of sub-systems, which does not alter the general overall pattern of society. By contrast, phase-shift processes are fundamental differential leaps or evolutionary breakthroughs, typically caused outside the social realm (e.g. in the realms of culture or personality) which reorient the social pattern.
>
> (Crooke *et al.* 1992: 5)

Here we find the language of complexity and chaos being used by contemporary commentators, as Hayles tells us we must reasonably expect to, given the current character of the Western episteme, but what really matters is that the perspective they are describing is so congruent with the approach, even though it predates chaos theory by many years.

And now for the naming of parts:

Small changes make for big differences and lots of things are out to play, together

Linearity in relationships is most simply expressed[7] in algebraic terms by the equation:

$$Y = a + bX$$

Here the interesting thing which statisticians want to determine when they construct a bivariate regression equation of this form, is the value of b. b gives the amount of change in Y when X changes by one unit. Every time X increases by one, Y increases by b. Of course, interpreted regression equations where X and Y stand for real variables do not produce exact predictions of real Ys. The degree to which the real Ys differ from those predicted by the regression equation is used in both simple bivariate models and in the multi-variate extension into the general linear model in which lots of variables are brought into play together, as a measure of strength of relationship and explanatory, if not causal, power.[8] It has been remarked that 'regression equations are the laws of Science' and indeed the search for laws in science has in essence consisted of attempts to find relationships which can be formalised in linear terms.

The search for linearly-founded laws is a search for predictive ability. If we can establish the relationships so that our formalised linear mathematical models are indeed isomorphic with the real world, and our ideal method for doing this is usually thought to be the controlled experiment,[9] then we can predict what will happen in a given set of circumstances, provided we have accurate measures of the initial state of the system. Once we can predict, we can engineer the world and make it work in the ways we want it to. We can turn from reflection to engagement. This is a wholly honourable project so far as I am concerned. It is the technological foundation of modernity itself.

The trouble is that much, and probably most, of the world doesn't work in this way. Most systems do not work in a simple linear fashion. There are two related issues here which derive from the non-linearity of reality, despite the availability of non-linear mathematical models which can sometimes be used in place of the general linear model and its derivatives. The first, which is generally discussed in the literature on chaos, is extreme sensitivity to initial conditions in non-linear systems. The classic, and by now well-known, expression of this is in relation to weather systems. Efforts to model weather systems in mathematical terms are faced with the major – and indeed essentially insurmountable – problem that variations in initial conditions of the scale of the force of a butterfly's wing beat can produce vastly different weather outcomes over quite short time periods.

The problem that this raises is one of measurement in terms of accuracy. Lorenz originally encountered the phenomenon when he re-ran some weather data by re-inputting print-out results which were accurate to three decimal places instead of to the six the computer used in internal calculations. Re-inputting data produced very different outcomes because the measures differed in the fourth decimal place. It has to be stressed that the existence of chaotic outcomes of this kind does not involve an abandonment of causality *in principle*. If we could measure to the degree of accuracy we need then we could model the system, albeit in non-linear terms, and then we could predict what the outcome of changes would be. *In practice* we can't. It is precisely this practical limit – that word: 'limit' – which seems to set a boundary on science and science-derived technology. This is why the idea of chaos is so attractive to postmodernists. Science seems to have come to the end of its capacities. Rationality seems to be exhausted as a general project. Is it hell as like!

Before turning to robust chaos, the basis of that robust rejection of postmodernism as state of mind,[10] I want to pick up on the social sciences' experience of non-linearity through encounters with interactions. The word 'interaction' here is not being used in the general sociological sense to describe social interactions among individuals, but in the statistical sense where in the simplest three variable case, the relationship between two variables is modified by the value of a third. This sort of thing crops up all the time in sociology.

The issue is that in the social world, and in much of reality including biological reality, causation is complex. Outcomes are determined not by single causes but by multiple causes, and these causes may, and usually do, interact in a non-additive fashion. In other words the combined effect is not necessarily the sum of the separate effects. It may be greater or less, because factors can reinforce or cancel out each other in non-linear ways. It should be noted that interactions are not confined to the second order. We can have higher order interactions and interactions among interactions. It is in principle possible of course to calculate interaction terms and enter them into linear models, and there are statistical programmes (elements in SPSS and the dedicated package GLIM) which exist to do exactly this. What this amounts to is the creation of new variables in the linear equation which represent the interaction among the measured variables. In essence the complexity is locked away in the interaction term. Once there are lots of variables in play this is, to say the least, a difficult business, and it always worries me because it seems to be a way of ignoring the complex character of the reality being investigated. In practical terms in contexts where chaos exists, the effect of interactions is to make the issue of precision of measurement even more important. The effects of interactions are not additive either in themselves or in relation to measurement errors. This means that complex causes can easily generate chaotic outcomes.

How and when things split

At this point we need to sort out some of the implications of the generally systemic character of chaos/complexity accounts. I want to do that by considering the difference between mechanics' Newtonian interest in trajectories and thermodynamics' interest in the behaviour of whole systems. The idea of a trajectory is generally to do with movements through space over time under the influence of forces. When I was doing A level Applied Maths we used to spend a lot of time working out the trajectories of artillery shells. Another applied example would be the kind of problems which had to be solved by a navigator in a coastal command plane flying blind by dead reckoning, i.e. without being able to fix position by reference to a fixed point achieved either by recognising a landmark or by getting a fix from either the sun or stars. The position of the plane would be a resultant of courses taken over time and wind speeds and directions.[11] The plane was within a system of wind, space and time, and had some autonomy (the effects of piloting and courses) within that system. What mattered was where it was as the result of its trajectory. When we come to look at individuals and households we will be interested in trajectories of just this kind within social systems.

However, here we are interested in the properties of the system as a whole. The nature of the kind of systems we are interested in will be considered subsequently, but we need a preliminary specification here. Prigogine and Stengers provide us with this:

> The study of the physical processes involving heat entails defining a system, not as in the case of dynamics, by the position and velocity of its constituents . . . but by a set of macroscopic parameters such as temperature, pressure, volume and so on. In addition, we have to take into account the boundary conditions that describe the relation of the system to its environment.
>
> (Prigogine and Stengers 1984: 105–6)

It is very important to note that whilst the state of the system may be described in terms of the values of a very large number of variables, it may be, and for the systems which interest us it is likely, that the actual character of that state is determined[12] by the value of a far smaller number (sometimes just one) of key control parameters. If the relationship of system form to the value of control parameter(s) is linear then small changes in them produce corresponding changes in the system, without a change in the system's form. In non-linear relations at crucial points something very different happens.

Prigogine and Stengers deal with this in a discussion of chemical systems by reference to the law of large numbers. Social scientists should be familiar with this in relation to the construction of sampling distributions. Its implication in that context is that when we draw samples of size n from a given population, provided that n is large, then the distribution of the sample estimates of a key population parameter (true population value) if we drew all possible samples of size n, would be normal with a standard deviation determined by the product of the actual population standard deviation and the value of $1/\sqrt{n}$. This holds regardless of whether the characteristic which is the basis of the measurement of that parameter is itself normally distributed in the population. The point is that as n gets large the effect of sampling fluctuations becomes small. This is broadly what happens in a linear system. Fluctuations are not important in relation to mean values and may be neglected.

However, close to bifurcation points the values of the fluctuations increase dramatically and can reach the order of magnitude of mean values of the parameters of interest. We need to think rather carefully about what is going on here. As Nicolis puts it:

> We have repeatedly stressed the difficulties arising in the solution of nonlinear problems. We therefore give up the idea of obtaining exact results of a global character and limit our attention to *the local behaviour* [original emphasis] of the solutions in the vicinity of the bifurcation point.
>
> (Nicolis 1995: 96)

What happens is that at these crucial transformation points the system seems to have two possible trajectories into which it can move and it 'chooses'[13] between them on the basis of very small differences in the values of controlling parameter(s) at the point of change. Peak and Frame (1994) offer an interesting introduction to this, based on the simple enough models in experimental mathematics. Here we need, first, to know that it happens and that it happens in real world systems as well as in abstraction.

The second thing that we need to know is that there seems to be an underlying fundamental character to the way in which such changes occur. This character is fundamental both in the mathematical models, and in the real systems which are isomorphic with them. Feigenbaum (1978) established that there is a period-doubling route towards chaos characterised by a series of 'Feigenbaum numbers' representing proportionate changes in the initial value of a controlling variable. There are two ways in which the term 'Feigenbaum number' seems to be used in chaos theory. The first is to describe a sequence of numbers representing proportionate changes in the control variable, which describe successive bifurcations and correspond to successive strange attractors. The second is the value to which the ratio of successive changes tends, which seems to be a universalistic constant describing chaos.

Here let us focus on the 'Feigenbaum sequence' which describes all systems (a very large set) in which there is a periodicity to bifurcation which doubles with each successive bifurcation. This represents a route from simple determination through a realm of complexity within which there are multiple but limited outcome situations towards a realm of chaos in which there are very large possible sets of outcomes.[14]

If we go back to Prigogine and Stengers' description of systems in physical chemistry but replace the term 'fluctuation' with that of 'perturbation', which implies disturbance in a way that fluctuation does not, we can begin to apply this sort of analysis to social systems. If we think of a system in equilibrium we should be able to recognise that it can absorb certain changes in key control variables but that there is a limit to this. Harvey and Reed put it like this:

> In the absence of significant perturbations, a dissipative system will usually follow a 'normal' linear trajectory. Of course there will be the usual boundary testing, but in the absence of any sustained increase in environmental energy, the system will return to its original point of reference. At some point, however, this stable regimen is disrupted, and, if the internal movement of the system is propitious, the system's stable behaviour gives way to random fluctuations.
>
> Abandoning its original trajectory, the system destabilizes and exhibits a so-called 'pitchfork bifurcation' pattern. . . . That is, once destabilized, the system begins to fluctuate between two or more new points. The oscillation continues until it abandons its original path and takes one or more of the alternative points as its path of development.
>
> (Harvey and Reed 1994: 385)

The most frequently modelled real world example of this sort of thing is provided by the world's climate. Let us think about what the word 'climate' means. It describes a set of weather systems bounded within a range of values. Expressed in a particular space, for example Northern Europe, it can be considered to be defined by a range of winter temperature values which does not pass over limits at either extreme. It seems clear from actual fossil and geological record that there are in fact two climate regimes which have applied here. One is the relatively warm one in which we live. The other is an ice age. The scary thing is that the transition from one to the other is not a gradual linear process. It happens suddenly as the result of small scale perturbations in controlling variables. This is an extreme example of the Lorenz or butterfly attractor which will be discussed in the next section. The point is that change is the result of perturbation beyond a boundary and there is a radical regime change.[15] The difference in the controlling parameters may in incremental terms be small. The outcome effect is enormous.

Let us go back to the implications of the quotation from Nicolis about the significance of understanding local behaviour at bifurcation points. We shall see subsequently that some argue that science founded in chaos/complexity can be historical and only historical. I want to suggest that it is precisely by focusing on understanding what happens at bifurcation points that we can do more than explain what has happened. As Peak and Frame put it: 'any system that obeys rules – even if the behaviour is chaotic – can be controlled once the rules are known' (1994: 233). I would suggest that for social systems such rules will include both the specification of the controlling parameters and an account of the non-linear effects of changes in them. In any event, even for understanding, points of change are the points of interest.

Phase space – time and space and all the rest

Adams (1994b, 1995), in asserting the social significance of time, has drawn explicitly on complexity theory, and in particular on the work of Prigogine, both directly and as mediated through Hayles. In this section I want to begin to deal with the issues she raises, although the main discussion of them will be in the next chapter. To do so we need to define the expression 'phase space', here equivalent to the idea of 'state space' as defined by Kauffman (1993: 174). The state space is all the possible states in which a system might exist in theoretical terms. Here we have operationalised our description of a system in terms of real values for a set of parameters and we locate either or both elements within the system and the general character of the system itself in relation to these parameters. We can think of this in system terms as defining the state of the system in terms of a set of n co-ordinates in n dimensional space when we have n parameters. I am well aware that I am here combining a discussion of the trajectory of objects within systems (individuals, households, neighbourhoods, localities, regions – when considered not in terms of their internal structure, when they are themselves to be thought of as systems, but as unitary wholes), with a discussion of system changes. Let us begin by concentrating on the character of systems.

In historical systems with an evolutionary character the key dimension of movement is change through time. Time can always be considered to be our fundamental axis. Poincaré described a way in which we can map things in time. We do this not by using time as a continuous axis measured in Newtonian terms, but rather by recording the character of the system at successive time points and presenting a description of it at the successive times we measure it.[16] This idea of representing systems through trends as a way of exploring longitudinal changes is of course inherent in social statistics. In the UK we have decennial censuses which record changes over time across a range of indicators of the nature of this society, and all advanced societies have something similar.

However, we are not dealing with single indicators when we want to describe the state of systems. Instead we want a description of the nature of the system in terms of all the variables which can be used to describe it.

We want it specified in terms of n co-ordinates in an n dimensional space, even if the form of the system is not determined by the value of all the variables describing it, but rather by the values of a much more limited number of control parameters. Thinking about n dimensional spaces is a good way to serious headaches,[17] but there are two methods regularly employed in social research which do deal with large scale dimensionality. The first, which is quite transparent, is the construction of contingency tables of a dimensionality of more than three. We should all be able to visualise a three dimensional contingency table. It can be represented by a cube drawn on a two dimensional blackboard, with the edges describing particular values for categorical variables. We can cross-tabulate age group against sex against class and draw the resulting 'two-way table'. What we can then do is add in another variable – say an ethnicity classification. We now have four dimensions on which our cases are measured and the cells in the contingency table in which they are located correspond exactly to co-ordinates specified in a four dimensional space defined by continuous variables.

In order to get such a table onto a two dimensional print-out we slice it up. We present a series of bivariate tables which can be printed in two dimensions for each, let us say, of the gender categories, further subdivided by age group. So we related age ethnicity to class for women over 60, men over 60, women aged 40 to 59, men aged 40 to 59, and so on. I want to come back to a complex way of thinking about where we find our cases in such n dimensional tables in the subsequent discussion of strange attractors in relation to a discussion of the quantitative programme in social science.

The less transparent n dimensional method involving the use of n dimensional spaces is cluster analysis in which we use continuous variables to measure cases (transforming categorical variables into binary attributes with the value of 1 if in the category and 0 if not in the category). Here we do create out of sight n dimensional spaces in which our cases are located. Again I want to come back to just what our clusters are, in discussing strange attractors and the quantitative programme in social science.

At this point I want to try to sort out something which has been puzzling me during the time I have been reading and thinking about chaos/complexity theory and trying to see how it can be used in relation to the social. This is the issue of levels and the relationship between spaces and the systems contained within those spaces. I have been troubled by the issue of whether the social constitutes a system or whether the social is the space within which that system is located. The only answer I can come up with is that it is both. In coming to this conclusion I have been helped by Reed and Harvey's (1994) discussion of nested ontologies, of which more subsequently. In other words, at one level of analysis social systems are located as entities with states describable by co-ordinates in n dimensional spaces. The time axis here is certainly not Newtonian and continuous but rather represents transitions in the forms of social orders. Within those social orders, and along a time axis contained within them, we can map social changes, especially if we consider the role of physical space as a hierarchy and relate movements in space to movements in time.

If the systems which interest us change through time, then we need to think about the character of those changes. Let us go back to our earlier discussion of linearity, chaos and complexity and remember that our discussion was of changes, which meant that it was inherently temporal. In linear systems changes over time in control parameters produce incremental and linear changes in the system. In 'absolute chaos' (popular chaos, postmodernism's vision of chaos) small changes through time produce indeterminate results: anything could happen. The interesting thing about complex solutions is that we can't predict what will happen, but we know that what will happen will be drawn from a set of alternatives greater than one but less than too many to cope with – the realm of determined chaos. The point about phase spaces is that we can map these changes out in them. Historically we can see what has happened. If we can deal with robust, determined, organised chaos, then we may be able not to predict, but to act so that some things happen and others don't happen. We may create – in the Judaeo-Christian-Islamic tradition we have free will for just that purpose. To be able to do that we have to realise what might happen. The route to that realisation (an interesting word – it means both to come to know and to make happen) is through strange attractors.

Strange attractors

There are several ways of thinking about attractors, but here it is best to begin by thinking about what happens to systems as they change over time in an n dimensional phase space. Let us take a simple example, that of a pendulum moving in three dimensional space. Over time the pendulum will stop swinging. It will become fixed in space at a single point. All the three dimensional spatial co-ordinates describing positions which it has previously occupied share the property that a pendulum situated in them will eventually come to rest at the attractor point. They constitute the attractor basin which 'drains' (see the geographic analogy) towards the point at which the pendulum is at rest.

26

The systems which interest us do not behave like pendulums. However, they do not behave in a random way either. If we map their movement over time in an n dimensional space whose co-ordinates are values on descriptor variables of interest to us, then in a system which was chaotic in the popular sense, the location of the system at successive time periods could be anywhere within the n dimensional phase space – Kauffman's expression of state space perhaps conveys the ideas rather better here. What we find when we have deterministic chaos is that the system's successive states are not anywhere but rather are to be found within a restricted set within the range of possible positions. Just to complicate matters the dimensionality of the figures generated in such cases may not only be less than that of the n dimensional state space, which is to be expected if the behaviour of the system is controlled by a limited set of a lot less than n control parameters, but may have a dimensionality which is not a whole number. It may be a fractal. We will return to a discussion of fractals subsequently and particularly in relation to socio-spatial systems.

There is a hierarchy of development of such strange attractors. Let us begin with the simplest – the torus or doughnut which is usually diagramatically represented as exactly that in a two dimensional diagram of the three dimensional thing, but which may have any dimensionality between two and three. If a system moves beyond stability, complete equilibrium as represented by a point attractor where nothing ever changes, through the domain of close to equilibrium where changes generally revert towards a single base state, then the next in the series is the torus. The torus describes the dynamics of self-similar systems. That means that over cycles of change such systems always end up somewhere within the bounding limits set by the surface of the doughnut. Things change from cycle to cycle, depending of course on changes in controlling parameters, but provided that those controlling parameters don't change too much, by less than the value of the first Feigenbaum number, then the system stays somewhere inside the doughnut. There is an interesting disagreement in the literature as to whether or not the torus is a strange attractor. It seems to me that it is because there is indeterminacy within the limiting boundaries, reflected in the possibility of fractal toruses with dimensionalities of between two and three. However, it is clearly the character of the boundaries which is of interest to us.

When I first read this the mental effect was certainly that of a resonance but the kind of resonance that comes from standing in the belfry itself, and there were two peels. The resonances were with two key Marxist contributions to the description of social systems. One was Raymond Williams' (1980) discussion of 'Base and superstructure in

Marxist cultural theory' where characteristically he analysed the use of words, and in particular of the word 'determine'. He concluded that the proper use of this is not to convey exact linear prediction but rather a setting of limits.[18] Lefebvre in his discussion of capitalist reproduction used a formulation which could have been drawn straight from chaos theory – social systems are reproduced from cycle to cycle but never in exactly the same way. These resonances prompted me to equate the Fordist mode of regulation with a system moving inside a torus attractor (see Byrne 1997a and Chapter 5 of this volume).

What happens next is particularly interesting for social scientists. When a key control parameter changes its value between cycles by an amount which is three times greater than the value in the previous cycle (the first ratio in the Feigenbaum series) then the torus attractor transforms into a butterfly or Lorenz attractor. This is Lorenz's description of weather systems. In the literature, discussion of this higher order attractor emphasises its fractal dimensionality. It should be noted that very small differences in the values of control parameters at the bifurcation point determine which of two radically different trajectories the system settles into. It is possible to think of these two trajectories as two toruses with a small area of inter-connectedness. The system in respective cycles is to be found in one or other of the toruses. In the sort of robust chaos which is of interest to us it may well be that there is a limited range of values of control parameters which can have the chaotic effect of assigning the system to one or the other trajectory. This seems to be what happens in reality with climate regimes at the planetary level. We don't cycle from ice age to temperate on a daily or annual basis, although the actual time period of changes is quite short. There is a stability for a period in one regime or the other.

Although the Lorenz or butterfly attractor is widely discussed in the literature, and there is an appealing metaphorical resonance between its binary character and contemporary social science's concern with social polarisation, it is important to note that it is simply a special case of dynamical bifurcation and may not actually be the form which is best used to describe social transformations. Brown (1995: 51) argues that catastrophic bifurcations are much more generally common. It is certainly possible to think of the kind of system change involved in the transition from Fordism to post-Fordism as involving a catastrophic transformation, without the second form being a 'butterfly attractor'.

When we are thinking of real complex systems it is important to consider that these are likely to be nested in the way described by Reed and Harvey (1994). What this means here is that the attractor space, the sub-domain of the phase or condition space represented by the strange attractor, constitutes the phase or condition space within which sub-systems of the whole system are located. Social and socio-spatial entities which are internally systemic, for example localities or households, can be considered to be located within the phase or condition space constituted by the higher order social system of which they are a part. It seems at least possible that we may have different kinds of bifurcation processes at different levels in the hierarchy. The butterfly attractor has great appeal as a description of the trajectories of individuals and households, whereas simple catastrophe might describe the evolution of the whole social order or of localities. Chapter 4 will be concerned exactly with the hierarchical form of social spaces nested in just this way.

In biology the idea of strange attractor has become associated with that of peaks in fitness landscapes. That concept will be discussed in a moment. Here we can simply say that the fitness landscape peak is in a sense the bottom of the attractor basin turned upside down. It represents a *for the moment* optimum form. What is interesting of course in biological evolution is that not all forms are possible. Rather there seem to be phenotypical expressions of possible attractors, observable not just in complex biochemistry but even at the level of gross anatomy, which show that whilst there is a great possible variation in body form, that variation is not infinite. The marsupial wolf looked very like a wolf, although the actual evolutionary gap between the two was far greater than that between a wolf and a human being. There is a strange attractor for that body form – this kind of thinking does tend to look very much like the Platonic conception of ideal forms towards which aspects of reality tend to approximate.[19]

The evolutionary process will be considered again in relation to a discussion of fitness landscapes. Now we need to take a European turn and consider the nature of the kind of systems which have evolutionary potential.

Far from equilibric systems

So far this chapter has followed the US style of thinking about chaos/complexity, although some mention has been made of the work of Prigogine. This approach was adopted because the US account is a good one for conveying the significance of change and change points for systems. We now need to consider, carefully, just what sort of systems we are dealing with. In this section the arguments of Prigogine and Stengers (1984) as developed by Reed and Harvey (1992) and Harvey and Reed (1994) will be outlined. Harvey and Reed describe the kind of systems we are dealing with:

Dissipative systems are the most general expressions of deterministic chaos found in nature. . . . Dissipative systems are
natural thermodynamic entities capable of evolutionary
behaviour. Two characteristics set dissipative systems off from
other natural entities: First, they have the capacity to import
energy from their immediate environment and transform that
energy into increasingly more complex, internal structuration.
By dint of their ability to increase metabolically their structural
and functional complexity over time, we can say that dissipative
systems are 'information accumulating' and 'information
preserving' configurations. Second, although all thermodynam-
ically ordered systems naturally accumulate increasing levels of
random disorder, dissipative systems have the capacity to offset
this tendency toward organisational decay by transporting their
internal disorder out to their environment. Hence, the dual
ability of dissipative systems to increase and store information in
the form of increasing levels of internal structuration, on the
one hand, and to export disorganisation to their immediate
environment, on the other, are their essential characteristics.

(Harvey and Reed 1994: 377–8)

Dissipative systems are clearly different from systems in complete equilibria or stasis, but have to be distinguished carefully from near to
equilibrium systems. Near to equilibrium systems are not static and
wholly isolated from their environment but their essential principle is
homeostasis. They return towards their general or ground state. The
mechanisms which operate to achieve this, work through negative feedback or damping of change. This kind of systemic description is, as
Harvey and Reed (1994) show, very much the description which informed
Parsons' work throughout most, if not all, of his career. It was precisely
the incapacity of such approaches for dealing with evolutionary
behaviour which was the basis of much critical rejection of them as the
basis of accounts of social reality.

Dissipative, far from equilibric systems, in contrast, are inherently
evolutionary. There are two sources of change which may operate inde-
pendently or together in relation to them. First, perturbations may be
externally engendered through the interaction of such systems with their
environment. Here the term 'environment' is being used in the general
sense to refer to all aspects of reality outside the system and with which it
has relationships, although it is clear that the more specific usage of
'natural environment' is one which is very generally a source of external
perturbation in human systems. A good example would be provided by

the impact of potato blight on nineteenth-century Ireland. Despite the best efforts of laissez-faire UK governments to assert landlord control over tenants in Ireland, as a foundation for the capitalist modernisation of agriculture, it took the intervention of an environmental change to transform the social system. Even then the attractor of capitalised agriculture under landlord control was not available. Instead, conacre potato growing became transformed politically over time into a system based on large peasant farmers becoming small capitalist farmers, raising cattle on standing grass. The perturbation was external to the system.

The other source of change is internal. Spontaneous internal fluctuations in far from equilibric systems test the boundaries of the system continuously. Either because of the occasional internal strength of such fluctuations, or because internal fluctuations interact with external perturbations, then the system's boundaries are breached and it is forced into a new and radically different trajectory. This is precisely what happens at bifurcation points, and the strength of internal fluctuations has to be considered in relation to Feigenbaum series numbers being exceeded by the value of changes in the system's control parameters.

In reality it would seem that internal and external always interact to some degree. In the case of the Irish famine the main perturbation was natural but radical system transformation was only possible because, instead of policy acting to damp out change, as it would have pre or post the dominance of laissez-faire, the British government continued with a policy regime which reinforced the destabilising effects of the famine itself. It has to be said that economic innovation, often of course driven by social conflicts within economic systems, seems to be a constant generator of fluctuations in capitalist social systems. This way of thinking is very close to the classic Marxist account of such transformational changes. Indeed, it is identical to it. It is absolutely a matter of the transformation of quantity into quality.

Harvey and Reed sum this up with reference to the history of systems thinking in sociology in this way:

> The dissipative social systems paradigm assumes social order is not always possible, nor is it necessarily desirable. It does not begin, as does the Parsonian project, by asking the Hobbesian question, 'How is order possible?' . . . Instead it addresses the more perplexing question, 'How do the mechanisms producing social order, periodically produce chaos and pave the way for radical social transformations?'
>
> (Harvey and Reed 1994: 390–1)

Porush spells out the implications of this approach very clearly:

> Although Prigogine's term 'dissipative structures' hasn't sold as well [as chaos] it is in most senses much more accurate. First, it focuses on the dynamic system which undergoes the sudden transformation from *apparently chaotic* to *increasingly ordered* on the other side of the bifurcation point. Second, it implies the structure in Prigogine's mathematical model which specifies when such orderliness is not only possible, but likely to arise.
>
> (Porush 1991: 59)

There is one additional element which must be added to the specification of the nature of dissipative social systems of interest to us. This has already been mentioned but is important and must be returned to. This is their nested character. Harvey and Reed (1994) argue for this most convincingly. The point is that we can see an evolutionary process not merely of specific dissipative systems, but of kinds of dissipative systems. The route which matters here is that which runs through the domains of deterministic chaos–dissipative systems–biological evolution–multilinear social evolution–dissipative social systems. These schemata are extremely important and will be further considered in Chapter 2. Here we have to note that this is not a hierarchy of progression and replacement, but rather represents the development of more specific sets which remain part of the larger sets from which they develop. This brings us up to the notion that evolution is a process which can occur at several levels. We can best develop this through a consideration of the idea of 'fitness landscapes'.

Fitness landscapes

The term 'fitness landscape' describes an approach derived from biology where possibilities in evolutionary terms are represented by a landscape of peaks and valleys. The peaks represent high fitness. The point about the landscape formulation is that it shows that where you start from is of great importance. It is much easier to go up a ridge to a local peak than to descend into a valley and ascend again towards a more remote and higher peak. Any fell walker will understand this immediately. Landscapes represent available options but can themselves be changed because evolution is not just a matter of change in single organisms but also reflects the impact of change in one organism on others – coevolution. There is a clear association between the imagery of fitness landscapes and the idea of far from equilibric time dependent systems.

You can only start from where you are and there are constraints on the range of movement, short of a revolutionary transformation which changes the whole character of the global social order.

Kauffman relates fitness landscapes and chaos thus:

> We will find . . . that whether we are talking about organisms or economies, surprisingly general laws govern adaptive processes on multipeaked fitness landscapes. . . . The edge-of-chaos theme also arises as a potential general law. In scaling the top of fitness peaks, adapting populations that are too methodical and timid in their explorations are likely to get stuck in the foothills, thinking that they have reached as high as they can go; but a search that is too wide-ranging is also likely to fail. The best exploration of evolutionary space occurs at a kind of phase transition between order and disorder when populations begin to melt off the local peaks they have become fixated on and flow along ridges toward distant regions of higher fitness.
>
> The edge-of-chaos image arises in coevolution as well, for as we evolve, so do our competitors; to remain fit, we must adapt to their adaptations. In coevolving systems, each partner clambers up its fitness landscape towards fitness peaks, even as that landscape is constantly deformed by the adaptive moves of its coevolutionary partners. Strikingly, such coevolving systems also behave in an ordered regime, a chaotic regime, and a transition regime. It is almost spooky that such systems seem to coevolve to the regime at the edge of chaos.
>
> (Kauffman 1995: 27)

Coevolution is not confined to binary pairs or even multiple combinations of organisms. The evolutionary impact of the development of a species can transform the whole eco-system of which it is a part. Human beings have been particularly good at this for a long time. Even in our supposedly benign role as hunter-gatherers we did for most of the megafauna of the paleo-Arctic in very short order. The landscapes can evolve. In a fascinating suggestion, highly reminiscent of the ideas of Teilhard de Chardin, Kauffman proposes that there is a third level which is the evolution of evolutionary mechanisms themselves. That is very important in relation to agency and we will return to it. But first to conclude this chapter.

Scientistic 'science' doesn't own it

In this chapter ideas which originate in the domain of traditionally conceived-of 'science' have been presented as the basis of a conceptual tool bag for the development of a complexity-founded approach to social science. It is perfectly true to say that those who are articulating these ideas are at the very least open to their use in this way. Prigogine and Stengers (1984) go much farther and recognise in the most explicit way the reflexive interplay between 'science' and the 'human sciences' in the development of these perspectives. This is perhaps the reason why so many US writers in the 'scientistic' tradition are uncomfortable with their work. However, Prigogine and Stengers are exceptional. It is still necessary to say something about the status of science in relation to these concepts and to say it somewhat brutally. Scientists of a scientistic bent do need to be telt, just as postmodernists are in for a telling in the next chapter.

Hayles has done this telling and her remarks are ones I would wish to endorse absolutely:

> It should not be surprising, then, to find other sites within the culture that also embody the presuppositions informing chaos theory. . . . The question of how such isomorphisms arise is not easily answered. Let me say at the outset, however, that I do not assume they are the result of direct influence between one site and another. In particular I am *not* [her emphasis] arguing that the science of chaos is the originary site from which chaotics emanates into the culture. Rather, both the literary and scientific manifestations of chaotics are involved in feedback loops with the culture. They help to create the context that energizes the questions they ask; at the same time they also ask questions energized by the context.
>
> (Hayles 1991: 7)

The foundation of that statement is, to my mind, although Hayles might not be happy with this interpretation, essentially a realist ontology which suggests that the 'obduracy of the world'[20] is imposing these forms of understanding on us as our knowledge of the world and our place in these forms develops (a very modernist notion) beyond simplicity and reductionism. The next chapter will be concerned with a development of this theme.

2

THE REALITY OF THE COMPLEX

The complexity of the real

> it is necessary to recall an absolutely founding presumption of
> materialism: that the natural world exists whether anyone signi-
> fies it or not.
>
> (Williams 1979: 167)

Introduction

The purpose of this chapter is to confront social theory with the implications of complexity. This is not a wholly original project. Reed and
Harvey (1992, 1996) have more than begun the ontological component
of the debate through an explicit assertion, endorsed absolutely here,
that Bhaskar's scientific realism provides a philosophical ontology which
fits pretty well exactly with the scientific ontology underpinning the
complexity programme. Adam (1994b, 1995) and Hayles (1990, 1991)
have, perhaps somewhat tentatively, and for Hayles even ambiguously,
picked up the gauntlet offered to any foundationalist theory by postmodernism, and done so from a complexity-informed position.
Complex accounts are foundationalist,[1] although they are absolutely
not reductionist and positivist. It is intended here to argue that they are
surely part of the modernist programme,[2] and really always have been
throughout the history of that programme. An understanding of this
will certainly put the kibosh[3] on postmodernism and poststructuralism.
Harvey and Reed (1994), as noted in Chapter 1, have pointed out the
way in which complexity provides us with the basis of a systemic
account of the social world which transcends the limitations of the
homeostatic systems model basic to Parsonian structural-functionalism.
From this we can argue that complexity enables us to deal with both of
the crucial problems identified for any sociological theory by Mouzelis
(1995). It provides a way of relating the macro and the micro which is
not inherently aggregative and reductionist and it provides a way of

describing the relationship between agency and structure which takes account of Elias' assertion of the fifth dimension of reflexive human consciousness.

Mouzelis (1995: 1–2) makes a useful distinction between two types of theory, contrasting theories of the first kind which constitute substantive accounts of the world and which are to be sustained or not by empirical investigation, on the one hand, with theories of the second kind which provide a set of tools on the basis of which theories of the first kind may be constructed. In reality the distinction is essentially heuristic. The practice of science always involves a mixing of the two, although Mouzelis makes a convincing argument for the value of sociological theory as a specific form of sociological practice concerned with the elaboration and elucidation of theories of the second kind. He also establishes that the value of theoretical formulations of the second kind is their heuristic utility – their capacity for 'generating interesting questions and for generally facilitating empirically oriented research' (1995: 2). One purpose of this chapter is to demonstrate that complexity theory satisfies this criterion, but that is not its only purpose. Mouzelis is much less convincing when he suggests that this sort of task may be undertaken separately from a sorting out of quite fundamental philosophical issues describing the metatheoretical content of any scientific project.[4] It really is necessary to consider the nature of the reality to which theoretical frameworks are being applied, however generally and heuristically. However, with the necessity of an ontological element asserted, *pace* Mouzelis, the subject matter of this chapter will be complexity considered somewhat as a theoretical programme of the second kind, i.e. as a conceptual framework founded on the centrality of the forms and processes of deterministic chaos. The ontological qualification is a very important one. It means that even here we are dealing with a substantive account of the world – ontological statements are statements about the nature of reality and it is difficult to be more substantive than that. Nonetheless, for the moment the programme will not be attached to accounts of specific historical reality, for me the demarcating characteristic of theories of Mouzelis' first kind.

This chapter will consist of three sections. First, it will seek to establish a clear ontological foundation for complexity as part of the general realist programme. Second, it will take up the discussion of chaos as a way of confronting the rational and modernist programme of complexity with the post- (and often ir-) rational programme of postmodernism/poststructuralism. Finally, it will develop the contrast between the close to equilibric and homeostatic account of Parsonian functionalism and its derivatives (which Mouzelis 1995 demonstrates includes much of contemporary social theory), begun in Chapter 1. This last element is important in itself, but becomes even more important when considered as representing a basis for the conceptual resolution of the structure/action, macro/micro dilemmas in the framing of social theory as a basis for informed social action.

The complex is real

Sometimes it is necessary to be abrupt. This section will begin with an abrupt statement. Positivism is dead. By now it has gone off and is beginning to smell. If, in the words of the Russian proverb, it is rotting from the head, that means that whilst there are those in science practice who *think that* it is still a valid metatheoretical position and foundation for a methodological programme[5] there are very few who *think about* the validity of metatheoretically-founded methodological programmes who still think this. The implication of this abrupt assertion is that it is not necessary to conduct a debate with positivism in this text. There are a number of good accounts of the demise of positivism and of its general replacement in science by a more or less realist programme and their content will not be reproduced here. However, it is necessary to say something about the range of dominance of realism. This is not total and it is weakest in sociology and those areas which share with an important and necessary version of sociology the notion that there is something distinctive about the social world and the products of human social action. The best way to illustrate this is by reference to the way in which geography became realist and then moved on to something else, and that will be done in the discussion of the relationship between postmodernism and chaos/complexity.

Let us, however, begin by specifying the essential content of the realist position. This has been most developed by Bhaskar (1986) but he is a notoriously opaque writer and there are much clearer summaries available in Sayer (1992), Outhwaite (1987), Reed and Harvey (1992) and Williams and May (1996). The essential elements in realism are the assertions that that which we observe in the world is real and that it is the product of complex and contingent causal mechanisms which may not be directly accessible to us. It has to be said that Bhaskar uses the term 'real' in a more restrictive sense than that applied here, and that there is some value in his usage. For him the term 'real' should be reserved for the complex and contingent causal mechanisms and the entities which compose them (although there is a clear holistic element in realism – mechanisms are not reducible to their components). The events which happen in the world are actual. Those things which we experience are empirical. The real may not become actual because the causal mechanisms are complex and contingent and the effects may be blocked. The actual may not become empirical because it is not necessarily observed.

Outhwaite summarises the implications of this in a way which is both clear and enormously suggestive for the complexity programme in general and for its social applications in particular:

> Unlike a constant conjunction analysis, which logically presupposes that the system within which 'causal' relations are observed is isolated from extraneous influences, a realist analysis of causality can account for the interaction of various causal tendencies within the complex and open systems among which we live, and which we ourselves are.
>
> The latter point is important, for it is a particular virtue of a realist analysis that it enables us to see the parallels between our own causal powers and liabilities and those of other physical objects. Like the higher animals, we can choose to initiate certain causal sequences made possible by our causal powers. Unlike them, we can reflect on those powers and formulate long term projects.
>
> (Outhwaite 1987: 22)

The best way to explain realism is through an example. I have a favourite. In the 1930s Bradbury, a prominent chest physician, carried out a study of the incidence and causes of tuberculosis on Tyneside (Bradbury 1933). He begins his book with a rhetorical question: why ask what causes TB? We all know what causes TB. It is the TB bacillus. However, the real problem is that not everybody exposed to the TB bacillus develops the clinical disease of tuberculosis. In fact, given that just about everybody on Tyneside in the 1930s was exposed to the TB bacillus, the issue was why did most people not get the disease?[6] In realist language, exposure to the TB bacillus was a necessary but not sufficient cause.

Bradbury's investigations led him to conclude that the actual development of clinical tuberculosis was the product of the interaction of three factors, namely poor housing conditions which led to overcrowding and facilitated transmission of the bacillus, poor feeding and in particular insufficient consumption of milk which facilitated the infection gaining hold, and being Irish. This last was a product of less generational exposure to the disease. TB, like any good parasite, bred for resistance. The Irish had two generations fewer of urban industrial

38

selection behind them. In other words the causal mechanisms for clinical TB were complex and contingent. Good housing and good food blocked the disease. The epidemiological support for this account is absolute. TB mortality rates declined dramatically over time in direct association with improvements in general living conditions. The introduction of effective antibiotics in the 1950s made very little difference to the rate of decline.[7]

Reed and Harvey describe realism as a 'philosophical ontology', complexity theory as a new 'scientific ontology', and suggest that the two may be combined as the basis of a new social ontology through: 'a modified naturalist perspective in which societies and institutions can be treated as if they were dissipative entities' (1992: 354). Their arguments for the congruence of realism and complexity theory seem wholly persuasive to me. As they put it, what is required is:

> a scientific ontology which fits Bhaskar's philosophical framework: one which treats nature and society as if they were ontologically open and historically constituted; hierarchically structured, yet interactively complex; non-reductive and indeterminate, yet amenable to rational explanation; capable of seeing nature as a 'self-organising' enterprise without succumbing to anthropomorphism or mystifying animism.
>
> (Reed and Harvey 1992: 359)

If we refer back to the description of complexity/chaos theory in Chapter 1, we should be able to agree with Reed and Harvey that it fits this bill very well indeed. Perhaps the crucial element to emphasise here is 'amenable to rational explanation'. We need to think about what that means and the possibilities of it quite carefully.

Here it is necessary to disagree with Stephen J. Gould and his account of the potential of historical explanation as present in *Wonderful Life* (1991). This is indeed a wonderful book and Gould's account of the contingent nature of the historical development of life provides a resounding refutation of the reductionist programme in general. His assertion of the historical nature of science is one which fits very well with the complexity programme. Harvey and Reed (1994) take it up in exactly that way. However, in this text Gould confines the potential of historical reconstruction to explanation and explicitly rules out the possibility of prediction in his extensive and fascinating discussion of the nature of history (1991: 277–91). For Gould, what matters is contingency interpreted as chance, which he counterposes to the reductionist laws of linear science. In a revealing passage he remarks:

Am I really arguing that nothing about life's history could be predicted, or might follow directly from the general laws of nature? Of course not; the question that we face is one of scale, or level of focus. Life exhibits a structure obedient to physical principles. We do not live amidst a chaos of historical circumstances unaffected by anything accessible to the 'scientific method' as traditionally conceived. . . .

But these phenomena, rich and extensive as they are, lie too far from the details that interest us about life's history. Invariant laws of nature impact the general forms and functions of organisms; they set the channels in which organic design must evolve. But the channels are so broad relative to the details that fascinate us! The physical channels do not specify. . . . When we set our focus upon the level of detail that regulates most common questions about the history of life, contingency dominates and the predictability of general form recedes to an irrelevant background.

(Gould 1991: 289–90)[8]

It is important to note that Gould does not equate contingency with randomness, explicitly differentiating the two thus:

I am not speaking of randomness . . . but of a central principle of all history – *contingency* [original emphasis]. A historical explanation does not rest on direct deductions from laws of nature, but on an unpredictable set of antecedent states, where any major change in any step of the sequence would have altered the final result. This final result is therefore dependent on, contingent on, everything that came before – the uneraseable and determining signature of history.

(Gould 1991: 283)

Gould's own brilliant citation of Capra's *It's a Wonderful Life* provides a good basis of argument with him, and a beautiful illustration of social bifurcation. The interesting thing here is that the decent humane co-operatively founded Bedford Falls on the one hand and the rentier-induced urban horror of Pottersville on the other are exactly the two sides of a bifurcation – the two wings of the butterfly attractor. The difference, the determining perturbation, is of course the wonderful life of George Bailey. Clarence the angel has to show George *what* he has done, but we should remember that George was shown *how* to do it long before and well understood what was to be done. He was imitating the actions of his father and took over the responsibility for the Savings and Loan when his father died, precisely because he had the same combination of moral values and general competence – the scene where he tells his mother what a decent man his father is, and is sharply told by the black maid that it is well time he realised it, sets that up, as does the subsequent scene where the directors of the Savings and Loan make it plain that it will fold unless he takes over as manager. All his actions were well understood by himself for exactly what they were. He was always conscious of why he acted. What he didn't see, until shown by Clarence, was the non-linear product of those small perturbations in the locality of the bifurcation.

Peak and Frame have asked the question to which Gould, in my view, provides the weak answer:

> We are accustomed to judging the worth of a scientific theory by its ability to synthesise data and organise observation *and* [original emphasis] by its ability to make accurate predictions. Does the existence of sensitive dependence on initial conditions mean that the science of chaotic systems is doomed to be purely taxonomic, devoid of predictive power?
>
> (Peak and Frame 1994: 151)

Gould makes a very powerful defence of the legitimacy and importance of taxonomy, of 'mere' stamp collecting, as the foundation of historical explanation. This in itself is an important statement to the effect that a historical conception of science takes us beyond classification to the possibility of retrospective explanation in historical terms. It is the weak programme of deterministic chaos. However, we still want to know where we might be not passively going, but actively getting to. If we can set up a strong programme we want it.

We can turn back to Peak and Frame for an optimistic position in their interesting discussion of 'controlling chaos'. As they say, if a system obeys rules we can control it once we know what those rules are. What they suggest is the possibility of gentle control of chaos by the introduction of small perturbations which maintain the stability of the system. I would go further. In the nature of bifurcation points, small perturbations can achieve not just stability, but the possible transformation of the system to a better of two alternatives. This requires knowledge of what to do, and a belief in the efficacy of the actions. George Bailey surely had the first. Clarence the angel had to show him the truth of the second.

That is the profoundly optimistic implication of the possibility of the understanding of the domain of complexity as characterised by robust chaos. We can come to see what makes the difference. And if we can see what makes the difference, then we can make the difference. It is, to quote O'Connor,[9] 'not a matter of what will happen, but of what will be made to happen' (1982: 328).

The similarity between the notion of crisis, as discussed by O'Connor, and the character of a bifurcation point is evident. This is yet another resonance between Marxist thought in the tradition of historical (absolutely not dialectical) materialism, and the complexity programme. Crises are turning points in which things cannot stay as they are. To quote the horrendous jargon of contemporary 'human resources' management when destroying the conditions of workers, status quo is not an option. However, there is more than one way in which things can go. Agency is the basis of that difference.

Complexity against postmodernism

> where scientists see chaos as the source of order, poststructural-
> ists appropriate it to subvert order.
>
> (Hayles 1990: 176)

Hayles begins her discussion of 'cultural postmodernism' with a definition of it as 'the realization that what has always been thought of as the essential, unvarying components of human experience are not natural facts of life but social constructions' (1990: 265). That seems absolutely correct, although it should be noted that if postmodernism is social constructionism it is a rather primitive version of what in sociology has been an interesting and important strand of the discipline's project. The reason for this is that all that interests postmodernism is the social construction of knowledge. The social constructionist position in sociology in its original form asserted the distinctiveness of social reality from physical reality, because the former was the product of human social action, including intentional social action. This ontological distinction had epistemological consequences, expressed in a general endorsement of Weber's principle of *verstehen* – interpretative understanding, in which we must understand people's actions in terms of the meanings that they themselves attach to them. In sociology the postmodern turn has taken the form of the reflexing of this metatheoretical account back onto the discipline itself, so that it too becomes a social construction to be understood in social terms. This is not a novel project. It is after all exactly what Karl Mannheim was engaged in fifty years ago. True, we might prefer not to turn to sociologists as Platonic guardians of truth, but the social nature of science cannot and should not be disputed.[10]

However, the original programme of social constructionism had relatively limited objectives and was still presented, perfectly correctly, as part of a programme of rational understanding. Its first objective was to dispute the territorial claims of positivism to stand as a meta-theory for all science. That fight is long over. Its second was to justify a sociological programme concerned with the creative capacity of human beings, not just as reflexive contemplative critics, as knowers, but even more as reflexive understanding actors, as doers. It seems perfectly proper that the social constructionist programme should have been extended as the basis of a sociology of science. The problem was that in so doing it met up with an anti-rationalist programme, much of whose ancestry is to be found in the work of Heidegger, which manifests itself under the title 'postmodernism'. The core of this position is well expressed in a quotation from Graham:

> knowledges are fully constitutive social processes rather than dependent reflections of an independent real. . . . Like other social processes, knowledges differ from each other in the ways in which they are constituted and in their social effects, but they cannot be ranked hierarchically on the basis of their closeness to or distance from a singular objective or unchanging 'reality'. In other words the truth of particular knowledges is not adjudicated in a universal setting but is particular to certain social settings and validation practices.
>
> (Graham 1992: 398)[11]

This absolute relativism in the essence of this 'grand narrative' – for postmodernism is itself a grand narrative despite its rejection of the possibility of grand narratives – can seem to resonate with non-linear science's rejection of general accounts and its emphasis on local under-standings. We certainly cannot have a linear, law derived, reductionist founded, version of the history of any process of evolutionary or other change. However, as Gould shows so clearly, we can have an under-standing of that process which can be 'tested' against reality by procedures which may indeed serve to privilege one account against another. Historical science remains science.[12]

It is revealing that Adam, whose work could on a superficial reading seem to be open to appropriation as part of the postmodern programme, is very careful to distinguish her approach from it:

I want to focus more explicitly on the principle of implication and show its relevance and utility for theorising temporal complexity. This revisionary concept, I suggest, is pivotal for a consistent and coherent dissent from the Enlightenment episteme. It transforms recognition of complexity from a rather non-committal and circumspect pluralism into a critical and radical social science criterion whose points of departure are both continuous with and distinct from allied postmodern and feminist critiques of that tradition of thought.

(Adam 1995: 151)

Actually this is too tentative on Adam's part. Her project centres on a reconceptualisation of the social nature of time, in a way wholly compatible with the rejection of linear Newtonian time as a universal principle which is such a central element of the conceptualisation of the evolution of dissipative systems, but a reconceptualisation is not a rejection. On the contrary, Adam's assertion of the centrality of time in the social is inherently evolutionary in its implications and as such is absolutely incompatible with postmodernism's essentially atemporal character.

I stated earlier in this chapter that Hayles, however tentatively and ambiguously, differentiates between the postmodern programme and chaos/complexity.[13] I certainly think this is the absolute implication of much of what she says, but when it comes to specification she actually identifies 'scientific chaos' as itself 'a' postmodernism:

To speak of the sciences of chaos as postmodern science is not in my view to speak incorrectly. It is to speak carelessly, however, unless one specifies the tensions that mark a specific site and re-mark it with the distinctive dynamics that characterise it. . . . Having acknowledged the importance of local differences, I should like to make a global conjecture about why the sciences of chaos have been so energised by cultural postmodernism. Many scientists have commented that working on chaos has allowed them to renew their sense of wonder. Although they do not put it in this way, they intimate that chaos has given them a sense of being in touch with the Lacanian real. For them, chaos is an image of what can be touched but not grasped, felt but not seen. At a time when resistance to mastery is so sophisticated that it cannot help but

be perceived as masterful, chaos presents them with a resistance that alleviates the fear of mastery.

(Hayles 1990: 292–3)

It is this issue of mastery which is offered so often as the crucial distinguishing difference between the postmodern and the modern. I want to
argue that the dichotomy between domination[14] of nature and the dena-
turing of the social is inherently false, even as we shall see in the
subsequent discussion of the character of medical knowledge, as a
description of the effective practices of modernity itself. It is even more
inappropriate as a description of the potential of complexity as a scientific
programme which realises the reality of nature and works with it rather
than attempting to wring truth from it and transform it without regard to
natural limits. Hayles is perfectly right to identify this retreat from domination as a possible postmodern element in the science of chaos/
complexity, but it is only one possibility. It is also possible that
chaos/complexity can serve as the basis of a different sort of rational
project which allows for, and indeed asserts, the absolute necessity of
conscious human agency in knowledge-based social transformation.

One way to conceptualise this would be to be explicitly dialectical –
to see the linear and reductionist as a thesis, postmodernism as an
antithesis and complexity as a synthesis. This formulation has its attractions, although it is not an historically accurate account of the nature of
either the general development of knowledge systems or of knowledge-
informed human social actions.[15] In any event it seems to me that there
is a radical and essential difference between chaos/complexity and the
postmodern programme. The quotation from Hayles which serves as an
epigraph to this section refers of course to the contemplative use of the
two programmes as means of understanding, but it also resonates with
their potentials as bases for social action expressed in terms of the
results of such social action. In the case of postmodernity we have to
accept that the form of social action is absolute social inaction – the
disengagement of the intellectual project from any commitment to any
social programme whatsoever – bone idleness promoted to a metatheoretical programme. Here we may interpret sloth, which after all is a
deadly sin and carries with it the implication of the exercise of free will,
as a form of action. Complexity/chaos offers the possibility of an
engaged science not founded in pride, in the assertion of an absolute
knowledge as the basis for social programmes, but rather in a humility
about the complexity of the world coupled with a hopeful belief in the
potential of human beings for doing something about it.

It is difficult to improve on the swingeing criticism mounted of the postmodernist project by Mouzelis, and I will not attempt to do so, not least because it provides an excellent link to the themes I want to pursue in the last section of this chapter:

> the poststructuralists' total rejection of the agency–structure and micro–macro distinctions, as well as their failure to show how discourses or texts are hierarchized via unequally empowered agents, has led to a systematic neglect of the hierarchical features of complex societies, as well as to the disconnection, or very tenuous connection, between theory and empirical research.
>
> (Mouzelis 1995: 6)

The objective of this book is precisely to present a 'theoretical framework' as a potential for empirical research and subsequent, or even simultaneous, action. To get on with that it is now necessary to turn towards sociological theory itself.

Sociological theory – another way to put it right

Mouzelis' timely book *Sociological Theory: What Went Wrong?* (1995) coherently and exactly identifies the two crucial criteria by which any theory must be judged. These are:

1 How adequate is it in relating the micro level of individual and individual action to the macro level of society as a whole?
2 How adequate is it in conceptualising the relationship between the conscious agency of individual and/or collective social actors and the social conceived of in terms of social structure?

We might add, as Mouzelis does in his general review of the Parsonian project, a third question:

3 How adequate is it in terms of providing an explanation for discontinuous and fundamental changes in the character of the social system as a whole?

The purpose of this section is to assert, and perhaps even demonstrate, that thinking in terms of society as constituted as a dissipative and evolutionary system, thinking about it in terms of the conceptual structure of chaos/complexity, is a good way of resolving these questions. The approach may not meet with Mouzelis' approval. It is inherently foundationalist. It makes very firm statements about the nature of reality itself. It is certainly not a modest project in any way. The combination of the philosophical ontology of critical realism and the scientific ontology of chaos/complexity constitutes a very general, indeed absolute, claim about the nature of scientific understanding and the character of scientific investigation. Yet, contrawise, this imperialistic and foundationalist project does start very much from the same premises asserted by Mouzelis as the basis of a modest and provisional programme:

> If, *contra* modernism,[16] we accept that the only interesting substantive generalizations . . . in the social sciences are those that take into full account context in terms of time and space; and if, *contra* postmodernism, we respect the autonomous logic of sociological theory, then we should put at the centre of our preoccupations the modest and ever provisional production of a set of interrelated tools that can prepare the ground for the empirical investigation of the social world.
>
> (Mouzelis 1995: 152)

Chaos/complexity, because it is founded in a recognition of the non-linear character of reality, is absolutely concerned with the implications of local context expressed in terms of time and space. Chaos/complexity, because it recognises the significance of emergent properties, asserts the emergent, distinctive and non-reducible character of the social, and thereby respects the autonomous logic of sociological theory.[17] Chaos/complexity, not least and perhaps most importantly, because it provides a basis for a new formulation of the quantitative programme in sociology, is a tool-making strategy par excellence. However, the assertive general conceptualisation of all systems as analogically dissipative is much more foundationalist and universal than Mouzelis might wish. We will return to this issue of analogy in a moment. For now, let us see what complexity/chaos has to say to Mouzelis' explicit and implicit questions.

Let us deal with them in the order 3–1–2. The adequacy of the dissipative systems account for handling the issue of discontinuous general systemic change has already been dealt with, following Reed and Harvey (1992, 1996), Harvey and Reed (1994) and Prigogine and Stengers (1984), in Chapter 1. What we have is exactly a theory which describes discontinuous general systemic change, precisely by distinguishing between close to equilibrium homeostatic systems of the kind which informed Parsons' formulation, and far from equilibrium dissipative and evolutionary systems. Change is no problem here.

The way in which we can use chaos/complexity as a framework for understanding micro/macro inter-relationships requires somewhat more elaboration. Here Mouzelis gives us a good kicking-off point in his criticism of the inadequacy of rational choice theory:

> rational choice theory tends to link micro with macro levels of analysis via logico-deductive methods that result in the neglect of 'emergent' phenomena and/or the various socio-historical contexts within which rationality takes its specific forms. In that sense it comes up against the following dilemma: in so far as its mainly logico-deductive theorising refuses to take into account 'emergence', history and context its statements (like all transhistorical, universalistic statements) tend to be either wrong or trivial. On the other hand, when rational-choice theory does seriously consider institutional context, it loses its distinctive profile and its logico-deductive elegance.
>
> (Mouzelis 1995: 5–6)

Chaos/complexity's capacity for handling issues of micro/macro inter-relationships lies exactly in its central concern with emergent order. The problem that rational choice theory (and any 'market'-founded social theory) faces, is that the best it can come up with as an account of the foundation of social action is the aggregation of individual actions in an additive/linear way. The technical foundations of modern economics lie exactly in the development of linear and integrable mathematical models which are asserted (not demonstrated, asserted) to be isomorphic with significant social reality. This provides no basis whatsoever for collective social actors whose character is not reducible to the sum of the entities constituting them. In statistics this is the general problem not just of hierarchically ordered data sets, but of a reality which is itself hierarchically ordered, and we will come back to this formulation of the issue in Chapters 3 and 4.

The point can be illustrated by reference to that simplest of social collectivities, the household. There are aspects of the household which can be understood in terms of the additive sum of its individual constituents – expenditure is the most obvious. There are other aspects, of great social significance, which cannot be so understood but where we have to think of the household as an emergent and historically contextualised system, composed of more than the sum of the individual social atoms who make it up. A good example is provided by the very important problem of assigning some operationalised version of 'social class' to a household and to its members. This has generally been done by using the occupation of the 'head' of the household understood as the male 'breadwinner'. The obsolescence of those terms illustrates the nature of the problem. If we take any Weberian conception of social hierarchy, we might consider that we could assign market-related class of a household on the basis of the compound sum of material resources available to it from individual income contributions and the composition of individual and collective wealth. However, we could not do this with status. Here we would have to deal with a complex and interactive set of factors, which would include the character of the relationships among household members and especially the socio-legal connections of adults to adults and adults to children. The single parent-headed household, the cohabitee-founded household and the 'married couple' represent three different forms with quite different implications, notably in terms of inherent stability as entities. The necessity for interaction terms in any quantitative model shows the existence of emergent properties.

This is not a problem if emergent properties are permitted. The essentially holistic conception of chaos/complexity descriptions of nested systems facilitates exactly this kind of account of micro/macro relations, which is of course extensible both to more complex levels (e.g. aggregations of households in space to constitute distinctive neighbourhoods – see my refutation of the conception that such an approach involves an ecological fallacy, in Byrne 1995a), and to other emergent complex formations. A good example of the latter is provided by the school where emergent properties are again the product of complex and essentially social interactions.

Newman has put this point well in general terms:

> Causal theories of emergence suggest that emergent properties are properties of structured wholes which have causal influence over the constituents of the whole . . . suggesting that one of the emergent properties that a system can have is the power to exert causal influence on the components of a system in a way that is consistent with, but different from, the causal influences that these components exert upon each other.
>
> (Newman 1996: 248)

If we turn to the relationships between agency and structure, conceived of in complex terms, then we need to have recourse to consciousness and reflexivity, to Elias' fifth dimension. Reed and Harvey comment:

> The questions of agency raised by the symbolic production of
> humans is quite another matter [from external perturbation],
> for in human societies we confront the possibility that the locus
> of perturbations in certain instances may be internal to society
> itself. As Nicolis and Prigogine (1989: 238) have suggested,
> human systems differ radically from nature on this point. In
> social systems, perturbations of far-from-equilibrium condi-
> tions can originate in the values and actions of humans
> themselves.
>
> (Reed and Harvey 1992: 370)

Again, this is best illustrated by example. Let me take one which is
central to the subject of social policy which I teach – the issue of the
emergence of 'welfare states' and the particular example of the British
welfare state as it was put together in the period 1945–50. If we look at
the form of the social structures of welfare which were created in that
period we can see the considerable extent to which they reflected the
character of pre-existing systems and the limits of the social and
economic context. What had gone before mattered. The general
economic and historical context mattered. However, there were crucial
demarcating differences between the system created post-war and its
precursors. There was a non-linear transformation of kind. This was
essentially value-driven and the product of collective actions. Hennessy
entitled his outstanding discussion of this period *Never Again* (1993). *Never
Again* is a statement of historically contextualised values. In the period
of reconstruction after a total war, the majority of the British electorate
(Labour and Liberal voters both voted for this sort of programme)
recognised that through an act, the way they cast their vote, they could
determine the kind of post-war society which would be created. It was
by no means inevitable that this would be the kind of welfare-oriented
system which was actually established. Barnett's *Audit of War* (1986)
argues that the wrong choice was made and that the prioritising of
economic development with a much more residual welfare function
would have led to a 'stronger Britain' in the post-war period. We may
well regard this as elitist tripe but the Conservative programme was
oriented in this direction.

Perhaps an electorate in general and one component of it in particular has never been so well informed about the nature of the choice
facing it. The British Armed Forces had available a programme of
education in the prospects of peace (debates and adult educational
classes were a far more acceptable way of occupying the enormous
amount of down time of a modern army than drink and whoring,

particularly acceptable to the decent and moderate generation who composed those troops: see Fraser 1992) and they made their choice voting against their war leader in the ratio of 9:1. That was George Bailey to the power of six million.

Social history at any scale is full of agency, of agency at any scale. At the moment we can see in the enormous individual agency of Rupert Murdoch an excellent illustration of the importance of Mouzelis' absolute insistence on the significance of mega-actors, 'individual actors in control of considerable resources whose decisions stretch widely in space and time' (1995: 16). The Murdoch empire is founded precisely on the capacity of Murdoch for recognising the key bifurcation points in terms of the inter-relationship between technology and communications systems, and achieving dominance, the attractor in which his companies control the media channels, through very direct actions in relation to political systems.

Conclusion

Chaos/complexity is of course inherently systemic. What is crucially important about it is that it is systemic without being conservative. On the contrary, the dynamics of complex systems are inherently dynamic and transformational. At the same time, even in its weaker retrospective form, it is foundationalist in that it does provide a basis for single knowledge claims. Of course it allows that there is a social element in scientific practice. Gould's *Wonderful Life* (1991) precisely locates the original interpretation put on the Burgess Shale fossils in relation to the socio-cultural milieu in which that interpretation was made. However, Gould does not fall into the postmodernist trap of saying that to recognise the social context is to relativise all knowledge. He regards contemporary interpretations as more closely aligned with the actual real natural world. There is a privileged truth, and that is to be established through empirical investigation.

At the same time, as Reed and Harvey demonstrate (1992: 370), chaos/complexity shares critical realism's insistence on the emergent material character of understanding in particular and social action in general. This means that it not only serves as a basis for demarcating the distinctive character of the social as an object of knowledge, but also allows for the reflexive, knowledge informed, reconstitution of the social order.

The next two chapters of this book will be concerned with the conceptual and practical possibilities of the quantitative programme in social science, as a basis for knowing the complex. Before proceeding to them there remains one issue which needs discussion here. That is the nature of analogy as understood in relation to dissipative, evolutionary systems. This term has to be distinguished very carefully from that of metaphor. Khalil (1996: 4–7) discusses the different forms of metaphor precisely in relation to this issue. He speaks of superficial (equivalent to simile), heterologous (or analogous), homologous and unificational. It is the last three types which concern us here. Khalil defines them thus:

> Heterologous likeness denotes a similarity arising from the resemblance of *analytical functions* [original emphasis], when the respective contexts are different. In contrast, homologous likeness designates a similarity emanating from the resemblance of *contexts* [original emphasis] even when, although it is not usually the case, the analytical functions are different. . . . The unificational metaphor expresses similarities when they arise from the same law.
>
> (Khalil 1996: 5–6)

The idea of analogy as it will be used in this book combines elements of the heterologous and unificational. It is heterologous because it describes similarity of function. It is not homologous because there is not necessary relationship of context. There is a unificational element, although not one that can be expressed in terms of a simple universal law. Rather the unificational element is the self-similarity of dissipative systems at whatever scale. A dissipative system is a dissipative system is a dissipative system, whether it is a cell, an organism or a city. This is not a statement of reductionism, nor is it a statement of the general applicability of a predictive law. There is no predictive covering rule here. Rather, the homologous character of dissipative systems – their generally similar propensities, possibilities, ways of becoming rather than being – reflects their character as both limit-bounded and limit-testing systems. In this context the operation of the Feigenbaum series does not represent a law but rather a universal. The controlling parameters are not bound to change by the necessary orders, but if they do, then the chain of bifurcations does occur. Cohen and Stewart describe this as 'a meta-law, a law about laws, a common pattern shared by an entire class of rules' (1995: 266).

Again, an example is necessary. There is a very obvious one to hand – that of a biological ecological system and a city considered as a system of neighbourhoods (see Byrne 1997a for a development of this). Note very carefully that the complex account of a biological ecology is not to be equated with the Spencerean crude and reductionist

52

Darwinism which underlay classical Chicago School urban ecology. Remember also that the periodicity of cycles in a city is constructed from a socially grounded time, whereas a simple natural ecology may even operate on an annual cycle, although ecologies too may have a non-Newtonian temporality. The point is that both an ecological system and a city system will change in ways which show the development of bifurcations if key controlling parameters are changed by the appropriate ratio. Both change in non-linear ways. Neighbourhoods 'flip' in terms of key descriptors, for example of order/criminality, if key order-maintaining parameters are changed. Ecologies flip in terms of species content if key resource inputs are transformed. The two systems work in the same sort of way because they are the same sort of system. They are far from equilibric dissipative systems. That is the meaning of analogy here.

3

COMPLEXITY AND THE QUANTITATIVE PROGRAMME IN SOCIAL SCIENCE

It is very striking that the classic technique developed in response to the impossibility of understanding contemporary society from experience, the statistical mode of analysis, had its precise origins within the period [early nineteenth century] of which you are speaking. For without the combination of statistical theory, which in a sense was already mathematically present,[1] and arrangements for the collection of statistical data, symbolised by the founding of the Manchester Statistical Society, the society that was emerging out of the industrial revolution was literally unknowable.

(Williams 1979: 170)

Introduction

The programme of chaos/complexity in science is clearly quantitative, although it is intimately linked with the recognition that the dominant form of the quantitative programme in science has limits and has reached those limits. It is necessary to say something about these limits before we go any further. There are three aspects to consider:

1 the limits to formalisation of any mathematical system established by Gödel;
2 the limits to capacity of measurement central to deterministic chaos; and
3 the working limits for the expression of mathematical formalism derived from the non-linearity of the real systems with which chaos/complexity is concerned.

We surely have a quantitative programme here, but equally surely that quantitative programme has uncertainty writ three times at its very

54

core. This is crucial and the development of the implications of this statement will form a large part of this chapter, but here it simply has to be said before we go on.[2]

Nonetheless chaos/complexity involves both quantitative measurement and the development of mathematically formalised accounts of reality based on those measurements – the twin essentials of any quantitative programme of scientific understanding. Quantitative work is clearly privileged in discussions of the application of chaos/complexity to any substantive area of science. Rumour has it that sociology is excluded from the Santa Fe Institute because it has no coherent quantitative programme. It is quite usual to encounter statements of the kind represented by Kiel and Elliott's remarks[3] to the effect that:

> The obvious metaphorical value of applying a theory of chaos to the social realm has served as an impetus for the emergence of the application of this theory to social phenomena. Yet chaos theory is founded on the mathematics of non-linear systems. Thus social scientists, in the efforts to match the mathematical rigour of the natural sciences, are increasingly applying this mathematics to a variety of social phenomena. Time-series analysis is essential to these efforts, as researchers strive to examine how non-linear and chaotic behaviour occurs and changes over time. . . . Economists and political scientists have applied chaos theory with considerable methodological rigor and success to the temporal dynamics of a variety of phenomena in their fields. Chaos theory has also been applied to sociology. In this field, however, more than in economics and political science, such efforts have tended towards metaphorical and postmodernist or poststructuralist usages. . . . Thus, while this volume does not include rigorous mathematical assessments of chaotic dynamics in the subject matter of sociology, the applications in political science and economics should serve as foundations for the development of such research in sociology.
>
> (Kiel and Elliott 1996: 2–3)

The purpose of this chapter is to suggest how we might conceptualise a chaos/complexity-founded quantitative programme in sociology. It will continue the already established motif of rejection of any kind of physics envy, by arguing first that central to any such project is the development of a coherent understanding of how we measure what is going on in the world, and second, that the quantitative methods through which we might do this are not necessarily those applied in physics, although they certainly will have to pay attention to changes through time. Indeed the actual superiority of the sociological programme in relation to the first of these elements needs stating clearly. Not only does sociology understand the social nature of the measurement process, but it has available a method which when understood for what it is and not regarded as some quasi or ersatz form of experiment, is actually capable of dealing with complex co-variation in reality and can relatively easily be extended to deal with such complex co-variation over time. That method is the social survey, and in particular those surveys which are longitudinal in form.

This chapter will be organised as follows. It will begin with a discussion of the general inductive problems for any quantitative programme which are related to the measurement uncertainty in chaotic/complex systems, and of the surprisingly similar deductive problems of any kind of mathematical formalism in the aftermath of Gödel's work. These come together, at least in principle, in the difficulties encountered in developing any but the most trivial of formal mechanisms for the solution of non-linear equations, the actual illustration not only of the limitations of Newton's mechanistic model of reality, but also of the adequacy of the differential calculus which he developed as a way of describing that reality. We will need to consider the implications of natural sciences' quantitative programme's turn to a strange mixture of brute computing force and qualitative[4] description as a way of handling accounts of non-linear systems.

The next section of the chapter will take the form of a re-examination of the quantitative programme in sociology from a chaos/complexity perspective. We will not attempt to fit sociological research into the methods used in the natural sciences, or rather more precisely in physics, physical chemistry and biochemistry. Rather the actual quantitative method of sociology, the social survey, will be considered in chaos/complexity terms.[5] This consideration will be methodological rather than method centred. It will attempt to explain what social surveys are actually doing and how they might serve as the basis of a causal account founded in an understanding of the nature of a social system which is subject to deterministic chaos.

The word 'system' is very important here. Far too often attempts at the development of a quantitatively founded causal account in sociology have really been relatively trivial models of the determinants of outcome for individuals or other entities within a social system. What is required is a return to the concern with the nature of the social system as a whole, the actual focus of the social statistics movement as it was originally conceived. This point may appear simple when baldly presented, but is absolutely fundamental in explaining the actual limitations of quantitative sociology as a project thus far. It will be elaborated with particular reference to the possible use of system descriptive secondary data sources.

It is important to establish a distinction between the content of this chapter and Chapter 4. Here the emphasis will be on a methodological justification of a complexity-founded quantitative programme in sociology. In Chapter 4 there will be a presentation of actual methods of quantitative analysis which might form the basis of such a programme.

The last element in this chapter will take up and generalise the question asked by Marsh in her seminal book on social surveys (Marsh 1982). Can any quantitative programme in sociology get beyond adequacy at the level of cause[6] and grapple with adequacy at the level of meaning? This is particularly important, not only because interpretative explanation is essential for any scientific account of the social, but because of the inter-relationship between meaning and reflexive social action founded in knowledge of the potentialities of the world – the basis of the programme of social intervention derived from the account of robust chaos presented in Chapters 1 and 2.

Mathematics as analogy

> Mathematical descriptions of nature are not fundamental truths about the world, but models. There are good models and bad models and indifferent models, and what model you use depends on the purposes for which you use it and the range of phenomena which you want to understand . . . reductionist rhetoric . . . claims a degree of correspondence between deep underlying rules and reality that is never justified by any actual calculation or experiment.
>
> (Cohen and Stewart 1995: 410)

> Mathematics is also seen by many as an analogy. But it is implicitly assumed to be the analogy which never breaks down.
>
> (Barrow 1992: 21)

The quantitative programme in any science has two forms. The first, simplest, and often best is the use of numbers to describe what is real. Even this simple descriptive programme has its very real problems. In particular it must always confront the issue of whether or not what is being measured is in any way really a measure of what is being thought to be measured. This is the fundamental problem of the validity of

57

operationalisations,[7] the issue of whether the way in which we describe some variable in terms of the procedure used to measure it does correspond to the actual concept we have generated on the one hand, and an aspect of reality on the other – the two-fold problem of reification and adequacy of measurement.[8] It is often asserted that we always measure by fiat,[9] by a simple declaration that we are measuring what we think we are measuring. These issues are important but we will not attempt to resolve them here. Instead, with a clear and absolute endorsement of the social character of the measurement process in terms of its 'emergent realism' (i.e. the view that measures are social constructs but are made out of something real rather than being reifications without any necessary correspondence with reality) having been declared, let us proceed to the next step – that of using formalised mathematical models to stand as accounts of causal processes in reality – the move beyond description to explanation.

There is one other aspect of the quantitative programme which we have to get out of the way before we can proceed with that discussion. Much of the application of statistical reasoning to the social world is concerned with problems of statistical inference, with attaching probability statements to things which are derived from samples. This can be distinguished from exploratory descriptive work by referring to it as involving a process of confirmation. Such confirmation is very important, but it is not the basis of quantitative causal reasoning in science. What it does is provide a way of handling the issues which arise when we want to say something about a whole (universe, population) on the basis of information about part of it (a sample). The measures that we have from the sample may be representative of the world or they may differ from the world because we have a sample which is not like the world from which it is drawn. The point about statistical inference is that it quantifies the likelihood that such 'sampling' Type I or Alpha errors have arisen.[10] Significance tests function as a way of deciding whether to accept or reject the sample's version of the world, but they are not in themselves an account of the world. This division is not as sharp in practice as it is conceptually. Not only must we always test for significance with any elements of a model which are sample derived, but analyses of contingency tables do often proceed by the use of significance measures. Nonetheless, inference is not about causality.[11]

At the level of description we simply attach the properties of a number (and the extent to which we attach those properties indicates the level at which we are measuring) to a case as that case's score on that variable. The next stage in the process of quantification is the actual formalising of a model of the world so that not only are the variables as measured considered to be valid quantitative descriptions of aspects of the world, but we can also describe the causal relationships among variables. Pure mathematics can be considered as consisting of a set of uninterpreted axiomatic systems[12] in which rules describe the relationships among abstract entities. When such a system is interpreted, when we consider that the entities correspond to something real and that the rules describe the relationships among the real things, then we have an interpreted axiomatic system – a mathematically formalised causal account of what reality is like. The pure example of such a formalised system is provided exactly by Newtonian mechanics. The point about such a description is that in principle it provides the basis for exact description forwards – for prediction. If we know the relevant things about an element in a mechanical system in terms of initial position, velocity and forces acting upon it, then we can predict exactly where it will be after a given time. Moreover, this runs in reverse. We can say exactly how things were backwards. There is no arrow of time.

The problem that the reality of chaos causes for such prediction has already been mentioned but bears repetition. If we cannot measure precisely enough in terms of initial conditions, then in any system which is non-linear our capacity to predict very rapidly breaks down. This is an inductive problem. Poincaré put it like this: 'A very small cause which escapes us, determines a considerable effect which we cannot ignore, and then we say that this effect is due to chance' (quoted in Ruelle 1991: 48).

It is clear that the existence of chaos means that the capacity of mathematical formalisation breaks down in practice. The way in which this is expressed is very interesting. Very few non-linear equations describing non-linear systems can be made to integrate. In other words, in contrast to descriptions of linear systems in which Newton's method of differentiation, in essence a way of specifying a momentary state of the system, can be reversed through integration to produce an account of the system's effects over all time, in non-linear systems such re-integration is not possible. The whole contains things which are not deducible from a description of any part of it. There is interaction. Superposition does not hold.

That is extremely important. What is even more interesting is that there is an analogue of this inductive adequacy in the formal processes of mathematical reasoning themselves, and that this analogue and the implications of real chaos do come together in terms of modern mathematical conceptions of processes of appropriate reasoning. This of course is Gödel's demonstration of the impossibility of a self-validating mathematical system. To quote Barrow's description of it as somewhat further developed:

> The upshot of this discovery is that logical and mathematical systems rich enough to contain arithmetic are not only formally incomplete, in the sense that some of their truths are unprovable using the paraphernalia of the system, but they are also semantically incomplete, in the sense that some of their concepts cannot be defined using the language and concepts within the system. One can always define them using a bigger system, but only at the expense of creating further undefinable concepts within the larger system. This means that there is no formal system in which the truth of all mathematical statements could be decided, or in which all mathematical concepts could be defined.
>
> (Barrow 1992: 125)

The significance of this is not that mathematics as we use it becomes uncertain, but that the ultimate project of mathematical description cannot turn to a logical and universal foundation in mathematics itself. It is another element in the episteme which is fracturing, and along lines which are intuitively closely related to those of chaos. Indeed the relationship is more than intuitive. Developments in considerations of the theoretical foundations of computing in terms of a consideration of the nature of algorithms and complexity of numbers have led to the identification of:

> a fascinating connection between the inability to predict *in practice* which chaos creates, and the inability to determine the solution of a problem *in principle* [original emphases] which Gödel undecidability forces us to contemplate. For it can be shown that there is no general algorithmic criterion which would enable us to determine whether any given system is chaotically random or not. Moreover, a whole host of related questions ... are in general undecidable. This is not the case for all chaotic systems, just as there are a host of statements about arithmetic which are decidable, but one cannot generate a catalogue of the ones about which there is decidability.
>
> (Barrow 1992: 241)

It is the actual breakdown of the linear model which matters for us when developing a quantitative account but the epistemic resonance is of profound significance. Before we turn to a methodological discussion of actual research programmes we must remind ourselves of what a linear law looks like. In general the model is that of mechanics. We attempt to determine a rule, expressed in terms of a mathematical equation or set of equations, which enables us to predict a future state of something given its present state and the effect of changes in the values of variables representing causal factors which affect the future state of that thing. A particularly interesting example is provided by epidemiological models because they do attempt to describe a characteristic of a whole social system rather than of elements in that system when they attempt to predict the incidence and prevalence of a disease in a population given knowledge about the original number of infective cases (I), infected but not yet infective (E), susceptibles (S) and recovered and immune (R), the SEIR model.[13] Linear solutions can work quite well but they break down when the exposure is a necessary but not sufficient cause for the development of the clinical symptoms; when there are complex and non-linear factors which may render exposure contingent. The obvious, historical and probably futurological example, is tuberculosis. The prevalence and incidence of tuberculosis changed in consequence of changes in the social system which were non-linear in terms of their impact.

Attempts through the development of regression methods to establish social laws analogous to the laws of mechanics have all collapsed. What is interesting is that so has the linear programme in areas of science where it was well established but it now cannot handle the problems of symmetry breaking and non-linear transformations. There have been two responses to this – brute force and what Reed and Harvey (1996: 309) call 'iconographic modelling'. Although Reed and Harvey associate this with the development of graphic computing packages, and the availability of such packages has certainly made such pictorial representation much easier, particularly in dynamic terms, Poincaré actually developed an approach in the form of the Poincaré map early in this century. Nicolis (1995: Chapter 7) includes a fascinating discussion of the movement between qualitative and iconographic presentation and attempts at mathematical formalising in a fully quantitative fashion. What matters is that only by a qualitative establishment of the nature of the local domain of bifurcation, can any quantitative description be developed. Reed and Harvey remark that 'the *gaze* [original emphasis] is more important than deductive logic in grasping the evolution of a chaotic structure' (1996: 310) but what really seems to be happening is that the gaze is an essential precursor of the local quantitative description of such evolution. Applications of mathematics are being forced back into description as a

61

precursor to algebraic reasoning. Stamp-collecting gets written into the heart of physics.

Brute force solutions consist in throwing computing power at a problem and attempting to generate a resolution. There are two classes of such approach which are of current interest to social scientists. One is simulation in which systems are modelled in abstraction and then driven onwards through time to see what happens. This approach has potential. Indeed its very development indicates the possibility of a new non-experimental 'emergent' science of prediction, precisely because such approaches allow for emergent properties in general and 'sociality' in particular (see Gilbert and Doran 1994; Gilbert and Conte 1995; Lam and Naroditsky 1992; Crutchfield 1992 and Byrne 1997c for further discussions of this).

The other approach is 'statistical modelling' which involves seeing what mathematical form will actually 'fit' available historical and time-ordered (longitudinal) data sets. One possible implication of the general chaos/complexity programme is that such historical reconstruction is possible but that it cannot serve as the basis of prediction. We may be quite certain about what has happened but we cannot say what will happen – the essence of Gould's position as discussed in Chapter 2. Such longitudinal models are important and we will consider them after a discussion of the social survey method which generates the data with which they deal. However, there is one aspect of them which we should consider here. This relates to Pearson's development of the notion of underlying continuity as a way of handling the reality of categorical variables in the world.

Categories are very important in the social and biological sciences. They represent breakdowns of linearity in and of themselves. A good biological example is provided by two UK species of gulls – the herring gull and the lesser black backed gull. The usual demarcation in biology of a species involves anatomical difference and non-interbreeding. The interesting thing about these two species is that they represent the points of a kind of torc or incomplete circle. There is a circumpolar distribution of largish gulls which differ slightly as you go west or east but where there is interbreeding at the boundary all the way round the circle until you get to the gap in the torc where the herring and lesser black backed gulls meet up and do not interbreed. Small quantitative differences have accumulated to produce a qualitative change. This is a discontinuity not expressible in linear terms.

MacKenzie (1979) shows very clearly how Karl Pearson, the founder of regression analysis, could not cope with this and had to invent a Platonic notion of underlying causal propensities which were continuous but which were manifest in the world as attributes – the tetrachoric method. This was necessary to get around the problem of qualitative and simply genetically determined inherited characteristics such as eye colour. Mathematics, which depends on underlying continuity, is not easily isomorphic with qualitative distinctions. Stamp-collecting rules, OK. Much of what interests us in the social sciences is best expressed mathematically at a simple nominal level – in terms of categories. It is true that we can develop linear models in which categorical properties can be handled but when we do this we continually find that we have to deal with interactions. Nicolis describes this as it is encountered in the physical sciences:

> A striking difference between linear and nonlinear laws is whether the property of superposition holds or breaks down. In a linear system the ultimate effect of the combined action of two different causes is merely the superposition of the effects of each cause taken individually. But in a nonlinear system adding two elementary actions to one another can induce dramatic new effects reflecting the onset of cooperativity between the constituent elements. This can give rise to unexpected structures and events whose properties can be quite different from those of the underlying elementary laws, in the form of abrupt transitions, a multiplicity of states, pattern formation, or an irregularly markedly unpredictable evolution of space and time referred to as deterministic chaos. Nonlinear science, is, therefore, the science of evolution and complexity.
>
> (Nicolis 1995: 1–2)

This is a description of interaction – of multiplicative relationships between variables rather than simple additive relationships, and of possible higher order interactions among variables, lower order interaction terms and higher order interaction terms. Sure the general linear model can incorporate interaction terms but the interactions often become the model. It should be noted how resonant the idea of interaction/non-superposition is with critical realism's conception of complex and contingent causation. To develop this argument further we need to turn to the actual way in which quantitative social science is done.

Why surveys are much better than experiments

The essence of the experiment is that it attempts to 'wring truth from nature'[14] through a process, ideally, of physical control of the world, by holding all constant other than a supposed cause which is caused to vary, and the effect of that cause. The essence of the notion of causality in the experiment is that causes are single and that there is a constant conjunction, in Galileo's sense, between causes and their effects. Of course this degree of actual control over nature is impossible outside the special conditions of the laboratory, and limited even there once the experimenter is dealing with any reasonably complex system. To handle this there have been developed a range of statistically-founded experimental designs in which randomisation of treatment is used as a method of controlling (or supposedly controlling) extraneous variation. The commonest example of that sort of approach is provided by the kind of analysis of variance-based models which underpins the present fashion for evidence-based medicine.

Such approaches work only if nature is both simple and unconscious. The requirement for unconsciousness refers to the difficulties posed for any experiments involving human beings by their human capacity to understand what is going on, attach meanings to it, and act according to their own purposes and meanings. The administration of placebos in clinical trials of drugs is the tribute reductionist simple linear science pays to the reflexive capacities of human beings. The reality of human agency and its creative capacity is the basis of the social constructionist metatheoretical project in sociology. The ontological premise of this project is that the social world has a different kind of causal nexus from the physical world (see MacIver 1942) because it is socially constructed, and that it must, therefore, be understood through a different epistemological and methodological programme emphasising, after Weber, the interpretative understanding of human action.

The critical realist metatheoretical programme which informs this text certainly recognises the reality of social construction – in Bhaskar's words it is 'emergent realist' – but it insists on the reality of the real and on the significance for the character of the real in relation to human actions. The problem it poses for a quantitative programme founded on the experimental method is that it argues against simple cause based on constant conjunction, and is concerned instead with complex and contingent causes. It is precisely for this reason that Reed and Harvey have, sensibly, seized on it as a philosophical ontology to correspond to the scientific ontology of chaos/complexity. It is this correspondence between the scientific and philosophical ontologies which is so threatening for experimentalism.

By its own criteria experimentalism only works when the world is linear and when causes are simple and single. It is true that interaction can be identified in more complicated developments of analysis of variance, but when it is, arguments that the accounts developed from the experiment can be used as the basis of prediction seem singularly specious. Certainly there can be valid historical statistical modelling. We can formalise what has happened. However, once linearity breaks down, it seems hard to say that we can formalise what will happen in the future. It is in the nature of interaction that superposition is not possible. We can specify the resultant form of past interaction effects, but we are being bold if we say that they will always take the same form in the future with other values of the interacting variables. Hellevik sums this up in a pertinent way:

> When interpreting the results of a causal analysis, interaction means that the overall effects are dependent not only on the strength of each partial effect, but also on the particular composition of the population under investigation, with regard to the multivariate distribution on the independent variables. If the composition is changed, the weights will change too, and this in turn may affect the weighted average even if all partial effects remain constant. This means that the overall effects cannot be presented as general 'causal laws', but as effects restricted in time and space to the particular population which is being analysed.
>
> (Hellevik 1984: 148)

It seems to me as if interaction provides a kind of road to fully developed emergent properties/symmetry breaking. If we do have emergent properties then the whole logic of the experimental method falls. There is a limited set of domains of social life where there is neither the potential for hostile and challenging human consciousness (no Hawthorn effects) nor non-linearity. These instances are not trivial but neither are they general. Even in the interaction between the social and the natural, for example in the development of health interventions, the really interesting and important innovations have been symmetry breaking and not experimentally founded.[15] Einstein once described the experiment as the nail that holds together science and reality. If it is so limited in its application do we have a quantitative method which does allow us to deal with messy, complex, symmetry breaking, contingent reality as it is? We do. It is the social survey.

Marsh (1982) made the most recent serious attempt to identify what social surveys actually are. She pointed out that they deal not with abstractions from reality, as is the case with any experiment, but with reality as it actually is. In other words they deal with complex co-variation as it operates in the real world. The central idea she used to express this was the notion that the surveys generate a case/variable matrix, i.e. a table in which the rows are cases, the columns are variables and the cells formed by the intersection of rows and columns contain either the value of that variable for that case or a missing data code. When this account is taken together with Bateson's seminal discussion of the social nature of the survey (1984) and the way in which the data is constructed as numbers from the real knowledge of the world held by respondents as information in the natural language of everyday life, then the non-positivist character of the enterprise can be seen for what it is.

Marsh specifically identified social surveys as inherently realist, and pointed out that they could successfully identify interactions and deal with them, not as awkward aberrations but as characteristic of the complex and contingent way in which the world worked. However, she was troubled, in the sense that she wrote a chapter dealing with the issue, as to whether social surveys could be adequate at the level of cause. For her the causal adequacy of the experiment arose because the experimenter introduced the variation into the experiment herself – control was the basis of specification of cause. In the survey the absence of control was exacerbated by the often literally coincidental measurement of variation. Things happened at the same time instead of in temporal sequence and time could not be used to order causes and effects.

The second problem is substantial and directs us towards longitudinally ordered survey generated data sets, but the first is in many ways trivial. Essentially what statisticians call 'the fallacy of affirming the consequent', and Popper identified as the logical problem of verification, means that no experiment can claim a deductive basis for the knowledge claims that derive from it. Experiments no less than surveys must turn to explicit theories as the basis of the construction of models of how the world is working. That form of words – how the world is working – was very deliberately chosen instead of the alternative of 'how the world works'. The latter suggests the possibility of universal and always existing fundamental laws. The former specifies the local and temporally specific character of causal knowledge. In this context Bhaskar's insistence that the generative mechanisms with which he deals are only 'relatively permanent' is of considerable importance. It resonates very well with the chaos/complexity programme and has been developed in interesting ways in relation to spatial debates (see Chapter 5).

Marsh's way of resolving the problem of 'adequacy at the level of cause' was to turn to explicit theoretical foundation, by a process of using existing knowledge in order to construct and justify the kind of flow-graph representations which were to be checked against the world as the data system described it. This is not a process of hypothesis testing as such. Neither is it the kind of abstracted empiricism which seeks to find the model which 'best fits' a data set. Rather it generates a reflexive process in which the theory serves as a basis for the organisation of the model but the data itself is also used to generate ideas in an exploratory way which are then taken back for further review. Note that this is not the business of repeat verification with different data sets which is necessary in statistical experimentation. Instead it is a reflexive relationship with the world and may well involve further modelling with the same data set.

The issue of time and changes in time is of course central to any consideration of the dynamics of complex social systems. Here it is helpful to consider the recent discussion of *Analyzing Social and Political Change* (Dale and Davies 1994) which has emerged from the UK Economic and Social Research Council's[16] interest in statistical methods of analysing change. This is an interesting and important text which represents a serious attempt at generating a quantitative programme in which temporal change has a central place. However, the title is absolutely misleading, for sociologists at any rate. The general character of the book's contents is well illustrated by this statement of the editors:

> Where individuals are surveyed at successive time points, then it is possible to investigate how individual outcomes or responses are related to the earlier circumstances *of the same individuals* [original emphasis]. This provides the framework for very powerful analyses of the processes experienced by individuals; it enables a model to be constructed which explicitly takes into account the earlier circumstances suspected to have an effect which carries through into later life.
>
> (Dale and Davies 1994: 2)

This is essentially a micro approach using micro data. Not only is there no resolution of the micro/macro issue,[17] there is no real sense of there being such an issue. Compare Dale and Davies' emphasis on the under-standing of causal processes as they affect individuals over time with this passage from Prigogine and Stengers which has already been quoted in Chapter 1.

> The study of the physical processes involving heat entails defining a system, not as in the case of dynamics, by the posi-tion and velocity of its constituents . . . but by a set of macroscopic parameters such as temperature, pressure, volume and so on. In addition, we have to take into account the boundary conditions that describe the relation of the system to its environment.
>
> (Prigogine and Stengers 1984: 105–6)

It is certainly possible to agree with Dale and Davies that: 'longitudinal data are essential if the temporal dependencies in micro-level behaviour are to be investigated in any analysis' (1994: 3), but micro-level behaviour is not the basis on which we can analyse changes in society and politics. We need to understand how the whole system within which the micro-level behaviour occurs is changing. We need descriptions of system characteristics which consist of something more than the mere addition of the properties of the elements which compose the system.

We can take this further by going back to the issue of hierarchies in data. Data is ordered hierarchically because the world does consist of things which contain things and we need to know both about the prop-erties of the things contained and the things containing, and how the one set relates to the other. In other words the hierarchical character of data is real. The relationship between the social order as a whole and its components in terms of individual and/or collective actors is expressed in data terms by the relationship between measures at the level of the actors and measures of the whole social order. Let us take an example drawn from Davies' (1994) discussion of 'How to get from cross-sectional to longitudinal analysis'. This is the substantively interesting and important discussion of the distinction between age effects and cohort effects in relation to patterns of employment by married women. If we have a cross-sectional micro-data set (one in which the measures are for individual cases rather than aggregates of them) then the relating of age of married women to their actual pattern of work compounds age effects and cohort effects. In other words if we find a difference in the employment patterns of married women in their thir-ties and married women in their fifties, we cannot, with cross-sectional data, distinguish between the effects of the twenty-year difference in ages and the effects of belonging to two cohorts separated by twenty years and therefore having had different experiences of labour market engagement over an adult lifetime. We cannot say that in twenty years' time the employment pattern of the 30-year-olds will be the same as that of the 50-year-olds, even in the extremely unlikely event of other things not changing over time. Now the question is, what are we interested in? Micro-data generated models tell us how to establish the present employment status of an individual married woman from an equation into which we can enter the values of the pertinent variables for her. The equation is probabilistically determinant, rather than absolutely determinant, but it remains determinant, although only as a description of historic status. Since we have not established an underlying time-independent law it cannot be used to predict forward.

What we need in order to be able to construct even a 'regressive-predictive'[18] equation is not only the current status of employment of married women in the sample, but also their historic status. We need to know the working pattern of the current 50-year-olds when they were in their thirties. From this we can construct a cohort effect. This is fine, but of course we aren't really interested in 'predicting' the employment status of individual married women. We are not in the business of sociologically constructing a quantified account of their individual historic trajectories. We are really interested in the way in which the domestic circumstances and available employment opportunities for married women in their thirties interacted with the relevant historic form of those relationships to set up a time-ordered systemic history. It is neither the individuals nor the simple aggregation of them which is of interest. It is the containing social system with properties which we can measure at a system level as well as in terms of the aggregate values for individuals. Sometimes the system measure is an aggregate value, but its systemic implication is different from that of any of the individual components which makes it up. The work relations of the women in their fifties, when they were in their thirties, were a product of the nature of the social order of which they were then a part. The cohort effect is simply a way of summarising this general experience. Sociologically, that is what matters.

This can be illustrated even better by a consideration of Wilkinson's work (1996) on the relationship between the pattern of general inequalities in societies and the mortality rates for those societies (standardised for age and gender composition). Wilkinson demonstrates that these two macro properties are related but we need to think about the micro implications. In other words, for individuals in the society, the degree of inequality, a property which can only exist at a macro level, has an effect on the likelihood of their dying. The death rate is simply the aggregate of individual deaths. The degree of inequality is not a property of individual income/wealth but is an emergent property of the relationship among individual incomes and wealth. The degree of social inequality is an extremely important system property, and there is good evidence to suggest that it is an important controlling parameter for social systems in general.

This brings us back to another problem we have already discussed in Chapters 1 and 2 and which we can now consider in principle in quantitative terms. If we follow Harvey and Reed's conception of nested far from equilibric systems, then one possible interpretation is to see the higher level as constituting the phase space for the levels contained within it. This is best expressed in relation to the idea of 'social polarisation'. It does seem (see Byrne 1997a) that much of our contemporary social order is characterised by the existence of two rather distinctive modes of existence – relative affluence and relative poverty, with a squeezing of the middle mass, which middle mass did dominate in the Fordist era.

It is interesting to realise that we do have the kind of systemic data we need to describe changes at this level. We do have aggregate data sets which describe containing systems, usually in terms of systems which have clear spatial boundaries. An illustration of how this can be utilised is provided by a consideration of the example of labour market participation by married women discussed above. If we consider that the labour market participation by the women is a function in part of the labour market characteristics of the localities in which they lived when they were 30, then ideally we need to know something about the characteristics both of the labour market and of the women's employment. We do have data sets which can enable us to relate the one to the other, but there is a problem in the way in which such data is generally treated. The easiest way to handle a hierarchical data set is to write all containing order properties to all contained cases as if they were individual values for those cases. Thus we would write something descriptive of the labour markets at the relevant time to the case whose trajectory we would pursue. The issue is that we are interested in all levels of change.

Conclusion

The materials reviewed in this chapter have several important implications for the quantitative programme in sociology in particular and for social science in general. First, they dismiss the effort at the establishment of general linear laws. Second, we can see that there are limitations to any mathematical formalism and that the implicit Platonism of quantitative science seems to be an impossible objective. Instead we can deal with the specific domains within which local accounts hold good. These domains are neither trivial nor infinite. Establishing local rules matters, but this is not a programme of always and everywhere.

The above remarks apply to all science. What is most interesting for the social sciences is that we can use the dynamic systemic approach of complexity theory as the basis of a different way of understanding our major quantitative investigatory procedure – the social survey. We can come to recognise it, not as an ersatz experiment, but rather as a technique which enables us to understand the changing social world. To do that we must explicitly reject the individualistic fallacy of almost all causal modelling in sociology. What matters is not the individual trajectory of social atoms, but rather the changing characteristics of the complex social order within which those trajectories occur. It must be remembered that individual interactions may constitute the source of changes in the social order itself. We have to understand how the micro is aggregated into something beyond the sum of its parts, to understand the nature of society as constituted by sets of attractors within the range of possible condition spaces, and to understand how changes in controlling variables for the whole system can come to reconstitute the form of that attractor set – to look in other words at real 'social and political change'.

In Chapter 4 we will examine how a rethinking of what a contingency table is, might help us to do exactly that. We will attempt a complex fix on the actual analytical methods of survey analysis. To that we now turn.

4

ANALYSING SOCIAL
COMPLEXITY

Introduction

In this chapter we will consider how to do quantitative work which will
help us to understand the complex social order. Let me make one thing
clear straight away. I am reasonably convinced that the least useful way
to do this is by attempting to import the quantitative methods of chaos
studies in the physical sciences into the social world. There are limited
areas of scientific, if not practical or mercenary significance,[1] where
this has some value, but in general it is not a good idea. Partly this is
because we seldom have enough time points for our measurements for
us usefully to engage in efforts to find order hidden within chaos
(although see McBurnett 1996 and Brown 1996 for examples of work
seeking to do just this). However, this is not the real issue. Rather it is
that in important work dealing with the social world and crucial aspects
of it, whilst we lack time points in relation to noisy data, we do have
very large amounts of information in terms of variable sets which
enable adequate descriptions of the whole social system and of its characteristics as they change over time. In other words, we can describe the
character of the system as a whole and seek to identify what key
changes in controlling variables led to changes in that character. We can
look at the long term transitions involved for both entire social systems
and for important sub-systems.

What we need to do is think about the tools that we have developed
for the analysis of data about the real world collected through survey
methods,[2] in complex terms. Here I am going to discuss three of those
methods: the analysis of contingency tables, cluster analysis and correspondence analysis. We will begin with a discussion of what a
contingency table actually is and examine how we might relate the
micro data derived from surveys to aggregate data describing characteristics of whole social systems. We will then proceed to a review of

cluster analysis, and return to consider how we might interpret advanced approaches to the analyses of contingency tables as part of a complexity programme. Finally, we will consider the potential of correspondence analysis as a social science-founded contribution to graphical methods in complexity.

For reasons only partly to do with space, instructions about how to use computer packages to carry out the sorts of analyses described here, do not form part of this chapter, although in the applied chapters reference will be made to the actual techniques employed in illustrative examples. Everything described here can be done using SPSS and the Advanced Statistics manuals for SPSS explain all the procedures other than correspondence analysis, although that is described in on-line help documentation. It seems to me that it is actually better for people to think about the techniques in relation to the argument rather than being given handout style instructions which can be followed without much recourse to thought on the part of the user.

The true nature of the contingency table

Let us begin by thinking about what a contingency table actually is. Everitt and Dunn define it thus: '*a contingency table*, where a sample of individuals are cross-classified with respect to two or more qualitative variables. The observations are the counts for each cell of the table' (1983: 117).

This is wrong because of the use of the word 'sample'. It is perfectly true that most of the time our data is derived from samples, although that is by no means always the case. However, whilst the requirement that we must use the techniques of statistical inference to handle data derived from samples is important, it has been so over-emphasised that we have forgotten what contingency tables are really about, if we think of them as describing social systems taken as a whole.

Let me illustrate by means of an example. In a study of household form based on data from the Cleveland Social Survey I was particularly interested in households which contained dependent children. This quite large sample survey (1,500 plus households overall) included a great deal of information about household structure and employment relations (see Byrne 1995 for a pre-complexity treatment of this material). I was interested in the relationship among the age of the household head by age category, whether the household was single or double parented, whether the household was 'work rich', 'work average' or 'work poor',[3] the tenure of the household, and the sex and Registrar General's social class of the household head, with the added category of no social class ascribable. This meant that there were six categorical variables.[4] The contingency table constructed was six dimensional. This could be reproduced here but it would take many pages because we would need to elaborate it and present it as a series of two dimensional tables relating, for example, age category to household work possession, for female single parents in Registrar General's Class 1 or 2 (taken together in this study), who were owner-occupiers.

The conventional treatment of a contingency table of this sort would be to try to develop some form of causal analysis in which we would use one of a range of techniques, for example logistic analysis, in order to construct a flowgraph which, with coefficients attached to arrows, would show us the effect of, say, the other variables, in 'causing' the work relation of the household. I am here arguing that to do that is to miss the real point. What we need to do is to think about the contingency table as an n dimensional condition space within which cases are found in certain sub-domains and not in others. If we have the enormous advantage of a time series of cross-sectional studies, which in the Cleveland case we have, then we can see how the form of that phase space changes over time. We can look at the strange attractors as they develop and change.

The best way to see what this means is to think about the commonest statistical procedure used in the analysis of contingency tables, chi-squared. Essentially this is a significance test used in statistical inference to test the null hypothesis of no relationship between two categorical variables. It compares the observed values in the cells of the contingency table with those that would be expected if there was no relationship. In practice chi-squared is widely employed as a scanning device in exploratory work. That is to say it is standard practice in an SPSS run to calculate the chi-squares for two-way tables of substantive interest and only to examine those which display a given (usually 5 per cent) level of statistical significance. Of course this is proper procedure but what is interesting is how often it is done when the tables relate to data which is not sample derived. This is on the face of it egregious ignorance, but in fact it is a use of chi-squared to do something other than support statistical inference. What chi-squared does in the simple two variable case is show which contingencies exist and which do not: it compares full(ish) cells with empty(ish) ones. It shows the condition states which are, and those which are not. In fact it is a weak device for doing this. If sample sizes are absolutely large,[5] differences which are not substantively significant can easily be statistically significant and for this reason we should consider the appropriate contingency coefficient, which gives a measure of the strength of relationship in traditional terms, or the degree to which areas of the possible condition space are empty relative to the degree to which things are concentrated in an attractor condition, in a complexity-founded imagery.

Chi-squared is not extendible beyond the two variable case. That is why complex tables are usually expressed in terms of simple cross-tabulations for defined condition states, for the social class 1 and 2, owner-occupying, female, single parents as above, the process of elaborating a table. The range of possible ways of elaborating a six variable tabulation is very large. It is not simply the fifteen possible two-way tables, but the very much larger number of two-way tables within condition states. What we need to do is to think about what is being elaborated. What we have in reality (an absolutely deliberate use of the phrase – in reality) is a six dimensional space in which the range of possible conditions is represented by the contingency states defined by values on the categorical variables. Let us see the nature of this condition space for the example chosen. In the form in which those variables were measured in the Cleveland study we had the following values.

Sex – two – male; female

Parenthood – two – single; double

Tenure – three – owner-occupier; social housing tenant; other

Work relation – three – work rich; work average; work poor

Social class – five – SC1 and 2; SC3 non-manual; SC3 manual; SC4 and 5; no SC

Age of household head – five – less than 25; 26 to 30; 31 to 40; 41 to 50; 50+

This gives 900 possible contingency states. In the sample there were some 800 households containing dependent children so it should be obvious that not all cells could have any entries. In one instance this is an obvious product of the way in which the variables were defined. No single parent household could be work rich because there would be only one adult in such a household and, given the definition of the variable work connection, the only possible values for such a variable would be work average (one full-time worker) or work poor. However, this is not an artefact of measurement. The impossibility of work rich single parent households is a reality and is socially significant because for most households in contemporary Cleveland relative affluence requires multiple earners. It is because this is impossible for the single parent household that single parent households are likely to be relatively deprived. This is the sociological expression of what in log-linear analysis are called 'structural values' (see Gilbert 1993: 85).

75

What I am suggesting is that we look at the pattern of cells with lots of entries against those with few and from that see what condition states are possible in Cleveland at a given point in time. This is certainly an exploratory procedure, that is to say it is serious as opposed to trivial statistical work from the point of view of substantive social science. In the example given we find some interesting concentrations. The work poor young, whether single or double parents, in the 1990s (time point), are very likely to be social housing tenants. There are few of them in owner-occupation. Likewise the work rich young are more likely to be owner-occupiers. What this expresses of course is the well known residualisation of social housing, although the work possession variable at a single time point is an inadequate measure here. We need some account of work relationship over time for the discrete households.

Because the Cleveland Social Survey was carried out on an annual basis from 1977 to 1995[6] it is possible to construct the condition space specified by the six variables as described above for a series of time points. We can thus examine the changes in condition space form over time for this locality as a whole socio-spatial system. It is obvious that there was a major shift in the composition of the attractor forms in that period. At the beginning social housing tenure was not associated with work poverty. Most very deprived households were female single parent headed. There were relatively few of them. By the end most work poor households (with children) were based on a male/female couple. The absolute numbers of such households had increased dramatically. They predominated among social housing tenants. The new class category of 'no social class assignable' because there was no employment-based occupational record on which to assign it, had become of considerable significance. If we use the vocabulary of social exclusion (see Levitas 1996; Byrne 1997b for a discussion of this), then we find that in the late 1970s the excluded attractor in Cleveland contained a relatively small minority of child containing households, which households were primarily female-headed. By the 1990s this attractor was much larger in terms of proportion of child containing households and contained more two parent households than single parent households. Exclusion had been significantly degendered and massively extended.

The Cleveland Social Survey was essentially a local version of the General Household Survey and early efforts at maintaining a panel of respondents were abandoned under cost pressures. This means that the study allows us to examine the form of the condition space constituted by the social system in that locality, but not to follow the trajectory of individual households within that changing system. For that we need a panel study of the kind represented by the British Household Panel and it is already apparent that the findings of that study are of interest if we think in complex terms (see Byrne 1997b for a very preliminary consideration). We can see how people and households move, and perhaps more importantly don't move, within the condition space of their social order.

The elaboration of high dimensional order cross-tabulations is probably not the best way of actually exploring the arrangement of cases within an overall changing system, although the log-linear approach does offer some interesting possibilities, as we shall see. Such high dimensional tables are easily enough produced in principle in SPSS[7] by the layered table command: variable by variable by variable by variable by variable by variable. That would produce a six dimensional table. However, printing out all possible arrangements and interpreting the results is very laborious and cluster analyses will achieve much the same results very much more easily.

Describing the system as a whole

The materials reviewed above do not constitute an account of the social system in terms of the defining parameters of that system. Rather they describe the elements within the system in relation to location and movement over time. What about the system as a whole? Again the Cleveland study provides an apposite example. We have measures of the state of the whole social system[8] in terms of key descriptive attributes. Let us consider what these general social indicators might represent in terms of the complexity programme. Conventionally we distinguish between micro data which describes individual cases in a study and comes in the form of variable values for those cases – and aggregate data which consists of total counts and averaged values for some larger set, usually defined geographically, which contains numbers of individual cases. We tend to make this distinction in relation to secondary data analysis (see Dale *et al.* 1988) because a great deal of accessible secondary data takes the form of sets giving aggregate values for geographical areas. The most important example in the UK is the small area statistics set derived from the population census. However, when we look at how such measures are employed we find that they are not actually used as simple aggregates. Rather they are, quite properly, used to demarcate the social characteristics of a socially significant space. It may well be that the actual spaces measured, enumeration districts and wards in particular, are not themselves socially significant spaces, but aggregates of them usually are. In other words 'New

Zones'[9] made by aggregating adjacent enumeration districts of the same type[10] do correspond very well to qualitatively established neighbourhoods. The quite conventional use of census defined 'Travel to Work Areas' as an operationalisation of the social geographical concept of locality is another example.

Let us take that 'pre-existing' level as an illustration. It is common to find localities described in terms of the changes in the character of their employment base over time. Such changes are associated with the idea that a combination of relative and absolute shifts in employment from production to services constitutes a process of 'deindustrialisation'. The data which is used to map these shifts is derived from the Census of Employment and is the result of the aggregation of individual employment records, but we do not think of the description as reflecting these individual statuses. Rather the pattern of employment is a property of the locality as a whole.

There is an all too common confusion between these properties of spaces and that special form of the problem of cross level inference known as the ecological fallacy. Ecological fallacies occur when we relate individual properties to individual properties through spatial association rather than direct measurement. The classic example is the interpretation of a correlation between the percentage of the population that is Japanese in Chicago Census Tracts, and the murder rates in those same tracts, as indicating that there is a direct association between Japanese and murderers/murder victims. No such relationship can be assumed because without direct measurement we may have spatial association when no murderer or murderee was Japanese. However, it does matter that the spaces (Zone of Transition in this classic example) contain both immigrants and violent crime. Unemployment rates, tenure patterns, mortality, and so on can be perfectly properly considered as system properties with social significance and social effects.

Wilkinson's (1996) extremely interesting work on the relationship between inequality and mortality has already been cited as significant for complexity interpretations. The idea of inequality generally is one which can only be understood as a system property. An individual case cannot be unequal. It is the relationship among cases which determines the extent of inequality. We can turn back to Bedford Falls and Pottersville here – the first was a civic society with clearly bounded inequalities. George Bailey's actions set those limits. The second was one of extremes of wealth and poverty, because George hadn't been there to do the business. Such differences are system properties. The lives of the townspeople were a function of the character of the place as a whole. What is important here is that since the early nineteenth century advanced industrial societies have had dials in place on their social systems and have recorded changes in these system properties over time. We have the records of the system's parameters and the time-ordered social surveys describe very adequately the position of the system's elements within that parameter determined system condition.

This can be illustrated by reference back to the Cleveland example. We can examine the characteristics of Cleveland as a system of employment by using a crude little device invented by the present author – the time engagement/gender/sector table. What this consists of is a record taken from the dial traces of the time engagement (full- or part-time), gender, and industrial sector of employed workers, together with the gender of unemployed workers,[11] recorded both as percentages of totally economically active workers and as absolute numbers, as recorded through time. The changes in that dial describe the changes in the system as a whole. The changes in the individual situation describe the way in which the social elements can be organised in space in relation to those changes in system form.

The actual statistical methods which can be used to construct such tables are very straightforward. They involve nothing more than the extraction of totals for a time point and the calculation of percentages for that time point. In the UK much of the relevant information can be derived from the NOMIS system[12] which gives detailed labour market and benefit receipt information. If the geographies are reasonably congruent NOMIS style information can be related to social conditions and economic status information derived from the population census. This is particularly easy to do for Travel to Work Areas which are census founded. This kind of approach is crude but it is very far from inaccurate.

It should be noted that working with variables describing the whole system state is in the general tradition of chaos/complexity analysis. We might seek to consider the condition state of a social system as a whole in terms of a set of indices of social integration (another index which can only exist at a whole system level) in relation to measures of inequality and economic engagement. Here we can use time series data to describe whole societies over periods of change and see if the changes are non-linear in form. This topic will be considered further in relation to the discussion of the use of complex approaches in application to urban and health issues.

Cluster analyses as a way of identifying attractors

The general set of numerical taxonomy techniques known popularly as 'cluster analysis' were originally developed by ecological biologists who wanted to extend their taxonomic approach in order to make use of the very large amounts of quantitative information generated by their research. No attempt will be made here to describe the mathematical intricacies of the approach, for which see Everitt (1974) and Everitt and Dunn (1983). Essentially the procedure is used to classify a set of cases into a number of relatively homogeneous subsets in which the members of these subsets are more like each other than they are like the members of other subsets. Unlike discriminant analysis there is no previous knowledge of set characteristics or even of numbers of significant sets which will emerge. The general method being discussed here is agglomerative hierarchical clustering in which all cases are originally treated as separate clusters and then cases are progressively grouped on the basis of some measure of similarity until all cases are in one single big cluster. A crucial element of information given in this agglomeration process is the distance between the most dissimilar elements of the clusters being combined at any given stage. It is useful to graph this out by stage and to regard a significant increase in the slope of the resulting graph as indicating the combination of very different clusters. In practice it makes sense to use a hierarchical procedure to establish which cluster level is of most interest and to use a quick cluster procedure to get a tighter fit of cases to clusters at this level.[13]

Cluster analysis is another example of thinking about cases as located within an n dimensional space. The dimensionality of that space is again equal to the number of the variables used for the clustering procedure. There is a range of methods used for these procedures[14] but all involve some method of calculating distances between clusters at successive steps. All incorporate the differences between cluster values for all n variables used in the clustering procedure and are therefore n dimensional. We could in other words graph the cases out with co-ordinates indicated by their value on n variables in an n dimensional space.

Seen in this way the clusters constitute attractors. There are certain combinations of state which seem to be possible and/or common and others which are impossible (in either the strong sense that they can't exist or the weaker sense that empirically they don't exist) or uncommon. We can visualise the clusters as full parts of the overall possible condition space which also contains empty parts. Sometimes clusters may overlap. That suggests that we are observing a time point when a bifurcation is in process. What is interesting is that the pattern of clusters which exists is not a product of individual case conditions but is determined by variable characteristics of the system as a whole. Moreover, it is both possible and likely that there are a restricted number of system descriptors which determine the form of the pattern – that there are control parameters.[15]

This suggests that simulations may be useful as a way of seeing whether we can move beyond retrospective histories to predictive accounts. We can certainly look at the past as a way of establishing the form of non-linear relations between changes in control parameters and the form of the elements in a condition space, and then seek to run changes forward with different data sets to see what results from changing the value of control parameters in a simulation exercise. The other device available to us is a complex usage of the comparative method. If we have household data sets and general system descriptor data sets for different social systems, with both having been measured over time, then we can examine the way in which changes in internal system structure are related to changes in whole system parameters. Of obvious theoretical interest here are the rates of unemployment and the degree of social inequality. The second of these at least is in principle subject to considerable modification by fiscal, employment and benefit policies. We can see what attractor states are available for societies as a whole, or for smaller systems such as regions or localities.

It should be recognised that when we relate changing system characteristics to the changing pattern of conditions of the elements within those systems, that we are engaged in hierarchical data analysis. This topic has been quite extensively discussed in relation to multi-level modelling, particularly of educational outcomes (see Goldstein 1987; Plewis 1994). The approaches adopted have essentially involved the generation of multi-level causal models in relation to dependent attainment variables. Although this is by no means a trivial exercise, it is not one which deals with social change as such. In other words it suffers from the general individualistic focus of such modelling approaches. What is interesting about it is the way in which it does treat higher level characteristics, for example LEA character or class teacher character, as something which can modify the relationships among individual level variables. This is very close to the notion of interaction. We will examine the relationship between these approaches and chaos/complexity perspectives in education in Chapter 7.

The kind of time-ordered typology generation which we can attempt using cluster analysis is clearly useful for historical reconstruction. However, can it be the basis of any sort of prediction? Clearly the development of predictive accounts is confined to the domain of robust chaos, but are such predictions possible? Let us now turn to procedures for the analyses of multi-dimensional contingency tables to see if they offer any assistance to us in the task of predicting what might be the results of our actions.

Log-linear techniques

Log-linear approaches to the analysis of contingency tables are of particular interest here, given the specification of the nature of such tables which has been presented above. Gilbert's (1993) general introduction to the topic is both practically useful, and highly suggestive, if read with a chaos/complexity frame of reference. Let us consider what the essential character of the log-linear approach is. It involves, as Gilbert puts it, the comparison of the 'real world' as represented by empirically collected/constructed data, and the 'imaginary world' as represented by values for the same variable set generated by some quantitative model building technique. Gilbert makes an important point about the use of statistical inference in relation to this process:

> the consequence of this more exploratory approach to analysis is that the tests of significance lose their original meaning, and the probabilities they generate cannot be relied on as indicators of the generalizability of the hypotheses being tested.[16] . . . Nonetheless, tests of significance do have an invaluable role in loglinear analysis because they provide the most convenient means of quantifying the comparison of a model table with data.
>
> (Gilbert 1993: 72–3)

The character of log-linear analysis is perhaps best demonstrated by comparing the two extreme models which can be specified for comparison with the actual data set. The first is the 'general mean' model in which cases are equally distributed around the contingency table cells. The second is the saturated model in which all possible single effects, bivariate relationships, and interactions are specified. The proper method of social scientific use of log-linear procedures is to compare theoretically meaningful models, specified to be more parsimonious in terms of specified relations than the fully saturated model, with the real situation, and find which are within statistically significant reach of it using the G2 measure which is closely analogous to chi-squared.

Let us return to the Cleveland Social Survey Household Data set, but now consider this as organised temporally with the addition of system descriptor variables written into the case file which describe the state of Cleveland as a locality at different time points. Let us add just one such variable which will be a description of Cleveland either as having only frictional male unemployment or as having 'reserve army generating male non-employment'. This is a whole locality property but we can write it to every case at the appropriate time point. In 1977 all cases will have frictional unemployment written to them. In 1991 all cases will have 'reserve army generating unemployment' written to them.[17] In other words we are adding a new variable – 'unemployment type' with two values. For the two time periods we now have a description of household characteristics and a system descriptor.

We can pool all the data with a time indicator variable and the system descriptor variable. What is interesting is the kind of model we need to specify to reconstruct a decent approximation to what actually happened in terms of household types. My bet is that this model will include a specification of gender of household head and time period and an interaction term between them, together with the work possession of the household, and that such a parsimonious reconstruction will be adequate. What does this mean? It means that the condition of possible household situations is determined by the unemployment type which characterises the locality as a whole.

Let us generalise from this example. What is being suggested is that the development of flat file[18] data sets includes temporally specific system specifications and the construction of log-linear models to see if these temporally specific system specifications are significant (in the exploratory use of significance measures suggested by Gilbert above) in the specification of good fits to the actual data which describes changes in reality. This approach seems to offer us the possibility of exploring, retrospectively of course, what system changes have produced the changes in social structure. It is quite important to distinguish this from regression based multi-level modelling. In that approach the characteristic (and non-trivial from a policy perspective) problem is to identify the effects of the nature of higher levels such as school or class on the lowest level such as pupil attainment. The task is to establish causality in relation to key single variable. The temporal and hierarchical use of log-linear approaches being suggested above is certainly concerned with causes but it is concerned with the way in which causes in the form of controlling system level parameters determine the character of the whole system rather than with modification of individual variable levels.

It is also important to distinguish this approach to the analysis of multi-way tables from that suggested by Payne *et al.* (1994). They describe their approach, which uses log-linear and logistic procedures, thus:

> Modelling allows us to test whether and how the relationship between variables changes over time. Sometimes we may be interested in whether there is a progressive change in the relationship over time. . . . In other cases time may be viewed as a proxy for underlying social, political or economic factors whose effects on the relationship between the variables are not necessarily monotonic . . . log-linear and logistic models for analyzing multi-way contingency tables can be used to test both types of hypothesis.
>
> (Payne *et al.* 1994: 43)

Of course this is true but it is not all that important. Sociologically there is certainly some interest in, to employ Payne *et al.*'s examples, the possibility of change over time in the relationship between social class and political allegiance, and in the notion that the relationship between employment prospects and qualification levels is different depending on the level of unemployment. However, the focus on 'causation' of specific variables distracts attention from the real character of system level social and political changes. What is constructed by this causal modelling of variable values is pieces of evidence which can then be interpreted and used as part of a general account of changes in the social and political order, but the actual use made of these apparently tight quantitative products is in reality rather unsystematic, precisely because the characteristics of the whole system are ignored. This is almost a classic illustration of the problem identified by Brown when he remarks:

> it is precisely because of the convenience of linear models (because of their mathematical simplicity and the ease with which probabilistic assumptions may be inserted into them) that researchers often depart from isomorphic parallels between social theory and nonlinear algebraic formalisms, leading them into the most dangerous of terrains.
>
> (Brown 1995: 6)

The approach I have suggested does quantify (descriptively) the whole system, and does allow for an exploration of the effect of key social factors on system form. In particular it allows us to handle ideas about social polarisation and social exclusion with the numbers being a good deal closer to the real social reasoning than is the case when the numbers are derived from variable centred causal models.

There is of course much in common between the temporally ordered cluster analyses which I suggested in the previous section, and temporally ordered log-linear approaches which incorporate system descriptor variables. Descriptively I think the cluster analyses have the edge, but the advantage of the log-linear approach is that it allows us to see what system characteristics do make a difference in our capacity to reproduce the character of the actual measured account we have of the world as it changes.

Correspondence analysis – social graphics as a complexity tool

Reference has already been made in Chapter 3 to Reed and Harvey's discussion of iconological modelling. They describe this approach in complexity in the following terms:

> Iconological modelling is rooted in a *pictorial method* [original emphasis], in visual correspondences rather than in deductive reasoning. Iconological modelling is a recent innovation, originating in the iterative mapping of complex systems of equations – such as the nonlinear differential equations that generate the quadratic iterator, or the so-called strange attractors. Iconological mapping arose in large part as a necessary response to the complexity of the patterns generated by the iterative analysis of these equations. Their evolution became so complex so rapidly that they overwhelm human comprehension. Thus, graphical techniques assist the researcher in visually tracing the chaotic trajectories of these iterative systems.
>
> (Reed and Harvey 1996: 309)

Reed and Harvey point out that they have borrowed the term 'iconological' from Panofsky's use of it in *Art History* (1972):

> The uniqueness of the iconological method lies in its ability to recognise how an aesthetic object's phenomenal appearance can communicate all aspects of itself, and the ways in which they express those different aspects. In a real sense Panofsky's aesthetic epistemology parallels the phenomenological and

analytic process the scientist uses when trying to interpret the meanings of the graphic images whose unfolding maps the chaotic evolution of a system.

(Reed and Harvey 1996: 310)

In keeping with the general approach of this text, it seemed worth reviewing the existing tools of quantitative social science to see if there was anything which might work in this iconological sort of way. An obvious possibility is correspondence analysis. Phillips describes this technique thus:

> Correspondence analysis seeks to represent the interrelationships of categories of row and column variables on a two dimensional map. It can be thought of as trying to plot a cloud of data points (the cloud having height, width, thickness) on a single plane to give a reasonable summary of the relationships and variation within them.
>
> (Phillips 1995: 2)

The essential point of the technique is that it produces quantitatively founded qualitative visual representations of relations. Phillips cites the example of the 'Lifestyle and Cultural Consumption' study (Featherstone *et al.* 1994) which was concerned with contributing to 'the discussion about the "postmodern" collapse of cultural barriers' (Phillips 1995: 5). The correspondence map presented is for a single time point based on a single survey. It seems quite proper to incorporate 'time' and 'system descriptor at time' elements into the correspondence analysis approach. At its simplest this would involve comparing a map looking at cultural relations at one time point with cultural relations at another subsequent time point. Indeed, such a temporal dimension would seem to be essential if there is to be any effort at understanding how things have changed, if indeed they have changed at all. This is what Phillips does descriptively when she comments that 'the cultural picture is quite unlike Bourdieu's frame of twenty years ago' (1995: 7). The point is that if we have time-ordered data we can see what the changes are.

The Cleveland study data can certainly be used to generate time differentiated correspondence maps which offer visual representations of the multi-dimensional relationships among household characteristics and the system descriptors at different time points. We might present this as one map with system descriptors and time specification included as variables or present it as two maps for the different time points, although we would certainly want to overlay the maps in the latter case.

There is an important difference between the use of correspondence analysis being suggested here and the usual form of graphic analysis in chaos/complexity work. The latter is inherently dynamic – it comes in the form of moving pictures.[19] The correspondence maps are at best frames in a cinema shot, although given sufficient of them they could be constructed into a filmic representation of dynamic change. More substantively many chaos graphics are in fact equation driven without real data points. They are simulations with abstract original data entries. The correspondence maps are inherently real.

Conclusion

I am always annoyed by superficial and ignorant dismissals of the quantitative possibilities of sociology. Regrettably, many of the dismal chorus are themselves sociologists. Statistics began as a way of using quantity to understand the complexity of social change. Statistical techniques were developed in order to handle the numbers being generated by such descriptions and only entered the 'hard' sciences by way of the life sciences, much later. The pursuit of linear prediction still remains strong in science, for many good and perhaps just as many bad reasons. Even when chaos renders prediction at least awkward, the tendency towards mathematical formalism remains very strong. The approach adopted in this chapter has been quite deliberately and unapologetically to assert that the quantitative methods of social science, founded as they are in efforts to understand a complex and changing reality, can actually – I was going to write be adapted, but on reflection I think it is better to say be understood for what they really are and what they can really do. We need to understand them as social products but as social products developed in a real effort to understand the world. Reality played a part in shaping them and they reflect the nature of that reality.

It seems appropriate to conclude this chapter with some abusive remarks directed at mathematical statisticians and their influence on social statistics. In his preface to *The Path to Rome* Belloc indicated that there were two possible ways in which the illustrations for the text might be obtained. He could either lead an artist on a rope behind him or he could do the pictures himself. The apparent third option that an artist could write a book was beyond the pale of possibility and good taste. Maybe social scientists have been letting the mathematical statisticians write the quantitative books for too long. Their proper place is plainly at the end of the rope but failing that we can draw the pictures ourselves.

At the risk of gilding the lily, let me continue in this vein. There has always seemed to me to be a strong connection between the art and science of navigation and the scientific use of chaos and complexity. Blue water navigation used to be able to proceed, decent seamanship taken for granted, on the basis of general principles, but for a lot of important stuff a pilot was required who knew detailed, changing, local conditions (they still are). Even then, general principles were inherently applied. This relates even more to the relationship between ship construction and ship use. Naval architecture has mathematical foundations. The most generous status I would give mathematical statisticians, and this is very generous because naval architects combine mathematical work with solid empirical evidence and can produce things of great beauty, is that of naval architect. In less generous moments I think of them as overblown slabbies, putting red lead on the bottom of the vessel. Even naval architects don't sail the ships. They have to be properly built but the navigators take them to sea and use them. That is our job.

5

COMPLEX SPACES

Regions, cities and neighbourhoods in a complex world

Introduction

Social science's engagement with 'the spatial' has had an interesting history since the 1970s. The discipline of geography shifted from being primarily descriptive with tendencies towards quantitatively-founded positivist explanation, through a period in which the dominant perspectives derived from Althusserian structuralism and claimed to represent a 'new' critical geography, to one in which postmodernist accounts are now presented as a 'new' 'new' geography founded on the assertion of the impossibility of general accounts of any kind. Geography being geography, none of these schools has ever been abandoned. Positivist number crunching continues unabated and certain spatially-oriented journals are full of it yet. However, the face geography has presented to the other social sciences has, more or less, followed the trajectory described above. It can be summarised in the overlapping careers of David Harvey from positivist law seeker to structuralist 'Marxist', and Doreen Massey's movement from structuralist Marxism to her present endorsement of postmodernist approaches. This matters because geography has profoundly influenced the general approach of social science to space for two decades, not just (rather oddly, perhaps least) in terms of accounts of the nature of social space(s), but by setting the character of theoretical debate.

What is particularly interesting about this is that the shifting debate has changed its use of measurement without ever quite abandoning it. The positivist period saw statistical number crunching, especially in the form of factor analyses, thrown at data in order to generate entities for ordering in causal models. This still goes on, of course. The structuralist, and even the postmodernist, approaches, whilst abandoning causal models, retained the use of quantitative descriptive indices as ways of describing social change and spatial variation in that change.

This was reasonable enough in epistemological terms for the structuralists, but it has to be said that postmodernists who should in principle discount such modernist products as statistical indices, don't half rely on them for the general representation of the world as having changed. Raymond Williams has already told us why that should be in the epigraph to Chapter 3 of this book. There is just no other way of grasping our sort of world in its complexity, even at the level of basic description.

I want to start this chapter by thinking about the measurement of spaces and of changes of spaces and in spaces over time. Geography and the other disciplines involved in 'urban and regional studies' work to a considerable degree in terms of a nested hierarchy of spaces comprising the world, blocks/regions1, nation states, regions2, localities and neighbourhoods. This is a relatively simple hierarchical structure. The only ambiguous level is the second, where the term 'block' is used to describe organised sub-world spaces, for example the European Union or the North American Free Trade Area, and the term region1 refers to sub-world but larger than nation states spaces defined primarily by spatial propinquity, for example the 'Mediterranean world'. Region2 here indicates sub-national but larger than local spatial units which in advanced industrial societies almost always have a clear administrative identity of some sort. The terms 'locality' and 'neighbourhood' will be unpicked subsequently.

What is interesting from a complexity position is that for spaces we have measurements over time. The measured account is certainly not simple. The actual spaces to which the measurements apply can shift boundaries, although there is an argument to be had about whether physical spatial reference matters all that much here.[1] This chapter will take the opportunity offered by the existence of this set of measurements and will suggest that thinking about what they are in relation to one of the central issues in contemporary spatial studies, that of sociospatial differentiation, shows the utility of the complexity approach in urban and regional studies as a whole.

These debates are by no means merely academic. There is a clear relationship between the forms of urban and regional policy and the character of academic understanding in these fields. Graham's (1992) account of the way in which 'regulation theory' in particular has informed the abandonment of any commitment to transformational social reform at the urban level, and led to a pessimistic endorsement of mere tendential modification, is wholly convincing. Chapter 8 of the thesis is exactly concerned with these sorts of issues of urban governance.

The hierarchy of spaces

The key word in contemporary spatial studies is 'globalisation'. The essential content of this idea seems correct. It describes a situation in which the world system which Wallerstein identifies as coming into being with the development of the seaborne European empires of the sixteenth century has become so generalised that all aspects of economic, and consequently social, life are interconnected on a global scale. It can certainly be argued that globalisation has not been a steady or indeed always forward moving process. The world of 1914 was probably more globalised than that of 1949, given the impossibility of free movement of capital into the Soviet bloc and China at the later date. Even within the West, the capacity of governments to regulate capital transfers remained significant from the First World War until the early 1980s. However, it now is true to say that finance capital is free in space in the very short term and industrial capital has much the same spatial mobility in the medium term, the length of which medium term is determined by the depreciation period of fixed capital assets.

Just as the productive capital assets of the system are spatially free, so are the products to be consumed, whether material or cultural. In their two books *The End of Organised Capitalism* (1987) and *The Economies of Signs and Space* (1994), Lash and Urry describe these developments. We have global consumption and a global culture. Urban theory has paid particular attention to 'world cities', i.e. to those cities which seem to function as key command and control centres within this global system and in which the virtual world of financial capital actually touches the earth in the form of the physical presence of the three key financial markets of Tokyo, New York and London. However, there is a real sense in which all cities and places are world cities and places, that is to say they are best understood in terms of their position within a world system, rather than in any spatial system constructed on a smaller scale.

It is possible to argue that this account is somewhat over-stated. The development of the European Community and of the North American Free Trade Area has involved the political construction of economic blocs which are quite big enough to be actors on a world scale. Much of world trade in commodities, as opposed to finance, is quite short distance and region1 centred. In the discussion of 'world cities' this is recognised by the specification of a first division below the premier league, including cities like Los Angeles, Miami, Hong Kong and Shanghai which mediate relations between regions and the world system. What is increasingly redundant in this formulation is of course the nation state which is subsumed into the bloc (or, as in the case of the federal US, subsumes other nation states, especially Canada, to it).

The next level down, region2, does have considerable significance. This sub-national level seems to be crucial for the effective sub-bloc organisation of the co-ordination of production and reproduction for a crucial level of enterprises and for policies relating to the organisation of space and the provision of trained labour. This is well recognised by the European Union with its commitment to a Europe of the regions rather than of the nations.[2]

Below the region2 level is that of the locality. This is a term which became very fashionable in spatial studies in the late 1980s and there is an extensive literature dealing with it (see Urry 1988; Duncan 1986). The term was developed to replace the astructural usage of 'community' as employed by the 1960s community studies of local social systems. The term is intrinsically, and usually explicitly, realist. Bagguley *et al.* assert that: 'the locality study as a *method* [original emphasis] has arisen from the attempt to address the complexity of spatially intersecting causal processes' (1990: 8). They develop their argument thus:

> We derive our sense of the local from a realist perspective, by paying attention to the *spatial ranges* [original emphasis] of the many causal elements that impinge on any chosen area. . . . All of these overlie each other and can enter into substantive relationships where they overlap, involving sometimes the same and sometimes different collections of individuals and other subjects. Social reality from this perspective, is made up of the totality of these significant inter-relationships over space.
>
> (Bagguley *et al.* 1990: 10)

Cochrane has developed the useful idea of 'micro-structuralism' as a way of identifying the core content of the notion of locality:

> The distinction between necessary and contingent relations which is so important to realism has been presented as a means of acknowledging the uniqueness of different places, without giving up the idea that their development also reflects general processes.
>
> (Cochrane 1987: 354)

This can be taken somewhat further. Duncan distinguishes between spatial differences which are mere spatial variation (a passive contingency effect) and another level at which:

> Over and above this contingency effect, causal effects may be locally derived. This is our second level. Furthermore a combination of these may create what can be called a 'locality' effect. The sum of locality derived causes is greater than the parts. In both these cases, our second and third levels of socio-spatial interaction, local variations are active in the sense of causally producing outcomes rather than just contingently affecting them.
>
> (Duncan 1986: 28)

The use of the word 'interaction' here is highly indicative. We are dealing with emergent properties of a system which can change. The level of region2 has been discussed in essentially similar terms, with the range of the two usually operationally distinguished in terms of level of economic integration. In other words, localities are usually operationalised in terms of local labour markets and regions in terms of aggregates of local labour markets which combine some socio-historical identity with being of an appropriate size for the essentially corporatist co-ordination of production and reproduction. It is very important to note the resonance between the usage of the term 'locality' by geographers and its usage by mathematicians interested in non-linear systems. The burden of Chapter 3's presentation of the mathematical accounts was precisely that general laws were not achievable, that what mattered was the local account.

Localities and regions are important in themselves and in policy terms. In other words they are real entities and they are the objects of active interventions by policy makers seeking to position them within the hierarchies of statuses available for each level on a world or smaller scale. Positioning policy is the crucial role of much of contemporary urban governance, at least of those aspects of governance which are in any way innovative as opposed to routinised continuation of existing reproductive policies.

'Neighbourhood' is simply the term I have chosen to use for the smallest significant socio-spatial scale. For me this is not described by function. Indeed, those parts of urban space which are not primarily residential lie outside the scheme of neighbourhoods. Neighbourhoods are the places where people of the same sort, in our world people sorted essentially by class but also by race/ethnicity, and to a much lesser degree by lifestyle,[3] all of which operate in a complex way, reside. This is the terrain of urban ecology, the baby thrown out with the bath water of Chicago School Spencerian social Darwinist determination of internal urban structure by Castells (1977). Although the term 'social ecology' is so taboo and polluting as to be almost never used, it is of course the basis of the contemporary and very proper interest in social polarisation in the 'divided city' and is integral to discussions of the development of a so-called 'underclass'[4] in advanced capitalist societies.

The hierarchy of spaces outlined above constitutes a set of nested systems each down from the world system, containing elements made up of the level below it. It may be that the bloc/region2 level, and is almost certainly the case that the nation state level, are dissolving systems, leaving a world system of regions, which in turn constitute systems of localities, which in turn constitute systems of neighbourhoods. Indeed, in the case of true world cities the locality and region2 levels may be identical. However, the systemic account still holds even in this more simplified form.

Here is where the measurements matter so much. We have measurements which describe the whole systems at any level and measurements which describe the sub-systems in terms of their position within the whole systems. We can think of the systems both as phase/condition spaces and as single entities. As an example of the latter we might consider the possible attractor states for the world system of Fordism and post-Fordism. We can see the hierarchy of positions for regions within the world system as representing a set of possible attractor states within a phase space constituted by the world system in its present form. Neighbourhoods within localities are entities within the phase space of localities which in turn are entities within the phase space of regions.

Local complexity – the 'locality'

The most systematic debate about the nature of space in recent years has focused on the level of locality. An extreme position in this is represented by Warf (1993) who seizes on the contextuality of the local as an essential component of any postmodernist account. In doing so he ignores completely the point about micro-structuralism made by Cochrane (1987) and seeks to assert the unique significance of the local against the kind of universalist political economy meta-narrative he identifies with the work of, for example, David Harvey. He constructs his argument around a prescription of the four essential elements of the general postmodernist account (which despite its generality cannot be considered, of course, to constitute any sort of meta-narrative at all). These are:

Complexity [original emphasis] – the explicit recognition that general metanarratives (including Marxism) have largely failed to capture the enormous variation within and among social formations . . . postmodern explanation rejects the assumption that explanation consists of showing particular events to be outcomes of wider processes.

Contextuality [original emphasis] – the reassertion of time and space into social theory (and an end of the primacy of time over space). Postmodern geography asserts that when and where things happen is central to *how* [original emphasis] they happen. Thus theory must acknowledge not only that knowledge is historically specific, but geographically specific as well, i.e. explanation must be tailored to the unique characteristics of places.

Contingency [original emphasis] – the stress upon intentionality and human consciousness. . . . Rejecting teleological explanation, postmodern geography posits that landscapes are fashioned through conscious human agents circumscribed within a finite, ever changing set of constraints. Such an approach accepts that history and geography could always be 'otherwise', i.e. that the present is by no means guaranteed by the past; *thus to know a society and a geography is to know how it could be different than it is* [original emphasis].[5]

Criticality [original emphasis] – the linkages between knowledge and power, the acknowledgement that every explanation is simultaneously a legitimation of a vested interest.

(Warf 1993: 166)[6]

It is important to note that Warf identifies the last as constituting an emancipatory principle in social science, although as he construes it, it cannot of course constitute a valid general emancipatory principle. Criticality is certainly important but it will perhaps be more useful if there is indeed some way in which its generality might be established. Here I want to suggest how, with an expansion of the notion of complexity (i.e. an assertion of the meaning given generally to that word in this book), a rejection of the absolute notion of contextuality, which nonetheless allows for the significance of the local, and a restating of the principle of contingency (à la Warf) in terms of the rather old-fashioned formulation that people make history, but not in circumstances of their own choosing, we might establish the basis for an emancipatory project which might actually work. Indeed, my

95

specification of contingency goes further here. Warf's understanding of this term is essentially the same as Gould's as discussed in Chapter 2. From a chaos/complexity-informed position it is certainly important to consider always how something could be other than it is, but it cannot be anything at all. Rather there are a limited set of possibilities constructed beyond bifurcation points. There is a range of others but not an infinity of others.

Let me focus on the idea of contextuality. Warf, in contrast with Cochrane's conception of the micro-structural character of locality, specifies the absolute uniqueness of each local context. He goes so far as to assert that: 'A postmodernist geography, structured epistemologically around the four sets of issues articulated above, recognises . . . that a theory of poverty in New York is fundamentally different from a theory of poverty in London' (1993: 167). Short's comment on this is worth quoting:

> This may be a rhetorical flourish. . . . But if he actually believes this and this represents a more general trend then I am worried. I can accept that poverty is different in different countries and different cities, the experience varies by time and place and person. General discussions of poverty need to be aware of such differences. But if we are going to try to generate fundamentally different theories about poverty in two capitalist cities then perhaps we need to redefine the word 'theory'.
>
> (Short 1994: 170)

Short's position is exactly equivalent to Cochrane's on micro-structuralism. Let us get a complexity fix on all of this by considering Teesside in the northeast of England. This industrial estuarine conurbation is a good example both because it constitutes a locality[7] and because there is a unique time series household-based data set describing the trajectory of forms of households within it from 1977 to 1995. Cleveland is located in the northern region of England which is a rather clear example of a region2. Within that region it is not the regional capital but rather an industrially specialised zone which serves as a sub-regional capital for retail and administrative functions. In turn the north of England is within the nation state of the UK, which is within the bloc of the European Union (although currently relatively immune from EU social policy forms), which is in a world system characterised by globalisation. That term stands for the relative freedom of capital in space and the hegemony of liberal free market ideology in political prescription. There is a direct and strong politico-economic link between it and the policy regimes of the UK state which is in turn rather directly transmitted to both the regional and locality levels, given that the former in the UK is run by civil servants in a prefectorial style and that the scope for autonomy at the latter has been enormously eroded through central financial control and the transfer of key areas of service and development activity from elected representatives to centrally appointed quangos.

Subsequently I want actually to go below the locality level and consider the case of East Middlesbrough, a neighbourhood which was the product of post-war left Keynesian housing policies and urban planning (see Byrne 1995b). Let us review the series of levels which operate here and see how they inter-relate. At the global level we can see how tendencies in the general organisation of capitalist production (technologically achieved massive increase in labour productivity) and the spatial reorientation of much basic department I (capital) goods production as part of the new international division of labour, have caused (a deliberate usage) the deindustrialisation of the Teesside area. In 1971 the locality contained 234,000 jobs, of which 58 per cent were industrial. In 1991 the locality contained 202,000 jobs, of which 40 per cent were industrial (see Byrne 1995b: 100). Over those twenty years, 54,000 industrial jobs were lost. This transition reflected both global changes, and the policy regime and general incompetence of UK national government over the period. Of particular national significance was the combination of high exchange rates in the early 1980s with both denationalisation and legislative weakening of the capacity of workers to defend themselves at the point of production (see Beynon et al. 1994 for an account of industrial changes in Teesside). However, these industrial changes do not constitute the whole of the national effect. Of just as much significance was the fiscal/social security policy of national government which massively reduced taxes on higher incomes and massively (in relative, if not absolute terms) reduced benefits paid to the poorest. It is the interactive effects among the factors of deindustrialisation and consequent job insecurity, low income substitution benefits, and high incomes for the secure owners and the higher service class which constitute the causal influence of national policies (see Byrne 1997b).

The significant locality level factor was the planning regime directed at consumption-oriented land development (see Byrne 1994 for a full account). This prioritised 'exclusive' schemes and channelled public resources towards a system of 'catalytic planning' which was supposed to stimulate a land market dependent on consumption by the beneficiaries of the Thatcher years. This project has been almost wholly unsuccessful in terms of its formal objectives, but distracted both political energies and funds from almost all other policy initiatives which might have addressed the social consequences of deindustrialisation. The effective operations of the region2 level over the period under review have simply been in support of this general programme of urban redevelopment.

We can measure the changes at all the spatial levels thus far defined. We can see changes in the state of the global system in terms of employment and production levels and patterns of trade and consumption. These change over time. We can see changes in the national level, particularly in terms of real levels of non-employment among men of working age and in relation to patterns of inequality in household incomes. Again these change over time. The global system constitutes a condition or phase space within which the nation state is located. During the period under review we can see the UK as being drawn towards a new form of 'welfare regime' (see Esping-Andersen 1990) which can be understood as one of the available attractor states for national economic and social polities. Of course the initial circumstances of the UK might well be considered to have predisposed it towards that attractor basin, but the historically contingent event of the Falklands War, coupled with actions of the establishers of the SDP who split the Labour Party at a crucial time, were at the very least significant political perturbations. This was robust chaos and here it is really quite possible to follow Warf's dictum and 'know how the society could be different than [sic] it is'. Here the meaning of 'how' is twofold. We can see what the different form might be – Sweden with a bit of luck and the wind in the right direction – and how that could have been got to – by a Labour victory in the 1983 election with the wind in the left's sails. There was another way to be.

What is interesting in the UK context is the way in which national government used the power of parliamentary sovereignty to limit the range of possible attractor states for localities in a very definite fashion. The elimination of local financial autonomy and the actual abolition of any subsidiary level which seemed to offer any kind of focus for resistance[8] meant that alternative local strategies could not be attempted. Urban governments were forced to go along with the catalytic planning approach embodied in the establishment of Urban Development Corporations (see Imrie and Thomas 1993) and generalised through the competitive scheme mechanisms of 'City Challenge' and 'the Single Regeneration Budget'. The only policy form that could be pursued was driven by the efforts to recreate an inner urban land market. This was justified ideologically by the continued assertion that more regulatory planning regimes had failed because they 'attempted to buck the market'. The general ineffectiveness of the consequent efforts at diverting land markets from their attraction for retail development to the edge city and for expensive residential development to the non-urban, demonstrates that bucking the market may have had its limitations, but they were considerably less than those involved in trying to fiddle it. The centrally determined policy regime eliminated the real other attractor, the just city, as a possibility. The attractor of the working market city just didn't exist. What we got was the unjust cocked-up city.

The emphasis here on the significance of relationships among the levels of the nested systems is of great importance. If it were not for these relations then Warf's account of the uniqueness of the local would stand – it would be exactly analogous to non-linear mathematics' insistence on the examination of local characteristics at bifurcation points. This remains crucial of course, but it is not enough. The real systems with which we are dealing are not isolated from other systems. They exist within them, are influenced by them, *and* influence them. The relationships are real and reflexive.

Let us look at the system characteristics of Teesside. One key variable here might be the proportion of adult males of working age who have been involuntarily displaced from being in full-time work. The definition suggested in the previous sentence is deliberate. It is not simply a matter of unemployment. There are two other possible statuses which can describe non-employed men of working age. The first is that they might be students. There has been an enormous growth in continuation in full-time education beyond the age of 16 (the minimum legal age for full-time work) in the UK. Of course part of this is certainly because people can't get jobs so they go for qualifications. However, I propose to treat this element as voluntary. The other element is the massive growth in the numbers of men of working age who self-classify themselves as 'permanently sick'. To a very considerable degree this is a product of the operation of benefit regulations during the 1980s and early 1990s when it was much better for a long term unemployed man to achieve the less regulated and better remunerated status of being in receipt of invalidity benefit rather than some form of unemployment benefit. Officials were encouraged to support such transitions as a way of reducing unemployment totals. Recent changes in benefit administration may well eliminate this, but over the period under consideration it is quite appropriate to treat the 'permanently sick' as really another component of the involuntarily unemployed.

Between 1971 and 1991 the number of men recording themselves on a census return as either unemployed or permanently sick on Teesside increased from 19,000 to 47,000. As a percentage of the adult male population this represented an increase from 10 per cent of the total of adult males of working age and not students involuntarily unemployed, to 30 per cent. This is exactly the Feigenbaum number, a change in a controlling parameter of three times, which suggests that a torus pattern of system states will become transformed into a butterfly attractor pattern. In Byrne (1997a) I have developed this account of both Teesside[9] and the Leicester urban area, and argued that it was this key control parameter shift which led to the development of both as 'divided cities' characterised by a high degree of internal social differentiation into two sets of affluent and deprived neighbourhoods. In this formulation the locality is seen as the phase space containing the neighbourhoods, but we can also regard the 'divided city' as a new attractor state in the phase space containing localities themselves

The most convenient tool for classificatory description here is the use of cluster analytical procedures at different time points. Given the existence of small area statistics sets for successive population censuses this is quite an easy thing to do (see Byrne 1989, 1995b and 1997 for examples). Essentially such analyses support an account of the polarisation of city space with the transition from a Fordist system based on full employment in an industrial system, to a post-Fordist one in which there is a re-creation of employment insecurity and a massive reduction both absolutely and relatively in industrial employment. We can see the city as coming to be a phase space in which neighbourhoods are located in one or the other of the wings of the butterfly. It is possible for neighbourhoods to shift position. This is the process of gentrification, most recently and systematically discussed by Smith (1996). Clearly the catalytic planning strategies attempted in Teesside were efforts at achieving gentrification. However, despite enormous energy inputs in the form of grant aid and the delivery of land to developers at negative costs (see Byrne 1994), this was not enough to achieve significant gentrification of these locales. Rather more common has been the transition to lower status which has characterised even formerly securely middle-class areas of West Newcastle, possibly the most disorganised social space in the whole of the UK. In the UK this is class mediated. In the penultimate section of this chapter I want to consider, using US examples, the role of ethnicity as a controlling parameter in urban systems. Before doing that let us turn to the last element in the urban system, the individual household.

Households as social atoms – the statistical mechanics of the urban system

The general complex account of social space presented in this chapter has at its core the notion that the successive spatial levels constitute the phase spaces of the levels below them. This stops with individual households, the significant social unit in which we spend our lives outside of work. All operational definitions of households centre on a combination of pooled consumption and shared residence. Household membership defines our class in Weberian terms since it is the resource base of the household which limits our capacity to consume[10] and residence fixes us in social space. However, we can move in space, either with our household or from it. Such movements require large energy inputs, but these are achievable. The divorced woman whose house is repossessed because of mortgage defaults by a departing husband, can easily pass down the system with her children. Very good academic achievement can bring a young adult up (although the schools they attend are not likely to be of much help here – see Byrne and Rogers 1996). A single parent can get a new partner and move from a household dependent on state benefits to one with one and a half wages, which can be enough to achieve movement into reasonable cheap owner-occupied housing. It is clear that these sorts of transitions can only really be mapped by a household panel study on the lines of the British Household Panel Study. However, even this has limitations, notably in terms of its spatial content. For anonymising reasons, and because the study is nationally founded, it is difficult, not to say impossible, to locate the households within their local social spaces at the times at which their measurements were taken. Regrettably, the Cleveland Social Survey abandoned its panel element very early on, so there is no local mapping of actual transitions directly available from it. It may prove possible to reconstruct earlier locations of people and their households from this data set but this is work for the future.

However, let us imagine that we did have a local panel study covering the period 1977 to 1995 (we should be so lucky). What this would enable us to do would be to plot the movements of households, and the new households which stemmed from them, over time and through social space, remembering of course that the character of social space itself might be changing in a non-linear way. We could see in some detail what exactly was associated with socio-spatial mobility. Of course, people would move to other localities, but, provided we knew their new addresses, we could locate them readily within the neighbourhood system of that new local phase space. In effect we would have an (almost certainly sample-based) account of the movement of social atoms within a social system. This would enable us to see the actual historical development of the system as it occurred and to map out the way households and people moved through it in the course of their lives.

This is all closely related to the criticisms of the general character of the quantitative programme in sociology which formed the substance of the previous two chapters. Essentially much of that criticism centred on the individualistic orientation of quantitative sociology. Enormous effort has been devoted to modelling how some person or household ended up in a given situation, without much thought being given to what produced the set of possible situations which there were to end up in. Given a data set of the kind described above, coupled with the system describing measures available from censuses of population and employment and a range of other descriptors of changes in the condition of the locality,[11] we can see both what the changing shape of the phase space is in terms of possible attractor sets, and what it is about changes in people's lives which facilitates their movement among that changing set of attractors over time.

Let us consider the case of East Middlesbrough. This large neighbourhood was the product of deliberate planning during and at the end of the Second World War. It represented a real social democratic commitment to the elimination of social and spatial inequalities. In an informative report researchers from the Centre for Environmental Studies (CES) concluded that:

> The pioneering 1946 Max Lock plan set out a very ambitious thirty year programme which involved the relocation of 50,000 people and heroically aimed at 'pulling together' the town which was at that time regarded as socially fragmented. Ironically, the thirty year building programme of East Middlesbrough's eleven neighbourhood estates put even more physical and social distance between East Middlesbrough's working class population and the rest of the town.
>
> (CES 1985: 1)

That statement is descriptively accurate and analytically inaccurate. In other words, as of 1985 it describes the situation pretty well exactly, but the actual planning and construction programme did not generate that situation – it did not 'put' it there. Rather, in the early 1970s, by which time the East Middlesbrough development was essentially complete, there was not a massive social distance between the people who lived there and the rest of the town. By the early 1990s, in the divided city of Teesside, there was. This is very easily illustrated by a comparison of social division on Teesside in 1977 with social division in 1991 (see Byrne 1995a). In 1977 just 10 per cent of Cleveland's households which contained dependent children were in a deprived category, when a cluster analysis was used to differentiate between deprived and non-deprived. By 1991, 30 per cent of such households were in this deprived category. In 1977 most deprived households were headed by a female single parent. In 1991 most were male headed, although most female headed households remained deprived. In 1977 a third of East Middlesbrough households were deprived. In 1991 two thirds were.

Clearly East Middlesbrough was less affluent than most parts of Cleveland in 1977 but most households resident there were not poor. By 1991 the area was essentially characterised by deprivation. That reflected the locality's phase space change from a Fordist torus to a post-Fordist, post-industrial butterfly. What would be really interesting would be to explore the trajectory of households into and out of East Middlesbrough as well as the change in the situation of the neighbour-hood within a changing locality, within a changing region2, within a changing nation state, within a changing bloc, within a changing world. There were certainly specific locality, and even neighbourhood, effects which set the situation for East Middlesbrough, but the general global context mattered too. It was interactions among globalisation, national policy shifts, local planning and development, and neighbourhood factors, which created the present situation of that place. When we come to the household level, the socio-spatial atoms, then we add in household factors as well, and all the interactions at and among these levels. That is what sets up the statistical mechanics of social space.

The US – race as an additional controlling parameter

The internal spatial ecology of cities in the United States is more complex than that of the UK because of the crucial role of 'race', and specifically of black American status, in constructing it. There is now good evidence from the 1991 census that the UK does not have ethni-cally constructed ghettos in any meaningful sense of that word (see Peach 1996b), but the situation in the US is one marked by: 'the unique segregation of black Americans . . . and the deleterious consequences they suffered as a result of this spatial isolation' (Massey and Denton 1993: viii).

Massey and Denton remark that:

> although we share William Julius Wilson's view that the struc-
> tural transformation of the economy played a crucial role in
> creating the urban underclass in the 1970s, we argue that what
> made it disproportionately a *black* [original emphasis] under-
> class was racial segregation.
>
> (Massey and Denton 1993: 136–7)

Massey and Denton's book summarises a very large number of studies
and uses census-derived materials to explore the extent of racial segregation in US cities. They note both that this has changed very little over
the twentieth century and that the black middle class is segregated
much more from its white equivalent than it is from the black poor.

There are three aspects to this from a complex systems view of the
city. The first relates to the character of the city as a phase system of
neighbourhoods. The residential space of UK cities can be understood
essentially in class terms. That of US cities must also take account of
race. Here what is being called the city might better be described as the
urban area. The phenomenon of white flight has rendered many urban
area cores primarily black, but the locality is properly considered as
including both the city and its suburban catchment area.[12] In seeking to
understand the patterning of US residential space, race is as important
as class.

The second aspect relates to the actual transformation process of US
residential neighbourhoods by realtors as block busters. Lemann (1991)
notes the inability of Saul Alinsky and progressive elements in 1960s
Chicago to create an ethnically mixed lower-middle-/upper-working-
class neighbourhood in the city. Instead, the entry of black families led
to the area becoming overwhelmingly black, by a process that could be
mathematically modelled in terms of catastrophe theory. In the UK the
ethnically mixed suburban area is a perfectly possible attractor. In the
US it is not.

This absence of the ethnically mixed middle-class neighbourhood as
a possible spatial attractor is crucial for the actual life trajectories of US
black households. Black people can achieve some social mobility but it
is very difficult for them to isolate their children from the disabling
characteristics of ghetto experience. White middle-class children attend
good public (in the real US sense) schools which contain very few children who are failing and who express deviant value systems. Black
middle-class children are far more likely to be in schools which draw on
areas of severe social deprivation.

The reasons for this saliency of race for black Americans, in marked
contrast to all other ethnic groups in the US, including Hispanics in the

main, but not those Puerto Ricans who are regarded by US whites as black, clearly lies in the cultural forms that became associated with the validation of chattel slavery before emancipation, and with racially-based exclusion from citizenship alongside economic domination, in the subsequent reconstruction system founded on sharecropping.

Morenoff and Tienda (1997) have recently reported the results of a very interesting study of the temporal dynamics in Chicago. This study is interesting both in terms of method and of substantive findings. The method used was precisely a time-ordered set of cluster analyses of the kind which it was suggested in Chapter 3 should be used as a way of exploring the history of dynamic qualitative change. The resulting account is one of considerable social polarisation. In particular transitional working-class neighbourhoods, which comprised 45 per cent of all census tracts in 1970, formed only 14 per cent of such tracts in 1990 (Morenoff and Tienda 1997: 67). Of considerable interest also is the way in which Hispanic immigration has modified the social ecology of Chicago with concentration of Hispanics leading to the transition of many stable middle-class neighbourhoods to the transitional working-class category. In Chicago 'underclass' neighbourhoods were overwhelmingly (90 per cent on average) black.

Ethnicity and its history is enormously important for the socio-spatial form of US cities but recent developments in the strategies of capital have also played a role which has occurred to a lesser degree in UK cities. Fitch (1993) provides a fascinating account of the 'Assassination of New York' which describes how the FIRE (Finance, Insurance and Real Estate) complex manipulated the urban planning system from the 1920s onwards in order to change designated land uses as a way of extracting more value from sites. What happened was that agency, much of it perpetrated by the Rockefeller family,[13] reconstructed the character of the whole urban space so as to preclude much industrial employment being possible. In the case of New York a complex and diversified employment system was actually simplified so as to exclude that part of it which generated decent blue collar incomes. This is of great significance in explaining New York's particularly high levels of real unemployment, which differentially affects black people.

I have argued before that the racialisation of 'the underclass' represents a process of assignation rather than something which is inherent in the urban system. What this means is that the processes of deindustrialisation, which as Fitch so convincingly demonstrates must be understood in local as well as global terms, create a series of positions. Ethnicity can function as a basis on which people are then assigned to those positions but processes of ethnic domination do not create them in the first place. Their origins lie with actions originating in relation to the systems of production and circulation.

It seems to me that this argument is essentially correct for the UK, but that in societies where ethnic domination is or has been integral to economic exploitation, then ethnicity has a determinant effect, in a complex and contingent form of course, of its own. The obvious example of such a system was apartheid-era South Africa where its spatial form in residential terms was ensured by the operation of the Group Areas Act. In the northern United States the cultural expressions of a uniquely exclusionary racism continue to be of enormous significance. It should prove possible to model the historical development of residential racial and class segregation in US cities through a process of quantitative historical exploration. This issue of the 'underclass' and its spatial constitution will be looked at again in Chapter 8.

6

THE COMPLEX
CHARACTER OF HEALTH
AND ILLNESS

Introduction

Mention has already been made of the work of Wilkinson (1996) on the inter-relationship between the extent of internal inequalities among different nation states and the comparative levels of mortality and consequent life expectancy in those states. This was cited as a particularly clear illustration of the inter-relationship between the levels of the hierarchy of nested social systems: here between the general social level and the actual health outcomes for individuals, since death rates and consequent life expectancies are generated by the aggregation of individual events, which in turn are in part the product of general social factors. It has also been suggested in a preliminary way that the level of inequality is a key controlling variable in determining the character, within the possible state spaces, of the attractor form describing a particular nation state. This is true for health but also can describe the social order in general. In this chapter the re-emergent social account of the origins of health and disease will be taken up in more detail. This exercise has two objectives. It is intended to reinforce the relevance of the chaos/complexity approach to social science in general by showing how it can be used to organise understanding about these socially important issues. It is also specifically addressed to the substantive concerns of Wilkinson and his associates about inequality and social exclusion.

The chapter starts with a discussion of the arguments presented in Blane *et al.* 1997. The general tenor of the book is illustrated by its title *Health and Social Organization* – it asserts that the health of people in a society is very largely a product of the character of the social organisation of that society. Whilst the contributors recognise the real achievements of clinical medicine in terms of reducing morbidity, this text is part of the strong social programme in the application of the social sciences to health issues – it says, modestly and quietly, but nonetheless firmly, that the biomechanically-founded programme of clinical intervention in the individual case is not what matters, and not what has made a difference. An immediate and superficial intellectual response to this would be to see it as part of a postmodernist attack on modernist rationality. Kelly *et al.* (1993) have perceptively pointed out that this is not so. Instead they identify the social account of health as an alternative modernist programme. I agree with this specification but do not follow Kelly *et al.* in their search for a postmodernist salutogenic programme. Rather it seems to me that the social model of health is not just any different modernist account. Understood as an implicitly complex account, it is the right account of health, and the policies which derive from it are the right policies. Specific aetiologies established by reductionist science may matter much less than biomechanical medicine thinks. Complex social aetiology matters a great deal. It is possible to be right about how the world works and to prescribe appropriate action to make it work differently.

The chapter will be organised around a scanning of the debate for signs of complexity. I will begin with a discussion of some of the ideas of contributors to Blane *et al.* (1997), continue with a consideration of the actual empirical study of *Health and Lifestyles* reported by Blaxter (1990) which brings in an individual dimension, and conclude with a confrontation of Kelly *et al*'s (1993) interesting attempt at a postmodernist critique with the chaos/complexity-founded fix on these issues and studies.

Understanding health

Population health can be conceptualized as three concentric rings of health determinants surrounding a central core that contains the population of people of concern. The inner or proximal ring refers to the immediate surrounding influences. . . . The second or intermediate ring refers to community or area influences. . . . The third or distal ring refers to macrosocial influences.

Within a ring the various features are highly interactive. Moreover, the rings are porous, allowing features of one ring to interact with features of another ring. Sometimes features of an inner ring interact with and influence features of an outer ring, although the predominant direction of influence is probably inward.

(Tarlov 1996: 82–3)

The central problem of medicine considered as a social science is how to get beyond the characteristics of the individual case. This is not merely a conceptual problem. It was of fundamental practical importance in the early years of the industrial revolution when the conditions of urban life were so inimical to human health, and in particular to the health of infants, that the actual physical survival of the industrial proletariat was at risk. This applied both to the absolute numbers of the population and to its general capacities. Infant and child mortality was so high in the industrial cities of Britain during the first half of the nineteenth century that the population could only grow by continuing immigration from the rural areas in general and Ireland in particular. By the early 1900s the minimum height requirement for admission to the volunteer British Army was five feet two inches, four inches less than it had been a hundred years earlier. Two thirds of the volunteers from industrial districts for service in the Boer War were wholly unfit for service. In the First World War special battalions of midgets, the bantam battalions, were raised from those who could not meet the height requirement.[1]

McKeown (1979) demonstrated that curative interventions based on treatments predicated on specific aetiologies have been almost wholly without significance in the development of the 'health transition' undergone by advanced industrial societies in which the infectious diseases have ceased to be the major cause of death.[2] Although he argued that public health improvements were of some but not great significance, this argument was predicated on the central role of clean water and sewerage as part of the public health programme and McKeown's view that air-borne rather than water-borne infections were the most significant killers. This account neglects several important factors. Simply it doesn't take enough account either of the enormous significance of summer diarrhoea as a killer of infants and children or of the role of changes in housing standards through construction by-laws, in improving ventilation in dwellings. In more complex terms it disregards the very real likelihood that the virulence of any infection is a function of the general state of health of the population exposed to it. This certainly means that diet matters, as McKeown contended, but it also means that exposure to any infection might weaken resistance to another. If the diarrhoea didn't get you, then the measles would, because the diarrhoea had softened you up.

The actual public health interventions of the first half of the nineteenth century were founded on a social understanding of the determinants of health. Indeed, insofar as they drew on a biological account, they drew on an erroneous one. Before Pasteur's work infectious diseases were understood as miasmic in origin. Bad smells and bad air caused disease. Eliminate the smell and the disease went with it. This worked of course because the ecological transformations created by the removal of human dung from the streets and the channelling of stagnant water ways[3] removed not only bad air, but also the locations of disease organisms and their vectors. It is clear that the urban-founded public health movement worked.

The aetiological programme of this early public health was necessarily complex. In other words it did not have a developed and specific account of the aetiology of infectious diseases. In its first phase practical intervention was dominated by administrators, particularly Chadwick, and civil engineers. The medical profession subsequently took control in part on the basis of the development of bacteriological science which provided specific and single causes for different infectious diseases. This doctrine of specific aetiology predicated a programme based on the removal of exposure and the development of immunities. In terms of the water-borne diseases, food poisoning and smallpox, and in the twentieth century measles and whooping cough, this programme worked quite well. However, it was never complete.

The most interesting case is that of tuberculosis – the major killer among infectious diseases of adults during the nineteenth and early twentieth centuries. Tuberculosis was endemic – always present in the population. In its normal pulmonary form cases lived for a long time in an infectious state. Certainly in realist terms exposure to the TB bacillus was a necessary cause, but it clearly was not sufficient. Many, most indeed, were exposed without developing any clinical disease. The decline in clinical incidence tracked both absolute improvements in living standards and reduced inequalities. The introduction of specific magic bullets in the 1950s, although plainly dramatic in the individual case, was of minimal significance in the reduction in incidence and prevalence of the disease.

Let us consider the example of TB with reference to the account of the 'social determinants of health' suggested by the quotation from Tarlov used as an epigraph to this section. First let us recognise that there is a specific biological aetiology. There must be exposure to the bacillus. Second, let us recognise a genetic component involving natural selection for resistance. It is plain that any such resistance is a matter of multiple gene inheritance; in Tarlov's terms (1996: 73) it is polygenetic. This means that it is not simply Mendelian and determinant. However, the phenotypical expression of resistance will be socially contingent. In a simple sense, in inter-war Tyneside the proximal ring was household circumstances. We do not need a very complicated account here. Being decently fed and housed made a hell of a difference. Beyond that was the nature of the immediate community. In Jarrow TB rates rose in the 1930s over the rates of the 1920s in contrast with a national decline. In the 1930s Jarrow was 'murdered' by the closure of Palmer's Shipyard and unemployment exceeded 70 per cent. This represented the intermediate ring. The distal ring was the character of national social and economic policy.

Here we have four systems in a nested hierarchy. The individual, the household, the community and the nation state. The outcome state of interest at the individual level is whether a person who will inevitably have been exposed to the TB bacillus develops the clinical disease. The possible attractor states at all levels involve bifurcation: for the individual having or not having TB; for the household containing or not containing a case of TB; for the community being riddled with TB cases or not; for the nation state containing TB-riddled communities or not. What I find very interesting is that we see action at all levels. It is perfectly clear that seeing your loved ones dying of TB in the inter-war years was a radicalising process. It made people truly hate inequality. It played a part in developing the grass roots of the socialist project, particularly for women.[4] It led to communal level action around housing provision and was plainly one of the factors in leading to a Labour victory in 1945. Here we find the interactive effects working outwards first, before coming back inwards.

It is worth taking this farther. It seems as if urban industrial societies have two possible states in relation to tuberculosis. In one it is a significant source of morbidity and mortality. In the other it is not. It is quite easy to see how this works. As with any infectious disease the prevalence of infectious cases is an important determinant of the incidence of new cases of the disease. However, the infectivity of TB is itself a function of the interaction between polyvalent genetic characteristics of individuals and those individuals' relationship with their social environment. This is interesting because it explains the two sorts of new case that actually occur. One is the case where either or both of weak immunity and weakening environment render someone liable to be infected. If the circumstances of inequality and immigration under which TB flourished are re-created, then the disease comes back (Wallace 1994). The other, which attracts more public attention, is when TB jumps over the gap in the divided city. The incidence of cases among the affluent will be much less, but there will be some because the rich are not wholly able to isolate themselves from the poor. This mode of relationship describes so many of the inter-relationships between wealth and poverty in a divided society.

Can we measure this? Tarlov remarks that:

> The capacities of the most often applied multi-variate analyses, including regression methodologies, are inadequate for the development of sound policy formulations to improve health. New hypotheses, and the development of new theories on the determinants of health, require new methodologies.
>
> (Tarlov 1996: 83)

Actually, whilst the methods may be new, in that they depend on the data mining and management capacities of electronic storage systems, the actual methodology is not. The origins of the statistical method, and of all stochastic reasoning, lie in nineteenth-century efforts at measuring a complex and changing world. What is required is a shift from the focus on the aggregation of individual case outcomes which has characterised the role of statistics as a tool of clinical science. Susser noted that: 'despite the epidemiologist's insistence on studying populations, his [sic] ultimate concern is with health, disease and death as it occurs in individuals' (1973: 59).

This perspective remains very powerful. Even Blane *et al.* (1997) seem to subscribe to it when discussing the possible difficulties of ecological reasoning, which are usually identified by reference to the 'ecological fallacy'.[5]

> can area correlations between deprivation and health be discounted on the grounds of the ecological fallacy? OPCS longitudinal study data were recently used to compare the effect of individual-level deprivation and area-level deprivation (Sloggett and Joshi 1994). The comparison indicated that the excess mortality in deprived areas is wholly explained by the concentration in those areas of individuals with adverse personal or household socio-economic factors. These results add weight to a substantial body of observation and they indicate that ecological correlation studies in which appropriate indices of deprivation have been used cannot be ignored on the ground of ecological fallacy.
>
> (Blane *et al.* 1997: 176–7)

This remains an individual-centred approach. It involves the 'excusing' of collective data, rather than a recognition of the effects of the social as perceived in the data, which jars with the explicit Durkheimian referent which generally informs these authors' arguments. In studies of the relationships among health and housing conditions (Byrne *et al.* 1985) we found that there was a real difference in the health of poor people depending on whether they lived in 'good' or 'bad' council estates. This was in addition to factors describing individual social circumstances and had a strong interactive relationship with those circumstances. In a range of studies Carstairs and her co-workers have shown the significance of immediate neighbourhood (Carstairs and Lowe 1986; Carstairs and Morris 1989). McIntyre *et al.* (1993) have argued for the general significance of place as a factor in health determination, remarking in a commentary on the Almeda County California study, that: 'it suggests that over and above individual level attributes of deprivation, people of low socio-economic status may have poorer health because they tend to live in areas which in some ways are health damaging' (1993: 217).

This is a matter of interaction among the levels of Tarlov's rings. Of course, my argument thus far has simply amounted to a demonstration of the necessity for thinking about health causes in complex and contingent terms – it has been at the level of the philosophical ontology of realism. The question remains as to whether we are dealing with complexity here. The simplest demonstration of this is achieved by considering the relationship between general socio-spatial inequalities and health inequalities. The divided city described in Chapter 5 is also the health divided city. When localities are treated as phase spaces of neighbourhoods and two attractor forms are identified within those phase spaces using socio-economic criteria for classification, then a radical health divide exists between the two sorts of neighbourhood within the cities. This is particularly apparent in relation to differential rates of premature mortality. When Townsend *et al.*'s (1988) wards on Tyneside, Wearside and Teesside are classified using socio-economic indicators and assigned to the different halves of their respective divided cities, this is evident despite the very real limitations imposed by relating mortality rates to final area of residence.[6] It seems that health bifurcates too in the transition from the Fordist to post-Fordist city.

However, we can do more with the data than this. We do have long runs of local and national vital statistics and we can examine the actual form of these as they change over time. The trail markers of complexity are visible in these data series and the evidence of bifurcation of health in the divided city is incontrovertible. We will return to this theme in the confrontation of complex modernism with postmodernism as modes of action for the achievement of healthy cities. What about the interaction between the individual and society as expressed in terms of individual health outcomes?

Lifestyles and health – constraint and choice in the formation of health attractors

Blaxter's report on the UK's first major investigation of *Health and Lifestyles* (1990) is a particularly useful study for consideration here. It is unashamedly quantitative and implicitly realist, emphasising the complex and interactive character of the causes of health and illness. It fits well with Tarlov's conception of the nested rings of health determination. As Blaxter puts it, 'The emphasis is on the individual, the single person with all his or her complicated pattern of circumstances' (1990: 12). The methods used for the causal analyses were Hellevik's, expanded with some log-linear modelling, which methods have already been discussed here in complex terms in Chapter 4. Although the study was not longitudinal, in other respects it represents a model of the kind of structurally informed quantitative social science in which the sociology of health is engaged, often it seems ignored by the 'mainstream' of the discipline [7]

What is particularly interesting here is the idea of lifestyle. Blaxter is careful in her specification:

> 'Lifestyle' is a vague term. Although it is a popular concept, what we mean by it has been questioned. . . . Often it is used to mean only voluntary lifestyles, the choices that people make about their behaviour and especially about their consumption patterns. In the context of health, choices about food, about smoking and drinking, and about the way in which leisure time is spent, are often thought to be the most relevant. Styles of living also have economic and cultural dimensions, however: the way of life of the city may inevitably be different from that of the country, the single from the married, the North from the South. There is overwhelming evidence for persistent socio-economic influences upon health: income, work, housing and the physical and social environments are also parts of ways of living. These have to be considered both as having a direct effect on health and as factors influencing behaviour. . . . This wide definition of lifestyle is the one which is used here, rather than one based on personal behaviours which are known to be risk factors.
>
> (Blaxter 1990: 5)

Blaxter points out the significance of this approach for the politics of health policy. The current emphasis on 'health maintenance' as opposed to cure is a reaction both to the escalating fiscal costs of expensive medical interventions and to the 'postmodernist' style crisis of confidence in the effectiveness of such procedures. However, there are two styles, indeed attractors, for such strategies. One emphasises the direct transformation of individual consumption and activity behaviours. The other by no means ignores these but regards such behaviours as themselves caused by social context, which social context has health consequences both indirectly through the behaviour sets and directly in terms of physical and social environment. Blaxter's conception of lifestyle is set in relation to the latter programme.

Obviously there is a substantial element of personal choice even in relation to the structural conception of lifestyle. A vegetarian diet is healthy, cheap and generally available, although there may be very real cultural constraints on accepting one in a culture where meat eating has had considerable status. However, individuals and households (there is of course a complex interactive relation between these levels) can make choices but within a system of constraints. The character of the constraints changes over time in two ways, both as a function of the social mobility of the individual within the social structure and as a function of changes in the social structure itself. The whole system is necessarily and intrinsically dynamic. Let us consider what the pattern of relationships among health and lifestyles might look like if we did have an adequate longitudinal data set covering the sorts of topics reviewed by Blaxter.

The easiest way to conceptualise what would be going on is by thinking of two inter-related systems which represent the set of possibilities for individuals as these sets change over time. One describes the possible lifestyle locations – the other the possible health locations. These lifestyle sets and health sets can be thought of as attractor states. If we think of lifestyles as sets involving all of individual characteristics, choices and structural constraints – that is to say if we think of them as co-ordinates in an n dimensional system where the dimensions are measures of individual characteristics, choices made and structural locations – then we will find sets of individuals in areas of the phase space of all possibilities, and not others. These attractors will be lifestyles. Similarly we can construct a health description based phase system.

Some things are possible and not others. It is impossible to combine affluence with poor social location. However, movement among locations, as these are stable, is possible, if difficult. What we have to consider is the intersection of two time flows. In one, society changes – the domain of history. In the other we are dealing with the time flow for specific individuals — biography. C. Wright Mills' remark that sociology deals with the intersection of biography and history seems especially pertinent in relation to this way of thinking about what is happening to people within society.

What the above amounts to is a kind of unpicking and heuristic separation of the two sets which constitute Blaxter's conception of lifestyle, individual choices and the social constraints within which those choices are made, together with a very firm emphasis on the temporally dynamic character of both along separate but related time paths. The individual attractors are lifestyles – the product of the interaction of constraint and volition. The social attractors are the grand social forms which pattern the possibilities of lifestyles. Even these may be embedded within a wider Gaian biosphere level of possibilities, which constitutes a ring enclosing all those specified by Tarpov and which is under serious perturbative assault from human industrial production and resource consumption.[8]

Complexity as modernity: the case of health

Conventional scientific research and the Healthy Cities concept belong to two fundamentally different worlds: the modern and the post-modern. Modernity is the world of conventional scientific research and rational administration applied to problems, physical or social. Post-modernity is a world of aesthetics, of the deconstruction of the conventional social arrangement, and of experimentation in cultural, artistic and life forms. . . . The core idea of post-modernity is that the social and moral conditions pertaining in the world at the present time mark a fundamental break with the past. In art, form displaces content; in philosophy, interpretation replaces system; in politics, pragmatism replaces principle; and in science chaos displaces order.

(Kelly *et al.* 1993: 159)

I greatly like the chapter from which the above quotation is taken. It is the most clearly written articulation of the postmodernist position in short form that I have ever encountered. It deals with a serious and substantive issue in an intellectually provoking way. And, the account it gives is absolutely wrong. In Chapter 2 of this book considerable effort has already been expended on asserting that if chaos/complexity has to be assigned to either modernism or postmodernism, then it can only be assigned to the former. It remains a programme of reason in understanding and of action informed by understanding. If ever there has

116

been a meta-narrative which is directed, contra Lyotard towards the speculative unity of knowledge and which might serve towards the liberation of humanity, then chaos/complexity is it. Let us take up the use made by Kelly *et al.* of Antonovsky's concept of 'salutogenesis' and, by identifying its central focus on emergent order, see how it is best understood in complex terms. Let us also rescue the social programme in health, the first and most effective health project of modernity, from Kelly *et al.*'s insertion of it into the positivist specific aetiological programme of 'scientific' (i.e. positivistic) medicine.

Salutogenesis is an interesting idea. It challenges the notion that health is the normal situation which is disrupted by disease. Instead it regards health as something which has to emerge from disorder. For Kelly *et al.* this makes it postmodern, but the resonance of the idea of health as emergent order with the general conception of complex emergence should indicate that this view is mistaken. Certainly salutogenesis' rejection of the notion that what signifies is system breakdown and resultant disease seems appropriate. In terms of the chaos/complexity vocabulary we can see this as involving a rejection of the notion that what we are dealing with are either equilibric or close to equilibric systems. If salutogenesis is concerned with: 'survival in spite of inbuilt tendencies to chaos, disorder and fragmentation' (Kelly *et al.* 1993: 160) then the importance of the *complex* analysis of health considered at both the individual and social levels as a property of far from equilibric systems is very great indeed.

Kelly *et al.*'s failure to recognise that the social programme in health is inherently founded on an idea of complex causes is crucial. It is a perfectly understandable failure, indeed an illuminating one, because it mirrors the development of public health medicine and epidemiology as the scientific basis of that public health medicine. The major distinction between the social programme in health and the biomechanical medical model lies precisely in the social programme's recognition that the causes of ill health are complex and contingent and cannot be identified in terms of a specific aetiology. It is perfectly true that the discourse of specific aetiology, fundamental to scientific medicine after Pasteur, dominated epidemiological work from the 1860s until the 1970s. However, it was a discourse which had to replace the earlier holistic and complex programme of understanding (and which never really replaced the earlier holistic and complex practices) of public health and which is now under serious challenge.

Charlton and Kelly (1993) assert that what is needed for the new public health is a form of understanding which does not take up the paradigmatic programme of 'normal science'[9] which they describe thus:

> Normal science is a puzzle-solving exercise which works within a strong and accepted paradigm where we know what the problem is, and that there is *an* [my emphasis] answer to it. The scientist's task is working out that answer.
>
> (Charlton and Kelly 1993: 83)

The significance of the chaos/complexity approach lies precisely in the recognition that whilst there is no inevitable outcome, no linear law, no single answer, we can nonetheless analyse in order to see what the possible set of outcomes might be, what the possible answers are, and, in situations of robust chaos, intervene in order to achieve those we want to see happen. We retain a programme of rational agency.

Let me come back to tuberculosis and consider it in salutogenic terms in the temporal context of the late twentieth century in New York. The specific aetiology of TB is bacterial causation and the social medical response to the disease is based on a single system intervention, the programme of immunisation through the BCG procedure, which is supposed to prevent infection given exposure. There is little evidence that this has ever had much effect at all. The clinical response is founded on the same aetiological account and is based on antibiotic treatment in the form of a magic bullet intended to kill the disease without killing the patient. This procedure was initially extremely effective but the value of clinical intervention is now under threat given the development of antibiotic resistant strains of the TB bacillus. A reductionist account has completed its story of the aetiology of TB when it describes the event of the exposure of a susceptible individual to infection, and the consequent development of clinical disease in that individual. The social account given by epidemiology is simply the result of the aggregate of such individual cases. We can go beyond this to a complex account of the genesis of individual cases – Bradbury's (1933) account in terms of diet, housing conditions and ethnicity. This is much better but it is not enough. For a salutogenic account we have to get beyond mere complex causation. We have to think of the interaction of the system levels.

Salutogenically it makes sense to assert that TB is a disease of society, not of individuals. We can be more specific. We can say that it is a disease of societies which are in the attractor state for societies of being relatively highly unequal. This makes its incidence a matter not of absolutes, but of the complex character of the system as a whole. The re-emergence of TB as a significant public health problem in New York is not merely a consequence of AIDS as a contingent factor. Indeed, we have to think about AIDS itself as a complex social product, given that one of the vectors for it, shared needle drug use, is a consequence of social alienation among the young. AIDS does matter but so do the effects of the withdrawal of fire companies for fiscal reasons from much of poor urban New York with a consequent loss of much housing stock in immigrant areas and a consequent increase in housing overcrowding. So does the relative collapse of public free hospital provision and health care. So does generic homelessness with its own complex origins in the de-institutionalisation of the mentally ill and the increase in housing costs in a world city. We can say here that an unequal world city will have a TB problem, but that it is possible for us to recast the city as more equal and in that attractor state there will not be a TB problem. This requires a combination of analysis and agency, but it remains rational. We do not have an infinity of competing truths about TB. There is a truth, albeit a complex truth. Yet again we see that chaos/complexity involves a rational programme focusing on determination. It just puts agency as central in that determination.

Outhwaite (1987) has remarked that one of the interesting distinguishing characteristics of realism as a meta-theory is its foundation in induction – in the actual sociology and history of science as it is and has been really done as a social practice. If we look at the social programme of public health in the original healthy towns movement[10] we find complex determination in operation through sanitation provision. If we look at the twentieth-century history of improved public health on a world scale we find that it is system re-specification – the achievement of the relatively equal attractor – which changes things.

The correct text for an understanding of why New York has a serious TB problem is not one written by a public health specialist. It is Fitch's *The Assassination of New York* (1993) in which he explains the current state of the city in terms of the planning ideologies, interests and actions of the 'Finance, Insurance and Real Estate' (FIRE) elite who have dominated its planning processes. Fitch wittily and clearly identifies 'post-industrial' New York as a 'mutation masquerading as a modernization . . . a "Throwback"' (1993: 235) to the preindustrial archaic urban form in which the city belonged to the elite consumers dominating and exploiting the producers placed outside it and somewhere else. I find his account of the agency-generated basis of this process wholly convincing – New York is a sort of Pottersville because the Potters have got their hands on it, not the working people. It is Gotham as Pottersville which gives Gotham its TB.

Conclusion

The strong social programme of the sociology of health is enormously important for public policy as a whole. This is not only because it has recognised the limitations of clinical procedures founded in the constant expansion of linear science-founded understanding of individual pathologies. That is indeed important for the development of health policy[11] and the reorganisation of power structures in health systems. This reorganisation of power is of course founded in large part on the informal redefinition of the status of linear basic and clinical medical science. It is precisely the realisation of the limitations of linear science-founded intervention which has shaken the knowledge-based authority of biomechanical medicine and, at least partially, invalidated its claims on public resources for the unquestioned funding of ever more 'expensive medical procedures'. One response to this has been an exaggerated assertion of the role of science in clinical practice: the move towards 'evidence based medicine' (see Sackett 1995; Sackett and Rosenberg 1995) in which a classical statistical interpretation of the results of clinical trials is used to inform practice in the individual case.[12] It is interesting that this involves an implicit abandonment of linear certainty in clinical determination in favour of a stochastically-founded probabilistic approach. There is nothing intrinsically wrong with this approach as a way of guiding clinical practice in secondary care but it is not a panacea for the problems of the biomechanical approach to human health in general. Here the potential for complex understanding as the basis of primary clinical practice is of considerable significance.

However, the most important consequence of a complex interpretation of the strong social programme in health is for the general orientation of politics in advanced 'postindustrial' societies. Equity in health outcomes has had particular political saliency in the post-war years. It remains almost the only shibboleth of the post-war political settlement in the UK not to have been ideologically challenged in the Thatcher years.[13] Only in the US do gross inequalities of health outcome seem politically acceptable. It is indicative that this acceptance is associated with a withdrawal of the poor from any real engagement with the political system. In societies where the majority of eligible adults remain politically active citizens, a gross health divide is, absolutely properly, understood as a crucial indicator of a fundamental fault in the character of the social order.

The crucial message of the complex account of 'health divided' societies is that this sort of Pottersville writ large is not a necessary state of postindustrial being. It is one of the possible states, one of the attractor forms, but it is not the only one. Changes in key control variables for the whole social system, evidentially[14] in the degree of income inequality, lead to a social form without such great internal variation in health states. The debate about the health divide has generally been conducted in a curious sort of parallel way to the overall debate about social exclusion. That is to say the debate about social exclusion has emphasised employment and lifestyle, rather than the gross exclusion represented by premature death. A good deal of real modelling needs to be done on this issue but the available evidence about the sources of that premature death seems overwhelming. This matters enormously. It matters intellectually because it provides such a clear illustration of how the social and the individual intersect, and how the nature of that intersection is best understood in terms of the dynamics of far from equilibrium nested systems. It matters politically because it is wrong.

7

COMPLEXITY, EDUCATION AND CHANGE

Introduction

The UK Economic and Social Research Council (ESRC) is currently funding a five-year programme dealing with 'the Analysis of Large and Complex Data Sets'. This is the largest programme in methodology ever commissioned by the ESRC and has been established to take advantage of the ESRC's holdings of such data sets. Clearly this is an extremely important initiative in social science. However, despite the presence of the word 'complex' in its title, it seems to be proceeding in a way which is not really connected with the implications of the chaos/complexity programme for quantitative social science.[1] This is a very great pity. To understand why this should be so it is necessary to work through an example of substantive significance. The example selected is that of the relationship among the educational achievement of children, the social characteristics of those children and their families, the character of the schools they attend, and the character of the neighbourhoods within which those schools are located. This has been the central concern of the nomothetic radical programme in the sociology of education (see Byrne *et al.* 1975) for many years, a programme which in the UK has focused on the effects of class and in the USA has been primarily concerned with the effects of race. In the UK this programme was displaced within the sociology of education by an originally Althusserian structuralist and subsequently postmodernist concern with the content of knowledge and the processes of the transmission of that knowledge. In the USA, because of the saliency of race for social structure, analyses founded in this programme have continued to be done.

Of course investigation of these issues has not stopped in the UK. Rather the investigations have been handed over to others, principally to educational statisticians with a mathematical rather than social scientific background. The result has been a considerable development in apparent methodological rigour associated with a distancing of the research programme from substantive sociological concerns. In the USA in contrast research conducted into these issues, and the closely related issue of racially constructed residential segregation, has been intimately associated with crucial developments in the theorisation of contemporary forms of social stratification.[2]

These issues have general significance in societies in which employment is increasingly dominated by service-class occupations requiring high levels of formal educational qualifications as entry tickets, and there has also been a massive decline in reasonably paid skilled manual employment which could be accessed without such qualifications. At the same time the development of social indicators as part of a programme for the evaluation of policy interventions which began in the USA in the early 1960s and was taken up in the UK in the 1970s (see Booth 1988; Rivlin 1971) has led to the use of published output measures of school performance – 'league tables' – as crucial 'facts' for parents in 'choosing' schools. The 1979–97 UK Tory government eliminated most of the control which elected Local Education Authorities were able to operate over state schools, absolutely for those schools which 'opted out', and introduced parental 'choice' of school alongside a formula funding system in which children became in effect walking vouchers for the schools which admitted them. This was associated with a tabloid press-supported campaign of denigration against the teaching profession in general, with teachers identified as 'trendy lefties' with low expectations of children and a generally bone idle attitude to work. The Office for Standards in Education (OFSTED) was established to replace the very widely respected Her Majesty's Inspectorate of Education and has been headed up by a repentant trendy, Chris Woodhead, who has made it his business to root out 'failing' teachers and 'failing' schools. Leading members of the Labour Party, including the present Prime Minister, have taken advantage of the opportunities offered by the Tory attack on comprehensive (equivalent to US high school) neighbourhood secondary education in order to achieve advantage for their own offspring, and have abandoned Labour's opposition to 'opting out' in order to permit this. The newly appointed Secretary of State for Education and Employment, David Blunkett, and his minister for schools have accepted the OFSTED line. The issue is very hot stuff.

This chapter will begin with a general consideration (referring back to Chapters 1 to 4), of the nature of 'large and complex' data sets, which will attempt to understand such data sets as descriptions of a social reality characterised by non-linear change, both globally and locally. This account will be illustrated by a careful examination of one of the most important studies to emerge from the ESRC programme, Goldstein and Spiegelhalter's examination of 'League tables and their limitations' (1996)[3] with reference both to the inadequacy of linear modelling as a way of dealing with these issues and to the significance of the neglect of emergent properties in this kind of quantitative social science. The illustrative value of the idea of fitness landscapes and evolutionary change in them, Kauffman's programme, will be considered through a consideration of the application of this approach to this issue by Byrne and Rogers (1996). Finally the chapter will attempt a complex account of the continuing discussion of the impact of residentially-mediated racial segregation in US high schools, with particular reference to the work of Bankston and Caldas (1996), and a series of contributions by Massey which are summarised in his presidential address to the Annual Meeting of the Population Association of America (1996).

Large and complex data sets

The data sets which the ESRC describes as 'large and complex' are large because they have many cases. The meaning of the word 'complex', however, cannot be so easily established. In the programme documentation the term sometimes seems to be used as synonymous with 'messy', for example: 'Longitudinal data generally exhibit a variety of sources of complexity, such as irregular spacing, measurement error, multiple instruments, informative censoring, and missing observations' (ALCD 1997a). However, here our attention will be directed at one particular aspect of ESRC 'complexity', that which derives from the fact that:

> Most social science data are structured hierarchically. Examples are the clustering of students within schools, individuals within households with neighbourhoods, and repeated measurements within individual subjects. . . . Researchers dealing with large and complex structures, such as longitudinal panel surveys or studies of educational performance, require modelling techniques which respect the hierarchical and cross-classified structures in their data.
>
> (ALCD 1997b)

The importance of the hierarchical structure of social science data sets matters because the data sets reflect the nature of the social world, of which they are descriptions. This is a crucial example of 'the obduracy of the world' in relation to science, and the issues which derive from this have already received considerable attention in this text. The important thing is that our data structures are hierarchical because they reflect the way in which the world is composed of a set of nested far from equilibric systems. This has been considered in general in the discussion of Reed and Harvey's ideas in Chapter 2, in relation to the quantitative programme in social science in Chapters 3 and 4, and in specific terms to do with space and health in Chapters 5 and 6. Themes which are part of this crucial topic include the idea of cluster sampling and the debate about cross level inference, usually referred to as 'the ecological fallacy'. If we take the significance of time as given, then we can agree with Skinner (1997) that we are dealing with those 'complex features of data sets, such as longitudinal or multilevel structures, [which] may be of intrinsic interest'. That they are, because so is the world.

Here the interesting complex aspect of the large data sets will be that they should take account of the dynamic character of the nested far from equilibric systems which make up the world. Let us illustrate by considering the educational data set analysed by Goldstein and Spiegelhalter (1996). In the educational part of this study, the authors use a simplified model. It involves only measurements of children and of the secondary schools they attend. In particular they note (1996: 390) that this ignores the problem of the contribution of primary schools to achievement which is a (resolvable) problem of cross-classification. In their simplified model there are two components in the variance around the level (average) performance of any individual student – an effect due to that student and an effect due to school attended. They then extend this by including two years' worth of results and considering the impact of variation between years. What concerns Goldstein and Spiegelhalter is that outcome indicators are used to generate ranking tables, despite the sensitivity of such ranks to sampling variability. In order to develop their argument they make a crucial, and dangerous, but explicit assumption:

> It is worth emphasising that we are regarding the set of students taking an examination as if they were a sample from a superpopulation since we wish to make inferences about the general 'effects' of institutions for *any* [original emphasis] group of students in the future.
>
> (Goldstein and Spiegelhalter 1996: 397)

Goldstein and Spiegelhalter draw on Raudenbush and Willms' (1995) distinction between two kinds of institutional comparisons. First, there are those made by those who are choosing between institutions for themselves:

> they wish to ascertain the expected output achievement conditionally on their own characteristics, such as their input achievement, social background, gender, etc. They will also be interested in whether there are interactions between their own characteristics and those of other students likely to attend any institution . . . there is some evidence . . . that, at certain intake achievement levels, attendance at a secondary school where the average intake score is higher than the student's leads to a raised output score compared with attendance at a school where the average is lower.
>
> (Goldstein and Spiegelhalter 1996: 396)

The second type of effects are 'the difference the institution makes'. Interestingly Goldstein and Spiegelhalter do not recognise the interaction effects among students as an institutional characteristic, but confine their discussion to the formal and informal arrangements of the institution per se. In their actual study Goldstein and Spiegelhalter adjust for intake variation by considering only students who scored in the middle half of the performance range at GCSE[4] level in relation to an output measure of A level performance. There is a good deal to be said against using this particular pair as any sensible measure of secondary school performance[5] but the end conclusion is that if evaluators are seeking to understand institution effects, added value in an input/throughput/output model, then the degree of sampling variation may be so great that a comparison of confidence intervals suggests that about two thirds of all possible comparisons between schools do not allow separation.

It seems to me that Goldstein and Spiegelhalter succeed pretty well in their main objective, which is to say that the measurement tools we have available are so imprecise, because of the possibility of sampling variability, that for most secondary schools we can't say that one set of school managers and teachers are doing better or worse than another, given the intakes they have: fine so far, but no farther and not adequate as a description of the social dynamics surrounding secondary schooling.

Let me pick up the hint offered by the reference made to interaction effects. Clearly there are two sorts of interaction effects which can be present. The first is the consequence of interactions among the students

– in everyday language people generally prefer to have their children educated alongside children who are well behaved and of the same or higher social status.[6] In a system where 'disruptive pupils' are an issue, such 'bad children' are to be avoided at all costs. The disruptive pupil issue illustrates these interactions rather well. One child making serious disturbances or even just excessive demands for attention or assistance, can disrupt the education of a whole class of other pupils.

The other kind of interaction effect is a consequence of the effect that the general character of pupils has on the institution's form. In the late 1980s I was Chair of the Board of Governors of an inner-city comprehensive which was situated in a Local Education Authority with a large amount of surplus places. This school served the poorest part of the inner-city area. Positive feedback (in the system sense of destabilising reinforcement) led to the numbers of pupils entering it falling dramatically – people who in formal terms should have sent their children there, sent them to more 'middle-class' schools in adjacent areas. The school differentially lost children who were higher achievers at age 11. In my opinion, and in the opinion of external inspectors, the school was actually doing the job it did of catering for a predominantly lower achieving intake very well indeed. The management and staff geared the school in that direction. There was an interaction effect between intake and internal form. These things were not independent. Although of course the school could have changed its form over a period of time, much as happened with the comprehensive reorganisation of UK secondary education in the 1970s, this would only have happened if the intake changed, and that would not have happened so long as the school was regarded as 'not for academic children'. Eventually numbers fell so low that the school was closed. This meant that many of the children who would have gone to it, now went to the more middle-class school which had previously received only the higher ability end of the first school's catchment group. This led to a change in the internal organisation of the second school which has had to respond to the intake it now has.

The point can be clearly illustrated by reference to the Ds to Cs programme of many state secondary schools in the contemporary UK. The key performance indicator for most schools is the percentage of a year group who achieve a score of five or more A to C grades in GCSE examinations. The easiest way for a school in the middle or lower ranks on this indicator to improve its performance is to concentrate resources on pupils who seem to be heading for D grades in order to ensure that those children get C grades. The effect of this pressure varies, given the 'achievement type' of the school. A school with a high rank will not change its programme in this way but will seek to get as many nine As or A*s as possible to show that it is a school suitable for very able children. A middle ranking school may well lose performances at A or A* because it concentrates its resources on middle achievers rather than high achievers.

These sorts of process cannot be modelled by linear models which assume independence between one year's results and the next year's. This point was cogently made in the discussion of the Goldstein and Spiegelhalter article:

> All the models in the paper treat the institutional effect as 'random', even though there is nothing random about the institutions involved: we typically have data on *all* the units . . . at *all* the institutions . . . *at one moment in time*, and our interest is in *these* [original emphases] institutions, not in any hypothetical population from which we might pretend these institutions were 'randomly' drawn. What, therefore, justifies the use of 'random effects' models in this case?
>
> (Draper 1996: 417)

Draper goes on to say that the possible justification lies exactly in the interest in future outcomes but that the models can only be justified in relation to that task if there is time homogeneity of the process under study: 'Shrinkage is of little value when the process under study is changing in ways that are not captured by your random effects model' (1996: 417).

This is precisely the issue. For the absence of time homogeneity, substitute non-linear change. For the notion that there is a continuous range of institutional forms, substitute the idea of a set of possible institutional types representing attractor states towards which institutions tend over time, and quite short times, and consider what perturbations might move them from one attractor state to another. Bring in the idea of a fitness landscape which itself can change given changes in defining rules – changes in the environment. This we will now do.

Schools in a fitness landscape

In England and Wales (Scotland and Northern Ireland have somewhat different systems) there are now four sorts of school providing education for children in their secondary years (mostly from 11 to 18). First, there are private schools. These vary from extraordinarily expensive and elitist residential institutions, some of great age, to hell holes provided on the cheap for the children of service personnel 'other ranks'. However, the most important group are not residential but are instead day schools, many formerly connected with the state system as 'direct grant schools' but which became private when their special privileged position was abolished in the 1970s. Then there are 'opted out schools' which left the control of their local educational authorities and receive funding from a centralised quango. These have considerable discretionary control over admissions policies and orientation. Associated with them are a small number of 'city technology colleges' which are recent new centrally-funded foundations. Then there are the 'county schools', those schools which remain under the general direction of the elected local councils as local education authorities, although with considerable devolved budgetary control and some devolved control over admissions. Finally there are the religious schools, overwhelmingly Catholic, which are essentially similar to the 'county schools' but which have to raise some of their own capital (but not current) funding and which have some greater degree of autonomy reflecting this. Some Catholic schools have 'opted out'.

If we ignore the boarding schools, which of course have traditionally educated the national elite, including the present Labour Prime Minister, then we can regard the day schools as competing with each other in a given locality. The introduction of an apparent right of 'parental choice' means that there is no centralised (at the locality level) mechanism for allocating children to schools and the private schools are in competition with the state schools to which parents might send their children free of charge instead of paying £5–7,000 per annum for private schooling. Schools want to attract children in general because formula funding means that every pupil represents income, even in the non-private system. This is a competitive ecology in which we are likely to see evolutionary change. It is a far from equilibric system as a whole, containing within it the far from equilibric systems which are individual schools.

The system of schooling is at least partially embedded within the socio-spatial system of the divided city which has been examined in Chapter 5. That embedding is only partial in that schools are of course physically located in space but can draw on pupils from varying spatial ranges. Those ranges can be very large for private schools and others which do not have a spatial element in their criteria for admission. They are quite large for Catholic schools given that Catholics form about 10 per cent of the English population[7] and are not residentially segregated in any way. However, most schools are to some degree 'neighbourhood' in character and have an initial intake base which reflects the character of their spatial location. We must remember of course that the socio-spatial system itself is dynamic and liable to change.

Goldstein and Spiegelhalter's account of a secondary school is that it can be anything and do anything within a continuous range of possible states defined by 'achievements' and that what it is in the future is quite independent of what it has been in the past. Draper's criticism of their paper was founded on a recognition that reality is not like that; that, to use the language of complexity, it consists of nested systems with a directional and evolutionary history. In order to get a 'complexity fix' we need to consider the actual possible range of forms of a school as constituting a multi-dimensional phase or condition space with the form at any given time point described by the co-ordinates on the variables which are the dimensions of that phase space. However, if we have a non-linear situation then we will not have a process of continuous and smooth transformation of possible states for schools. Instead there will be attractor states towards which they will tend. They can't be anything. They can only be certain things and with a given evolutionary context or fitness landscape, they will move towards the attractor which is closest to their initial starting condition and can only move to another in a way which reflects the energy/resource character of the fitness landscape of the system of all schools in their locality or which derives from a massive energy/information input into that particular school.

Together with my colleague Tim Rogers, I recently examined the pattern of output performance for secondary schools in England and Wales (Byrne and Rogers 1996) using the published league table data. This was not a dynamic examination in that it looked only at the system as a whole in one year, although with more resources a dynamic examination is now possible since the league tables are published for all schools every year and detailed trajectories can be established. What we attempted was in a sort of way a Poincaré section of the system as a whole. This was very much a 'sort of'. We were not attempting to establish even a local description in terms of a fully formalised mathematical representation. Rather we used clustering techniques, numerical taxonomy, applied stamp-collecting, to generate a typology and to assign individual schools to that typology. A dynamic account would chart both changes in the typological character of the system as a whole over time and shifts in type form by individual schools, the nested systems within the system, with particular attention paid to the nature of internal system shifts within school systems which led to the relocation of that school in terms of attractor association. In other words, what could happen to schools which would lead to a change in the sort of schools they are. The crucial thing here is the notion that what matters is not incremental change along a continuum, quantitative change, but radical change of form, qualitative change. Of course in a non-linear world we are always dealing with the reality of the transformation of quantity into quality.

We found three sorts of school in a complex fitness landscape which can be represented by the frequency polygons for each cluster in the form of histograms. Interestingly the overall distribution is plainly bimodal with the higher mode being 100 per cent achievement of the five A–C standard and with that being occupied by high achieving private schools. We can see a fitness landscape in which movement from low achievement to moderate achievement and from moderate achievement to the lower end of the high achievement category is possible, but in which initial selection seems the absolute condition for movement into the top end of the high achievement pattern. Of course we don't know how or if movements occur. That is why we need a dynamic examination of the process. It may also be that the appropriate scale for studies of this kind is not national, but rather that of the locality as discussed in Chapter 5. Indeed, when we turned to an examination of a specific locality, the Tyne and Wear conurbation together with the adjacent county of Northumberland, we found a slightly different speciation with an important and distinctive group of high achieving state schools.

When we related, very crudely, the social characteristics of the area within which the school was located to the achievement type to which it belonged, we found that with the exception of one selective anomaly, all the high achieving schools by national type were located in affluent areas. In contrast, of those schools which were low achieving by national type, all but one were physically located in deprived areas and that one drew its actual catchment from deprived areas rather than from the affluent ward within which it was situated (see Byrne and Rogers 1996). This is scarcely a surprising result but it does need to be thought about in relation to the inter-connection between local social area and educational opportunity.

The processes of positive feedback which are so important in non-linear systems are very well illustrated by this issue, as is the significance of categorical status in understanding social processes. Let me deal with the latter first. Schools are not best understood by their apparent location on some continuous dimension. Rather they are socially located in a classificatory schema which is derived from the complex effect of a set of categorising variables. In some cases physical location is not really very important, although interestingly very few high status private day schools, many of which were historically located in what are now poor inner-city areas, remain in such places. They are now usually located in affluent suburbs. However, for English urban 'county' schools physical location is crucial because it determines the character of the original core stock of pupils. Schools in poor areas have deprived core catchment areas, and the characters of the schools are very much affected (not absolutely determined in a linear sense, but certainly bounded within a range of possibilities) by the general character of the pupils coming from that deprived catchment area. The positive feedback comes from the flight of the children of parents who have ambitions for them towards 'good' schools in nicer areas. This issue is central to the extremely important politics of race and schooling in the USA. Let us turn to that context in order to develop the argument further.

Segregation and education – the interaction of race and space

Segregation in education was the key issue around which African Americans conducted the legally-founded programme which rejected the doctrine that it was constitutionally acceptable for US states and localities to provide 'separate but equal' facilities. Following the decision of the US Supreme Court in the case of Brown vs. Topeka 1955, educational segregation on racial grounds was outlawed in principle. However, it has persisted in practice given the residential segregation of blacks and whites in the US (see Massey and Denton 1993). Bankston and Caldas (1996) have examined both the conceptual debate which surrounds this issue and important empirical evidence relating to the effects of racial segregation on educational attainment.

The key issue here is 'equality of opportunity'. The major contributor to the discussion of the meaning of this vexed expression has been Coleman who has considered it in a series of works over some thirty years (see Coleman 1990). The formal objective of US policy in relation to educational equality of opportunity seems to have always related to Coleman's: 'fourth type of inequality [which] may be defined in terms of consequences of the school for individuals with equal backgrounds and abilities. In this definition equality of educational opportunity is equality of results given the same individual input' (1966: 14).

However, we have to ask 'what are schools?' They are not simply aggregations of resources, nor even best understood as the consequences of the organisational management of such aggregations of resources. We have to take account of the interaction effects among students identified by Raudenbush and Willms (1995) as considered earlier in this chapter. Bankston and Caldas comment on this most pertinently:

To argue that students are social resources for one another is to argue that schools are social environments that are, to some extent, independent of the families that supply the students. . . . Having brought behavioral and attitudinal 'capital' from the family to the school, students establish a peer society that makes their forms of behaviour and attitude a part of the common holdings. Parents who send their children to 'good' schools provide the children with the advantage of associating with 'good' students, advantages that may outweigh those of superior school facilities, and even those of quality teachers.

(Bankston and Caldas 1996: 536)

In the US, bussing, the movement of children away from their own neighbourhood for educational purposes, has been used in large urban centres as a method of trying to achieve some sort of racial balance in practice. This has led to a heated debate in two domains. The first is in relation to principles of distributional justice; the second concerns the actual outcome effects of such movement. Coleman (1990) has drawn on the contrasting positions of Rawls and Nozick as a way of defining the character of the dispute about distributional justice. Nozick would agree with, and perhaps was even the inspiration for, Margaret Thatcher's notorious assertion that 'There is no such thing as society; there are only individuals and families.' Rawls in contrast sees all resources as the product of social relations and argues that inequalities are only justifiable if they have the effect of increasing the absolute resource position of the poorest in consequence of higher overall social production – a notion very much equivalent to J. S. Mill's conception of the optimal utilitarian outcome.

Bankston and Caldas summarise Coleman's translation of this dispute into educational terms:

From the Nozickian perspective, since all resources, immaterial as well as material, belong to individuals and their families, parents have the right to invest and pool these resources as they see fit, and to educate their own children with an eye specifically towards maximising the children's own opportunities. From a Rawlsian perspective, on the other hand, allowing the concentration of advantaged children, and as a necessary consequence, also the concentration of disadvantaged children,

133

simply perpetuates unacceptable imbalances of abundance and deprivation.

(Bankston and Caldas 1996: 536)

In the UK the Blairs are clearly proponents of the Nozickian position.

In the US there are three positions on racial integration in schools. There is a position justified formally by Nozickian-style arguments and adopted in practice by most whites who can manage it, of maintaining de facto educational separation from blacks through residential segregation. There is a liberal/reformist position which argues for real integration despite residential segregation. Finally there is a black separatist position which argues for black schools informed by a black cultural ethos and which argues that the subordination of black children to a white majority culture is damaging to them. There are echoes of this debate in the UK but the proportion of 'other than whites' outside a few major urban centres is so small, residential segregation is so much less (see Peach 1996a), and the crucial issue is religious (Muslim schools) rather than racial, that in consequence these echoes remain rather faint.

Bankston and Caldas' study (1996) is a linear model-based examination of the impact of 'minority concentration' on the educational achievement of both black and white children. It is based on a single year's achievement measures and employs cross-sectional data which is hierarchical in form in that it includes measures both of the attributes of individual students and of the attributes of the schools which they attend. Bankston and Caldas include in the latter set summary characteristics of all students in the school and find that these sometimes have a more important effect than the actual measure of that characteristic for the individual student. For example, the mean number of hours of homework done in the school is more important for the achievement of individual students than the hours of homework done individually by those students. Ultimately the linear models demonstrate that segregation disadvantages black students more than the reversal of segregation would disadvantage white students, although such a reversal would imply costs for white students.

This is an important and interesting study but a consideration of the processes investigated in complex terms, rather than in linear terms, might be particularly productive. This is not just a matter of knowledge generation, but relates also to the crucial social issue specified by Bankston and Caldas in terms of a utilitarian effort to identify:

a 'threshold' effect associated with school racial integration. That is, is there an optimal school percentage of African American and white students where the benefits of a racially integrated school environment contribute most to African American academic achievement, while at the same time not detracting from white student achievement? If such a threshold could be identified, school systems would then have theoretically defensible racial integration target levels to aim for, and maintain.

(Bankston and Caldas 1996: 553)[8]

Let me suggest that we are not dealing with linear effects in relation to black/white segregation in US schooling (as we are not with regard to all other aspects of black/white segregation in the US). Instead we are dealing with discontinuities, with non-linearities, and the non-linear consideration of data sets of the form of that employed by Bankston and Caldas will be most productive. Such a consideration must begin with the establishment of a socio-spatial school landscape using school characteristics as inputs into numerical taxonomy procedures. This is not a preliminary process. In other words it rejects absolutely the privileging of linear models suggested by Clarke:

One of the classic debates in the history of science turns around the proper role of typologies in the development of theory. While in principle it may be apparent that the very existence of a reasoned typology ought to imply a set of inter-related propositions, and the associated conditions under which they hold – that is a theory – not a few observers have been convinced that in practice typological construction often distracts attention from the formulation of more explicit, more powerful, and more precise propositions.

(Clarke 1971: 7)

This is not just an abstract issue. It means that however much one may sympathise with Bankston and Caldas' objective of establishing a single level of integrated educational experience which in the best, and wholly honourable, liberal tradition achieves the greatest good of the greatest number, this may not be possible. If the situation is non-linear then the whole 'fitness landscape' will have to be transformed if Rawlsian criteria of social justice are to be achieved. In other words 'education cannot compensate for society'.

Conclusion

Massey has pessimistically identified the future as an 'Age of Extremes'. Let me quote from his presidential address to the Population Association of America given under that title:

> In the coming century, the fundamental condition thát enabled social order to be maintained in the past – the occurrence of affluence and poverty at low geographic densities – will no longer hold. In the future, most of the world's impoverished people will live in urban areas, and within these places they will inhabit neighbourhoods characterised by extreme poverty. A small stratum of rich families meanwhile will cluster in enclaves of affluence, creating an unprecedented spatial intensification of both privilege and poverty.
>
> (Massey 1996: 395)

Actually I think this is wrong in two important respects, even if the general account is correct. It is much more likely that we will, in Therborn's words, see a 'Brazilianisation of advanced capitalism' (1985) with a threefold division among the very affluent, ordinary and poor. It is also untrue that such a division is unprecedented. It was the European norm before the development of the Keynes/Beveridge and/or Christian Democratic welfare states founded on Fordism and it seems to be returning as the Fordist system collapses. However, Massey's overall story does seem correct. We are seeing increasing socio-spatial segregation within cities and that is the basis of many of the problems of social order and realities of social injustice in our world.

Education matters enormously in relation to this because it is the most important means for individual social mobility, more important in economies of signs and space than ever it was when the coalminer could earn the top dollar, however brutish the conditions of his working life. In the last 'liberal hour' in the US and the UK, the mid-1960s, improvement of educational opportunity was seen as the central mechanism for achieving a more just society. Central to this approach was the notion of the significance of 'positive discrimination' in which education resources were to be distributed as negative feedback against the trend of general social inequalities. However, as many critics of that time noted (see Byrne *et al.* 1975), education cannot compensate for all social inequalities. Indeed the development of divided cities, in the US so apparently divided to the disadvantage of African Americans, elsewhere divided on the basis of more complex interactions of class and ethnicity, means that the level of resource transformations required to overcome disadvantages is now enormous. This seems to me to draw us towards the issue of 'empowerment' as discussed by Freire in a range of works. We will return to this approach in Chapter 8 with regard to issues of planning, but some discussion of the educational implications of this term are appropriate here.

It was a hard learned truism of the 1960s that 'education cannot compensate for society' and that was a truism expressed within a social order in which inequalities were stepped rather than radically discontinuous and in which educational resources were distributed as negative feedback through programmes of compensatory education which, in the long run, have demonstrated considerable effectiveness, particularly in the case of 'Head-Start' in the United States. Now we have a discontinuous/polarised pattern of inequality and the tendency in educational systems to reward high achievement and penalise failure operates as positive feedback in intensifying social divisions. In advanced industrial societies we have nominal universalism in education but a reality of the engenderment of increasing social division.

Here the experience of Britain's Catholic schools becomes interesting. Religion, especially Catholicism, is not a significant social divisor in contemporary Britain (Northern Ireland is a very different story), whatever the historical salience of 'Rome on the rates'. The ethnic underpinnings of Catholicism by a 200-year process of Irish immigration are not particularly salient when this white (few whiter) Christian English-speaking group is so assimilated by inter-marriage over several generations. The existence of separate Catholic schools does not reinforce any particular line of fissure in contemporary British society.

Catholic schools were historically distinguished by their association with religious observance. In general the children of even minimally observant Catholics tended to go to them. Because Catholicism is not a principle of spatial segregation the catchment areas of these schools are substantially larger than is the case for the county schools. Contingently, when 'direct grant' status was abolished most of the Catholic direct grant grammar schools opted to become comprehensives rather than going into the elitist private sector.

The consequence of the combination of the contingency of an original high quality component and generally mixed catchment areas in which bussing is a voluntary activity is schools which are widely regarded as considerably superior to the state norm and with far fewer in the 'deprived and depriving' category. The problem is that the underpinning element in all this is the assertion of a distinctive identity. In contemporary Britain this particular segmented and partial assertion is without any wider significance but it has to be there. The Catholic schools in summary are the Rawlsian element in an increasingly Nozickian system, but only on the basis of particularistic common identity.

However, whilst the nature of the Catholic schools does represent a universalistic target, very much what Bankston and Caldas' work points us towards as a socially just resolution, it is a lot harder to see how it might be the object of a general and universalistic social programme. How can the torus frame be re-established? This issue will be re-addressed in explicitly complex terms in the Conclusion, following on from a discussion of 'empowerment in planning' in Chapter 8.

8

COMPLEXITY AND POLICY

The limits to urban governance

Urban development models focus on urban development processes as if intentional action – plans – and regulation were an exogenous disturbance to be contended with unhappily. Most urban economic models conclude that the development process will work fine if left alone because of the assumptions built into the models. Planning is of value precisely because the presumed natural equilibrium processes of such models cannot be relied upon to yield desired outcomes through sequences of decisions made myopically.

(*Environment and Planning B* 1997: 318)

Introduction

There are few better established illustrations of the inanity of 'free market' modelling than the history of cities, but of course the ideologues of the New Right forget everything and learn nothing, so the UK is perhaps just about to emerge from a seventeen-year period (beginning in legislative terms with the Local Government Planning and Land Act 1980) during which public policy has formally asserted that the future of cities must be determined by market mechanisms. As usual the formal assertion served in reality as a smokescreen behind which enormous sums of public money were placed at the disposal of land development capital, under the heading of 'catalytic planning',[1] and 'free markets' have had very little to do with developments, which have been far more the product of authoritarian centralism informed by a deliberate anti-industrialism. However, the Hayekian rhetoric was loud indeed. The crucial lesson of the 1840s, that a general urbanised form of life for the mass of humanity is biologically impossible without collective and informed public interventions (see Ashton 1988 for a history of the old and the new public health), was ignored. In the

139

United States this sort of right libertarian ranting as a basis for policy has led to the successful breeding of multiple drug resistant tuberculosis and the re-emergence of the white plague as a serious public health hazard. In the UK urban system breakdowns have, so far, been at the level of order rather than of public health.

In the urbanised world created by the development of an industrially-founded world system cities do not work unless they are governed in a way which directs their development. Urban governance can never be about the maintenance of equilibrium. In systemic terms cities are necessarily complex and evolving far from equilibrium systems with an evolutionary character. Jane Jacobs put it like this: 'Cities happen to be problems in organised complexity. . . . They present situations in which half a dozen or even several dozen quantities are all varying simultaneously and in subtly interconnected ways' (quoted in Batty 1995: 469).

To say that cities are complex is to say what has already been said in theoretical terms about localities in Chapter 5 in a slightly different way. The difference arises because the discussion in that chapter, founded as it was in the debates of a geography which even in its 'new new' postmodernist form remains profoundly influenced by structuralism, was mostly about the evolution of socio-spatial structures. In this chapter the emphasis is on conscious and informed agency, on the processes of planning which shape the development of urban space.

The term 'planning' is interesting and multi-layered. Hall begins his overview of UK and US land use planning systems with a discussion of the content of the process and concludes that: 'planning is concerned with deliberately achieving some objective, and it proceeds by assembling actions into some orderly sequence' (1992: 1). We have to recognise, as Ambrose (1994) demonstrates, that planning processes in a world which is both urban and capitalist are always about some combination of other objectives with the realisation of profit from land development. There are really two 'other than profit' sorts of objective sets. One is the general interest of the system, expressed through technically qualified professionals who assert the rationality of their technical projects. Of course, just as free market liberalism has discredited planning in political terms, so the postmodernist turn in the academy has discredited it in intellectual terms, precisely because of planning's claims to a rational foundation. However, what is more interesting than the postmodern gibe against all rationality is the wider question of rationality for what? Note that this question is being asked here in a structurally located way. It is not a matter of free standing competing discourses but rather of the relationship between technocratic planning and the social system, and in particular the classes, generated by capitalism. Capitalism needs planning – it really does sometimes need the state to function as the executive committee of the whole bourgeoisie and do that which the individual capitalist will not. Even neo-classical economics allows for externalities and public goods as the bases for collective rather than individual optimising decisions.

At one level planning might be thought to be a stabilising corrective. It can be interpreted in system terms as negative feedback which keeps things steady against the creative destruction which characterises the drive of capitalist innovation. But, of course, it is not really that at all. Planning is about change. This means that it is embedded as an integral and inseparable part within the capitalist development process itself. It is neither an external corrective and control element, nor something which can be analysed out of the development process. Hall talks of three stages in planning theory – an original stage lasting until the 1960s in which plans were literally blueprints, a subsequent systems-oriented phase, and a current understanding which sees: 'planning as continuous participation in conflict' (1992: 27). The last recognises development as inherently political. It is perfectly true that any review of UK and US planning history shows that when planning has been at its most technocratically authoritarian is when it has most damaged urban working-class interests and community forms. Only when a democratic culture has been able to achieve hegemony, even if only at the level of locality, has planning served working-class interests. This is particularly well illustrated by the history of design policy for UK social housing (see Byrne 1989). However, planning has been forced into the service of collectivism and universal social interests at important points in history. It has that potential, and the historical reality represents the other objective set, that of inclusive Keynesianism to combine the system description of regulation theory with the contemporary gloss on the Marshallian notion of citizenship.

Hall's account of the history of planning theory is worth some more attention before we go further. Planning is almost the archetype of modernity as process. Its origins lie in the development beyond epidemiologically-founded public health interventions of what was orig-inally an architectural/civil engineering-based interest in the foundation of the 'good city'. Utopian ideas, particularly those of Ebenezer Howard, were of great importance but Howard was a rational and scientific utopian. His notion of the garden city was well founded in the science available to him. Perhaps the main reason for planning theory's original emphasis on the 'blueprint' was the perfectly sound idea that land use planning was an effective mechanism for achieving physical health through the separation of people from pollution, a notion of considerable contemporary relevance in the late twentieth century, and for achieving social health through the provision of a decent and humane environment in which people were not absolutely separated from nature. The utopian planners invented the suburb and those of us who live in them have cause to be grateful.

The move in the post-Second World War period towards a system conception of planning, embodied in the UK's planning system by a shift from map-based land use planning to the document-founded structure plans, was a perfectly logical development of planning as practice. Planners as engineers were aware of the potential of system theory, although they usually took up its more simplistic and linear versions and were generally incapable of marshalling social understanding and social evidence in the formation of objectives (see Dennis 1970, 1972; Davies 1972). Indeed, the previous generation of planners had generally been far more competent at incorporating social evidence in Geddes' process of survey–plan–implement. However, the structure planning process was in formal terms democratic and included a considerable element of public consultation, if not of participation. Ultimately there was a representative democratic element to it. Actually systems-based structure planning was not a disaster. It never really had the chance to be. The planning disasters which played a by no means unimportant part in the discrediting of planning as part of collective intervention, were largely the work of simplistic architects and road engineers, both in cahoots with civil engineering capital. In practice structure plans have been replaced by *ad hoc* idiocy under the direction of quangos, particularly the urban development corporations (see Imrie and Thomas 1993), whose operations have been characterised by neither system nor accountability, and have been validated by absurd claims as to the efficacy of market mechanisms as social optimisers.

The failure of planning as a practice is important. It was a crucial part of the post-war Keynes/Beveridge style social politics of the United Kingdom and the devaluing of it matters. For now I would simply want to make a clear distinction between the radical modernist critique of planning mounted from both Marxist and Weberian informed frames of reference in the 1960s and 1970s, and the contemporary postmodernist critique. The radical modernist critique did not challenge the progressive/systems rationalism on which planning was founded. Rather it asserted that that rationalism was incomplete. It was a critique of content, not of form. In particular 1960s and 1970s systems planning ignored the rationality which interpreted working-class action as the universal basis of progress in the extreme theoretical form, and as a legitimate interest among others in practice. Planning asserted value neutrality, but in fact served capitalist development interests. To say that is not to reject progress, but to argue that there are alternatives for progress; there is more than one possible trajectory. The issue is progress for whom?

This review of urban governance will proceed by looking in some detail at the content of the chaos/complexity influenced revival of systems perspectives in planning theory. It will then turn to a consideration of how contemporary urban systems generate information which can be the basis of a rational understanding of how urban policy might be constructed. Central to the discussion will be a recognition of the absolutely essential characteristic of planning as a human activity. It is about alternatives, about different ways in which things might be done in order that different sorts of futures might come into being. It is always about people making history, even if not in circumstances of their own choosing. The important thing about planning is that it is about choices. The important thing about the chaos/complexity programme in relation to planning is that it provides a rational framework which is not based on simplistic determinism but rather is explicitly founded on reflexive social action. The condition space defines the possibilities – the plural is crucial – planning is about which outcome is achieved. What is interesting is that a chaos/complexity perspective on the governance of cities suggests that mass democratic participatory processes are not only morally preferable but actually represent the only process through which the achievement of unificational non-divisive urban forms may be possible. The chapter will conclude with a discussion of participatory planning as a process of empowerment in the real sense of that word as Freire meant it to be employed.

Rational planning is complex planning

Unlike their academic cousins, planning practitioners have seldom had the luxury of 'retreating from rationality'. They had always had a job to do, rationally; in this job they were once comprehensively assisted by researchers into computer-aided planning techniques. Yet the intensity of academia's retreat from rationality and the popularity of its rejection of 'rational comprehensiveness' have tended to inhibit such assistance for at least two decades.

(Wyatt 1996: 639)

143

Wyatt continues his trenchant remarks in a guest editorial in the journal *Environment and Planning B – Planning and Design* by remarking that whatever may be wrong with 'reasoned thinking', it is certainly far better than 'the alternative – abandonment to unbridled subjectivity and fickleness of politics, personality and fashion' (1996: 641). That and subsequent issues of this planning theory-oriented journal have very interestingly turned to the kind of computer-based simulation modelling discussed in Chapter 4, as the basis for a new systems-founded rationalism in planning as a process. This is based on a precise recognition of the non-linear character of city systems. To quote again from Wyatt:

> It should be fairly obvious that such a computationally intensive approach [back propagation neural networks] is far more flexible and adaptive than traditional modelling methods. Hence, it is probably much better at accommodating massive nonlinearities and threshold phenomena. For example, if some input parameter does not affect the final NN (neural network) output until it or other parameters attain some threshold value(s), then the richness and malleability of the interconnection weights, in combination with the variability of values on hidden neurodes, can probably simulate this effect – unlike regression analysis and other conventional statistical techniques.
>
> (Wyatt 1996: 650)

In a subsequent issue of the same journal devoted to the use of cellular automata as simulation devices the editors remark:

> In a world where global interventions fuse in subtle and diverse ways with local action, CA (cellular automata) looks like a paradigm for the 21st century, resonating with everything from the postmodern mathematics of fractals and chaos to the cry of development theorists 'Think globally, Act locally'. The really great attraction of CA is that it gives equal weight to the importance of space, time, and system attributes, thus imposing a frame which forces researchers to think very hard about representing any system where the importance of one of these elements becomes emphasised relative to the others.
>
> (Batty *et al.* 1997: 160–1)

Whilst rejecting their characterisation of chaos as 'postmodern' I wholeheartedly endorse the use of that crucial word 'resonate'. It is worth exploring these contributions to planning theory for resonances, both explicitly- and implicitly-founded, with the chaos/complexity account. There is of course a very important resonance in the actual passage quoted, in the assertion of the crucial requirement to consider time and space and the specific interactive attributes of the system altogether and at the same time – an absolutely holistic notion which resonates with Adams' views (see the discussion in Chapter 2).

A further and crucially important resonance resounds in the article by Batty and Xie when they remark that:

> science is not simply about the study of actual phenomena but about potential or possible phenomena. This notion is central to design but the prospect of a new science through computation which enables systematic and formal studies of 'possible worlds' has clear reference to the scientific understanding of human systems such as cities.
>
> (Batty and Xie 1997: 175)

Of course these pieces are by authors who are familiar with the ideas of Prigogine and even refer back to the significance of D'Arcy Thompson's ideas on morphology! It does seem to me that these are important if not as yet fully developed elements in a programme of complexity in action. The crucial notion is that of alternative futures and the recognition of the possibility of progress informed by reason. What is different is precisely the recognition of alternatives and of the role of purposeful action in achieving different alternatives. *Pace* Portugali *et al.*, this is not about the hermeneutics of interpretation. They are off down the wrong track when they:

> suggest that heuristic urban models can be subject to hermeneutics in the sense that every model is an interpretation of some urban phenomenon and that the aim of our research is not to achieve 'best fits' with reality but to provide a test – albeit of a new type – which must be interpreted. We use the notion of hermeneutics to emphasise that in both cases there may be more than one 'correct' interpretation.
>
> (Portugali *et al.* 1997: 263)

The article from which this is taken is a very useful and important contribution but this hermeneutic turn is absolutely in the wrong direction. As 'science' it is wrong about regress, about the establishment of what has been. There is (see the discussion of Gould on contingency in Chapter 2) a truth, however important the social context of the interpretation of that truth is. As 'planning theory' it is wrong because it misunderstands the materiality of the outcomes of the planning process. Human beings make their future world. The issue is not interpretation but doing. The philosophers have described the world. The point, however, is to change it.

Before leaving this complexity-founded new systems planning it is important to note that there is another view on the implications of chaos theory for planning. Whilst the authors cited above are generally inclined towards the possibility of a new comprehensive planning founded on complex and non-linear modelling, Cartwright uses chaos theory to deny this and to argue for a kind of Oakshottian incrementalism as the only appropriate planning approach:

> perhaps most important of all for planners, is the fact that chaotic systems are predictable only on an incremental or local basis. . . . On a global or comprehensive basis, chaotic systems are unpredictable because of the cumulative effects of various kinds of feedback. But on an incremental or local basis, the effects of feedback from one time period to another are perfectly clear. This is a powerful argument for planning strategies that are incremental rather than comprehensive in scope and that rely on a capacity for adaptation rather than on blueprints of results.
>
> (Cartwright 1991: 54)

Indeed Batty (1995), who specifically addresses the chaos/complexity literature and argues persuasively for the need to understand cities as complex dynamic systems, still seems to see understanding as based on the detailed analysis of micro behaviour. What is missing from his discussion is the idea of attractor states as sets of possible futures and of the possibility of robust chaos and the role of agency in steering the course of emergent development. Batty argues persuasively for the use of simulation as a tool here (see 1995: 484–5) but does so in a way which does not include the possibility of imagined futures as objectives of human action. What we are looking at in contrasting Cartwright's view with that of, say, Wyatt, is essentially the difference between the US emphasis on chaos and transitions from order, and the Prigogine conception of complexity and the importance of transitions to complex order. This present text is firmly in the latter camp and its tent is pitched pretty far to the left in that camp.

Reading the dials and steering the ship

Social researchers in public sector organisations are fortunate in working in increasingly rich information environments. Modern public administration involves very large flows and exchanges of information, mostly administrative data. Research, however, produces a particular type of information which is *meaningful* [original emphasis] to the policy makers and service planners, and hence is often termed 'intelligence'. . . . A particularly useful contribution made by research is to antici-pate change.

(Blackman 1995: 166)

The very word 'cybernetic' has its origins in the Greek for 'steersman' so it seems entirely appropriate to use the conning of a ship as an image for thinking about the management of modern cities in the immediate short term. I am going to take this analogy (definitely one of heterolo-gous affinity) even further by considering the ships in the form of 'general systems vehicles'[2] described as the key actors in Iain M. Banks' imagined future of 'the culture'. That means I am going to get beyond conning to actual reconstruction.

If we examine the bridge of a ship we find that it is equipped with instrumentation which describes both the state of the ship as a system and the state of environment in which that ship is located. The descrip-tions of the state of the ship come in the form of engine telegraphs recording engine power and propeller direction (full ahead both) and in the compass bearing of the course. Modern vessels have vastly more information than this, including exact satellite position references. The ship's pilot (officer of the watch) reads the instrumentation and adjusts parameters (engine speed and direction) in order to achieve an objec-tive, the maintenance of a course. In a modern vessel, as with a modern plane, the information is likely to come in the form of computer read-outs. Data streams are constant internally (or at least take the form of very rapid sampling of relevant states). Likewise the external is sampled. Of particular significance for the pilot of a ship (or aircraft, of course – these processes have a homologous affinity) is the state of currents in the media in which the vessel is operating. An onshore tide race and an onshore wind cannot be ignored! Indeed, in unfamiliar complex regions, harbour approaches, control has to be handed over to

147

those with exact and specific local knowledge (harbour pilots, air traffic controllers) who either completely (the harbour pilot) or partially (air traffic control) bring the vessel in.

The vessels of earlier modern eras, literal bearers of Wallerstein's world system, had equivalents of this instrumentation, but were much more dependent on the human element expressed through manual labour for their effective functioning. This meant that the reports of the surgeon as to the health of the crew and of the mate of the hold as to the amount of fresh water were as important as those of the bosun as to the state of the rigging or of the carpenter as to the state of the hull.

Cities are very like ships. Indeed social statistics, as has already been asserted almost ad nauseam, were developed as indicator systems in the nineteenth century in an almost exact, and certainly well understood, correspondence with the sick report of a ship's surgeon. Vital statistics were based on an exact, homologous and heterologous, analogy between the labour force (both present and potential) of an industrial city and the crew of a ship. As social statistics extended their range of coverage, so more and more aspects of social life were monitored. The state of industry in a city, as monitored by censuses of employment or production (or the sample based equivalents thereof), represents accounts of currents in the environment of the government of the city. Administrative data frequently takes the form of feedback on operations of city governance understood as steering commands. There are continuous and rapid samples of crucial sub-system states, for example housing management data on turnover on council estates; regular accounts of environment states, for example the results of decennial population censuses; and special investigations of particular issues (Blackman's research as intelligence).

The oldest modern reactive element in urban governance is the implementation of public health measures in response to deaths or notified notifiable infectious diseases. These represent indications of change from one state to another. Blackman *et al.* (1994) have shown how the now extremely fashionable Geographical Information Systems (GIS – essentially spatially located and spatially correlated data sets – lots of information for the same spatial points, preferably measured over time) can be used to indicate when council estates are about to 'go bad' in management terms. The key indicator is a sudden rise in the turnover of tenants who have lived on the estate for five or more years. When they bail out the place is becoming something other than orderly and acceptable. Prompt action may make a difference by acting to reinforce the trajectory of the estate in a different direction. Sometimes the

action may be something as simple as the eviction of a single household. Since the social dissolution of council estates generally leads
ultimately to their demolition and the writing off as a dead loss of very
substantial public assets, this sort of close in steering is far from trivial as
a practical exercise. Clearly school performance and attendance indicators are now being used in the same sort of way (see Byrne and Rogers
1996).

What interests me here is the use of GIS (Geographical Information
Systems) style data sets as the basis of the construction of quantified
histories, which 'regresses' can then serve as part of the information
required in public debate about the future trajectories of urban sets. In
Byrne (1997a) I documented the development towards 'postindustri-
alism' of two large UK industrial cities, the conurbation of Cleveland
County and the Leicester Urban Area. In other words, using the
numerical taxonomy across time method (sequential cluster analyses as
discussed in Chapter 4) for the level of neighbourhood elements, I
showed how the deindustrialisation of these cities was the precursor to
social polarisation and the generation of divided cities. 'Post-Fordist'
cities are divided cities. It is clear that the loss of blue collar industrial
employment (both male *and* female) has generated the urban form as
'butterfly attractor' in which neighbourhoods are either relatively secure
and prosperous or socially excluded and deprived. As a regress, as an
account of developments over the past twenty-five years, this model
stands. It stands triangulated in that it fits the data, the documents and
the actual accounts of change given by people who have experienced it.
It is very important to know how we got to where we are now and the
model of a bifurcating torus becoming a butterfly describes that process
very clearly.

What we need to be able to do is to work out what policy changes
will do in terms of their effect on the future trajectory of urban systems.
Notice that even to say that this is useful and necessary knowledge is to
be quite provocative. The thesis that 'globalisation accounts for everything' now being asserted by New Labour's intellectual gurus,[3] explicitly
denies the significance of local actions in determining the character of
local socio-spatial systems. Even the contributors to Brotchie *et al.*'s
interesting book on *Cities in Competition* (1995) intended, as the subtitle
indicates, to establish a foundation for 'Productive and sustainable cities
for the 21st century', take the notion of a globalised hierarchy of cities
for granted and really talk only about policies which are to do with positioning particular cities in more favourable slots in that hierarchy.
Certainly global tendencies, which are much more political than simply
the inherent product of anonymous system forces (see Therborn 1985),

are driving local social systems towards the generation of inequality. However, it is possible to envisage local policies which would act against this. It is even possible to illustrate this through tuning the parameters of non-linear iconological models and seeing what might happen. Note that this does not constitute the establishment of predictive laws, the pursuit of which has been the downfall of economic modelling, but rather is about the illustration of the range of possibilities. This is what Banks' general systems vehicles can do. They can reflexively remake themselves to fit the tasks they have and the conditions under which they are going to carry them out. A cruise liner can become a warship if it has to.

The actual planning area in which this kind of thing is being thought about is ecological in the fullest sense. It deals with social and biological ecologies and with their interaction in the complex socio-biological systems which are human cities. The key idea is that of the sustainable city, with sustainability understood as implying: 'that if some process is continued into the future, the conditions necessary to support that process will not be impaired. In particular it suggests that the process itself will not undermine the conditions which sustain it' (Harris 1995: 445).

Let us see what that idea looks like from a chaos/complexity perspective.

Sustainable cities

Sustainable development is not something to be achieved on the margins, as an add-on to current policies, but requires a fundamental and revolutionary change in the way economies and societies are developed and managed. Sustainable development is an integrating concept, bringing together local and global, short and long term and environment and development. It argues for the need for action *now* [original emphasis] to defend the future. Continuation of current paths will eventually bring disaster in various forms including depletion of the ozone layer, global warming, nuclear proliferation, loss of biodiversity and desertification. . . . The Town and Country Planning Association has for almost a century campaigned for the principles of environmental conservation and the balanced development of town and country. It is concerned about the relationship between environmental quality and social equality and the need to promote public participation to the fullest possible extent. The TCPA believes that these objectives can be secured only through effective, long term and strategic plan-

ning of environmental management and development. . . .
These enduring concerns of the TCPA are at the heart of
contemporary concern with sustainable development.

(Blowers 1993: xi–xii)

I was attracted to the idea of the 'sustainable city' as a peg on which to hang the last part of this chapter, by a remark at an Economic and Social Research Council funded seminar on 'Evaluating Urban Policy' made by the 'Sustainable City' Manager for Bristol. She observed that the sustainable city was not simply ecologically sustainable. It had to be socially sustainable, and it could only be socially sustainable if equal. I think that is right. The implications of this are absolutely global. If capital is a globalised system and the nation state is increasingly irrelevant to the operations of both global finance and global production, and if 'history has ended' in the sense that there is no clear competitive pattern of social organisation other than global market capitalism, then there is a crisis of engagement of people with politics. The idea of citizenship must include within it the possibility that the political actions of citizens matter in terms of determining the course of events. Increasingly this is not true. There is a crisis of political engagement, both in terms of visible actions by people, most notably in declines in voting, and in relation to the actual content of politics itself. Politics has, as Bookchin (1995) puts it, become a kind of unpopular state-craft conducted by professionals, most of whom are not elected. It is indicative that the UK's 'New Labour' party developed much of the actual political programme on which it was elected through the use of that favourite market researcher's technique 'focus groups', and is seeking to replace the deliberative democracy of its annual policy forming conference with a combination of fan club rally and 'policy forums' [sic]. In office it is now proposing to steer the ship of state exactly by this kind of market research process (see *The Guardian* 14 July 1997). In these processes the citizen who acts becomes replaced by the passive consumer whose action is confined to choice among available product suppliers, with the product being distinguished by superficial packaging rather than essential content.

There is a crisis in the cities of the industrial world. The word 'crisis' of course means 'turning point' (see O'Connor 1982) and describes a situation in which things cannot go on as they are. Crisis is exactly the period leading up to change of kind. It is the 'local' time of most interest to us when we study the transformation of complex systems. The expressions of urban crisis have so far been managed by the traditional linear methods of control through negative feedback, mainly through policing, but also including calls for the reassertion of traditional values through traditional methods in education. Etzioni's (1995) inane programme of communitarianism is the sociological expression of this sort of control orientation as a general social principle.

However, it is not possible to restore the status quo ante if there are changes in the underlying causal structural nexuses. Cities do change, precisely through a process of development. Even simple market led development is change. Such development is of course justified in Schumpeterian terms on the grounds that it is a process of creative destruction, but in terms of social integration it is generally a process of destructive destruction. Moreover, this social disintegration is accompanied by resource claims on nature which are of such an order as to hazard the ecological basis of urban systems themselves. Actually, I do not really think the issue which is being addressed by sustainable city programmes is really sustainable versus unsustainable, at least in social terms. Rather it is about the sort of sustainability which can be the stable attractor for the next 100-odd years. Lovelock reminds us that systems are pretty well always sustainable. The issue is in what state they are sustained.

Let me illustrate by an example. Newcastle City Council has recently submitted its Unitary Development Plan to the Department of the Environment. Newcastle is a city characterised by extreme urban disintegration in its 'West End', where a previously stable if poor set of inner suburbs have become disordered and dangerous. Interestingly, the best indicator of this is the collapse of property values in this locale for owner-occupied housing, but there are a range of others, including crime levels. Most of the riverfront areas of the city, and the city exists precisely because of its relationship with the River Tyne, are under the planning control of an Urban Development Corporation which is the local planning authority for its territory and which is able to specify the planning proposals for its area ahead of the development of the whole city plan. The local political branches of the Labour Party, which firmly controls Newcastle City, argued very strongly for a strategy directed towards ensuring that development was in the inner nineteenth-century suburbs and in relation to existing social housing outer estates to which inner area poorer residents had been moved in slum clearances since the 1950s. The controlling Labour group instead opted for what was essentially the preferred approach of private sector developers, and proposed massive development into the Green Belt towards the airport to the northwest of the city. Actually the Green Belt issue was not the crucial one here. There is Green Belt to the northwest of Newcastle all the way to the Edinburgh outer suburbs. Rather it was the issue of whether the objective of the new plan was to have a city which was more equal or not.

Of course the peripheral development proposal was ecologically damaging. It reached into agricultural and amenity land of high quality and would increase the level of car usage, particularly as at the same time the Urban Development Corporation which combined the roles of developer and planning authority was putting as much office park employment onto its central sites as possible. In this scenario the inner suburbs would be what the cars of the suburban office workers went through on their way to riverside office parks. The outer estates would be ghettoised and separated in space from the suburbs of affluence. At the same time 'edge city' development is occurring under real market pressures so the city would take the form of a segmented external zone in which roads linked locales of affluent residence and employment but did not connect to the 'outer estate' ghettos, most of the inner suburbs would be poor and deteriorating except for one affluent wedge (very unusually for European cities this is in the centre/east of the city), and there would be an affluent core of riverside office parks, leisure and cultural uses, and 'new' urban dwellers in loft living-style conversions and central city flats. Interestingly, the inner suburbs are now disconnected from the centre by orbital roads and especially the 'central motorway east'. The city's zones really are bounded.

Conclusion

In an interesting article Rose has argued that contemporary governance is marked by the death of the social in which: 'neither the included nor the excluded are governed as social citizens' (1996: 327). It is important to clarify what Rose means by being governed as 'social citizens'. For him:

> Social government was expert government. The devices of 'the welfare state' opened up a multitude of new locales for the operation of expert judgements, based on knowledge, training, professional and bureaucratic ethics and specialist skills.
>
> (Rose 1996: 349)

Plainly urban planning and the planning of services were both part of this domain of expertise. However, it is very important to remember that the operation of expertise was a contested process. The history of UK social housing is one in which, when it was being built for the poor, it was built to designs and standards imposed by a kind of expertise (see

Dunleavy 1981), but when it was being built for the respectable and organised working class the criteria derived from expertise could never be imposed. Social government had to be responsive to active citizen pressure, usually expressed through the local institutional processes of organised labour. Indeed, the institutional vision of those engaged collectively in such processes was frequently informed by a radical and contrasting combination of knowledge and aesthetic about the appropriate form of urban development. This was most often effective in relation to the planning of public sector housing and was generally least effective in the related domains of urban land use planning and economic development. Nonetheless, it was there.

What this chapter has argued for is the development in urban governance of radical forms of empowerment, and that term here certainly does not comprise:

> experts teaching, coaxing, requiring their clients to conduct themselves within particular cultural communities of ethics and lifestyle, according to certain specified arts of active personal responsibility [nor] . . . a range of interventions to transmit under tutelage, certain professionally ratified mental, ethical and practical techniques for active self-management.
>
> (Rose 1996: 348)

although that is a perfectly accurate account of much of 'empowerment' as professional practice. In Freire's view empowerment was about giving people tools for knowledge and understanding so that they could act. The radical end of urban governance in a complex world consists in a commitment to the rationality of complexity and the maintenance of collective mechanisms for the development of understanding based on that rationality and for the implementation of projects based on collective will.

The planning failures of the 1960s and 1970s were the consequence of the imposition of simple system based programmes of rational action which were asserted to be the 'scientifically founded' only way forward, when in reality they represented one way forward which served the interests of a particular fraction of capitalists, those involved with the construction and development industry. This is the political economy gloss on Dennis' account of the way in which people experienced planning as a process (1970, 1972), although Dennis himself advanced an account based on professional ideologies which would square remarkably well with postmodernist narratives of discourse.

Planners are not complete fools. The Skeffington Committee

reported on the necessity for participation in planning as a way of avoiding both intense political conflict and errors based on incomplete, and by implication, 'mere', technical knowledge. Participatory practices were developed in some contexts, particularly in relation to the area-based housing improvement strategies which were adopted as a popular and relatively successful alternative to massive clearance and replacement with system built engineering solutions, much of which resultant 'mass housing' has now been cleared, whilst the dwellings it was meant to replace continue in use.

However, participation was only ever really tried as a solution at the spatial level of neighbourhood. There was formal participation in structure plan development, the planning process which was intended to address the spatial level of locality, but the first round of structure planning remained a largely technical exercise. Despite the intervention of both community workers and 'technical aid' workers, the support systems for mass public participation were minimal and the political processes were not really understood as such by most people.

The ideology of non-planning and the substitution of market led decision making in the 1980s was a manifest failure, largely because those operating at the meso-level so misread the actual market direction in land and land development. This is a good thing, because successful development would have been profoundly exclusionary in its effects, as Eversley (1990) so pertinently and bitterly observed. Eversley himself was almost the ideal type of the technically (and for him technically included socially) informed planner *for* rather than planner *with*, but his modernist social democratic programme was one which in its day had done much good. He saw the role of planning in the service of development capital for what it was.

By the late 1980s Heseltine, back at the Department of the Environment and no fool, recognised that future strategies would have to incorporate some public participation. The resulting 'City Challenge' programme, funded yet again by top-slicing existing funding for inner cities, employed a rhetoric of 'community participation' in order to lessen still further the control of local government over the planning process (see Byrne 1994). In effect local community groups, often with extremely questionable status as representatives of the community as a whole, were co-opted into the process after the key strategic decisions had already been taken, and allowed to comment on and tangentially influence the details of implementation.

It cannot be pretended that the actual development of a proper participatory programme for planning will ever be easy. The whole formal process of political determination is now so avowedly short-termist and the poor in particular have been so disenchanted with any kind of political engagement that getting people to act is extremely difficult.

Moreover, basing popular participation on the application of the 'chaos/complexity' programme is perhaps not the easiest of exercises in social pedagogy. It was perfectly plain that most elected councillors did not understand the basis of the regression models, the essence of linearity, which were used to specify the range of alternative futures in the structure planning process of the 1970s. Nonetheless, the idea of choice is a reasonable one which is readily grasped by people. Here we can have recourse to the epistemological consequences of realism. For realists the world speaks to us. Resonance of scientific description with the way people themselves understand the world, an understanding absolutely necessary for survival in it, because that is what the world is like, is at least a basis for beginning to act.

All this begins to sound rather like a programme developed by John Stuart Mill but there are worse starting points, both for scientific under-standing and for the development of an informed programme for the encouragement of active citizenship. On the sound basis that one should practice what one preaches I am going to start rolling again the programme of the most stimulating adult education group I have ever had the privilege of being involved with, Tyne–Wear 2000. With less than two years to go to the millennium, serious debate about the possible forms of our futures and the kind of actions we need to take to get the one which most people want, seems to be rather timely.

9

CONCLUSION

The growth and development of the social sciences in the UK higher education system has not simply paralleled the growth in that system as a whole. On the contrary there has been a massive absolute and relative expansion in student numbers, departments and even 'disciplines' and 'fields'. This expansion has occurred during my adult life and for most of the period I have been working as either or both teacher and researcher in social science. Fortuitously, genuinely contingently, I took a first degree in sociology and social administration because that was what was available at the university which I had entered as a medical student and it was much easier to change courses within my university than to change to another university altogether. There was nothing contingent about the sociology. As soon as I was made aware that it was possible to study such a thing in a world available to me, I wanted to do it.

The contingency was the social administration. The course I entered had previously been one in 'social studies' geared absolutely to the turning of middle-class young women who were a cut above nursing and a cut below medicine, into social workers. The 'social administration' was a continuing genuflection in this direction. At the time I bitterly resented this. I really wanted to do a joint honours degree in politics and sociology, and to all intents and purposes I did, by careful choice of options. Social administration was something I had to do – like it or lump it. Well, along with the compulsory statistics – which I took willingly because I had far more of a mathematical background than any of my fellow students and could easily get high marks – it has been the compulsory social administration which has shaped my working life.

The effect of having a joint degree in sociology and social administration is that you can never really be happy with the idea of social science as a contemplative exercise. The knowledge has to be of some use. As an undergraduate in the 1960s, of course, I was made very well aware of the political form and relevance of knowledge, but in those pre-postmodernist days we used to say 'knowledge is power' and mean it in an implicitly realist sense. When, just five years after getting my first degree, I was working as a researcher in community development, I knew very well that knowledge was power. The two most useful things we did as community workers in North Shields were first to replicate the organisational forms of the labour movement around issues of social reproduction (a necessary re-invention of the wheel if ever there was one) and second, systematically to research the immediate local history and contemporary context of the issues which people in the 'action groups' wanted to know about and felt were relevant to their lives.

We found things out by a combination of documentary-based historical research into the very recent past and survey research on a large scale. And what we found out was what was really going on. Of course there was no necessary and simple pattern to what was going on. Outcomes were a product of actions – we were dealing with a dynamic and changing social system, one experiencing the first pangs of the dreadful process of deindustrialisation which has so immiserated so many people, in resource terms and far more in cultural terms (see Byrne 1989 for a later reflection on this). We saw that the system was one which had possible trajectories. We certainly worked locally and together with local people succeeded in achieving some better outcomes on a small scale, although most of our joint efforts were really a matter of pissing to windwards in the face of the global[1] gale of industrial and consequent social destruction.

What we were doing was 'action research'. The content of this expression has always fascinated me. I wrote a Master's dissertation on the process in 1970, arguing that action research was exactly the programme by which social scientists should engage in the world. When I became an action researcher I had to confront people who really believe that controlled experimental designs were the proper basis for applied social research. Fortunately they were generally a lot less numerate than I was so they weren't too hard to see off, although the myth of the experiment keeps coming back in applied policy research. Our programme was always reflexive. We fed back as we went along and evaluated through the generation of a historical account.

The point of this potted biography is to emphasise that the reason the chaos/complexity programme is so attractive to me is because I see social science as a way of informing our approaches to changing the world – absolute and unregenerate progressive modernism.[2] And yet in the time I have been in the game that has become a very unfashionable view. In part this is to do with the death of positivism, although as a 1960s radical with a very good grounding in historical materialism that death is not mourned by me. What died with positivism – to mix metaphors the baby thrown out with the bath water – was the notion that there was any method of grasping the character of the dynamics of social systems in a way which might inform the character of social action for change.

For me the big thing about all the stuff dealt with in this book is the clear message it delivers to the effect that the days of pessimism, pretentiousness and plain bone idleness are done. In the rest of this conclusion I want to say something about how and why they are done, beginning with an emphatic endorsement of the message Prigogine wrote into the report of the Gulbenkian Committee on the restructuring of the social sciences (1996) and going on to say something more about the future trajectory of applied social science as a social practice for adults with brains in their heads.

Postgraduate revolution?

> We come from a past of conflicting certitudes, be they related to science, ethics or social systems, to a present of considerable questioning, including questioning about the intrinsic possibility of certainties. Perhaps we are witnessing the end of a type of rationality that is no longer appropriate to our time. The accent we call for is one placed on the complex, the temporal and the unstable, which corresponds today to a transdisciplinary movement gaining in vigor. This is not by any means a call to abandon the concept of substantive rationality. . . . The project which remains central to both the students of human social life and to the natural scientists is the intelligibility of the world.
>
> (Gulbenkian Commission 1996: 79)

The implications of what the Gulbenkian Commission describes as the explosion of 'the long-simmering discontents with Newtonian assumptions in the natural sciences' (1996: 60) are profound. They really do seem to me to mean that the notion of separate and distinct fields of science no longer has any validity as an intellectual position and should not serve as the basis for academic organisation. The distinction between the nomothetic and the ideographic, between the quantitative and the qualitative[3] does not matter any more.

It would have been almost inconceivable even ten years ago to

159

suggest that it is not only possible, but desirable, and even perhaps essential for universities to consider the mounting of a common core course for all doctoral students in sciences of all kinds – in all the fields which in Slav languages would be prefaced by the term Nauk. In practice it is hard enough to mount a common core course for social scientists. Certainly the UK Economic and Social Research Council guidelines for postgraduate training continue to demonstrate only too clearly the role of disciplinary territorialism in the definition of the appropriate base of postgraduate study. And yet I am arguing that such a programme is exactly what is required.

There are weak and strong versions of this argument. Even the weak version is likely to provoke a good deal of resistance from two quarters, allied on the good tactical principle that my enemy's enemy is my friend if on no other conceivable basis. Reductionists, including those in the social sciences attached to the reductionist programme of rational choice theory and related approaches, are likely to make common cause with absolute relativists in the postmodern camp, against any argument that the 'chaos/complexity' programme is even generally interesting as a topic for consideration. Synthesis is frequently anathema to both thesis and antithesis. The most sensible response to this is inductively founded. If natural and social scientists, and others in the 'human sciences' beyond the social sciences as normally delimited, are using a common vocabulary and talking about things in the same sort of way, then something interesting is going on. I want to go further.

In an interesting think piece on simulation Halfpenny (1997) argues that unless simulators are prepared to argue that the mechanisms represented by the algorithms represent real generative mechanisms, then they are really not engaged in realist projects but are actually confined to:

> conventionalism, which makes no claim as to real existents. It merely maintains that its formulae provide a convenient way of calculating one set of observations from another, without any claim that they represent the way the world works.
>
> (Halfpenny 1997: para. 5.5)

But, if we accept that the description of the character of far from equilibric systems does constitute a general covering law of type, that heterologous analogies hold because the generative mechanisms are of the same general form, then we do indeed argue that 'this is the way the world works'.

That is the strong programme of 'chaos/complexity' as developed in a realist frame. Reed and Harvey in the articles and chapters cited in this text have pointed us in this direction and they are absolutely right in the indication they have given. My argument is that postgraduate students must study these things in a generic way because if they don't then much of what they are doing will be a waste of time. So my first loose end in this conclusion would be to promote a strong programme. Every PhD student in everything should get to grips with the 'chaos/complexity' programme, not for reasons of fashion or even legitimate career building but because this is the way the world works and we need to understand that.

Applied social science

Let me turn to the idea of 'applied social science'. This is a dirty and dangerous expression in many academic circles – a truly bizarre situation when we have been turning out massive numbers of social science graduates from universities for three decades in the UK and for far longer in the US. Those disciplinary purists, particularly but not exclusively located in sociology, who so dislike the very idea of application, ignore the existence of massive applied programmes of social science in the specific educational and practice domains of business, health, social and community work, education and planning/urban management. In the UK there are probably now more sociologists researching health issues and/or teaching courses in health studies, a product of the central place of social sciences in the development of nursing as a graduate profession, than in any other field (perhaps than in all other fields put together), of the discipline. However, even the most sociological of the journals covering this field, *Sociology of Health and Illness*, is set off on one side from the mainstream of professional engagement and interest. Applied is dodgy always.

It is just about academically respectable to engage in 'strong programmes' in applied areas, to use the tools of disciplines in order to challenge the assumptions and social locations of professionals and managers. Interestingly the postmodernist version of such strong programmes is of course confined to discourses, to language games as a basis for power, without any real sense of the relations of such things to social structures, and in particular structures of inequality, the point made so cogently by Mouzelis in the passage quoted in Chapter 2. Such deconstructions can be very useful, the more useful the more they employ notions of structure as well as the frames of discourse analysis. The analysis of 'knowledges' does serve a purpose.

However, such strong programmes can be allowed to run away with themselves. If social constructionism is taken to its extreme then we can never conceive of any knowledge which might serve as a basis for coherent and progressive social action. All we can do is deconstruct. There are no performers, only critics. Oh-hoh.

A way out of this dead-end is provided by a turn to Gramsci, that is to Gramsci the thoughtful and analytical Western Marxist as he wrote himself, not the re-interpreted and revised object of a certain strand in cultural studies. The interesting idea Gramsci offers to us is his distinction between traditional and organic intellectuals. The analogy should be obvious. Traditional intellectuals are contemplatives dealing with knowledge for its own sake in the institutions of knowledge, just as contemplative clergy dealt with God for his own sake in the institutions of prayer. Organic intellectuals are friars, not monks. They are in the world for the world. Their knowledge is analogous with pastoral theology. It is to be used.

What Gramsci wanted, of course, was organic intellectuals of the proletariat to stand against the organic intellectuals of the bourgeoisie. This was not a matter of knowledges constituted from one obvious mechanistic rationality, the Engels-derived foundation of Leninism as political practice. The concept is far more fluid and local, but it is nonetheless real. If for Gramsci in the important expression 'historical materialism' we must always in real circumstances place our emphasis on the absolute specificity of the historical, that did not make the historical any the less real.

My intention is to use the idea of organic intellectual activity as a licence for specifying the way in which knowledge of systems and their potentials, note: of whole systems including interactions and multiple potentials, not of simple laws and specific predictions, can be the basis of applied social science. This project will of course be socially located and contextual but it will be connected with the real, with the way the world works.

An illustration is in order. Let me pick up my current main substantive, as opposed to methodological, concern as a sociologist working in the field of social policy – the issue of social exclusion. It can readily be argued that social exclusion is as Lee puts it: 'endemic in the contemporary regime of accumulation within Europe' (1995: 1585). What is at issue is the necessary character of that regime. We can pick this up at two of the spatial levels which were discussed in Chapter 5 – that of bloc, which is the level of the determination of broad social and economic policy, and that of locality, which is the level of operation of the specification of the use of land for social objectives.

If we take the level of bloc then we find we are dealing with two proposed attractor states. One is that of 'the flexible labour market' as proposed by the market-oriented right represented in Europe by Blair, following the example of transformed antipodean Labour. The other is that of the 'social market economy' as originally developed by German Christian Democracy but now commanding the support of both Christian and Social Democrats. Of course there are important national distinctions representing specific national histories, the level addressed by Esping-Andersen's identification of 'welfare regimes', but the future trajectory of the European bloc will be described by one or the other of the above attractor forms.

In this context the nature and character of social exclusion as an attractor state for individuals, households and even neighbourhoods (as systems nested within spatially more extensive containing systems) matters a good deal. The neo-liberals argue that social exclusion is a function of personal capacities or lack of them, that all that is needed is an active supply side labour market-oriented set of policies, welfare into work, and then social exclusion will be resolved by getting people into employment.

Although the Christian Democratic approach does assert what Levitas (1996) has described as the Durkheimian imperative of organic inclusion through work, it also includes a recognition that work per se is not enough. Indeed, work too can be excluding if it is grossly exploitative. Even the organic intellectuals of the main agency of the states of global capitalism, the Organisation for Economic Cooperation and Development (OECD), have recently recognised that work paid at a rate below the cost of the social reproduction of the labour power employed might be better regarded as concealed unemployment (OECD 1997). Another, older, way of looking at it would be to regard it as absolute and immiserating exploitation.

There is more to this from a complexity viewpoint than the use of the idea of attractors to describe the range of possible trajectories of Social Europe as a bloc. Applied social science has a role in describing the actual character of social exclusion as an experience. Such descriptions matter precisely because there is a real way in which people live and if it does not correspond to the account which underpins supply side labour market policies then we can know that such approaches will not resolve the issue of social exclusion. We can identify what purposes such policy strategies might actually be serving, in marked contrast to their rhetorical content.

There are two crucial and intrinsically inter-related issues about the characteristics of the dynamics of social exclusion. The first is the actual relative scale of exclusion as opposed to inclusion as a dynamic

163

process, scale here being understood in terms of the relative numbers of people/households who are excluded as opposed to included. The other is the actual character of the individual dynamics of exclusion as personal trajectory.

The arguments which centre on labour preparation measures as a route to employment are premised on the notions that exclusion is experienced by a minority of individuals/households, and that the experience of exclusion cannot be described by a trajectory which includes experience of employment. Although social scientists (see Room 1995) are now well aware that it is trajectories which matter, that exclusion is a dynamic process rather than a static condition, those who argue for a flexible labour market ignore the reality indicated by the fact that 40 per cent of all the unemployed who find jobs become unemployed again within one year.

Of course, the above is simply an argument for a dynamic understanding of social processes, and hardly an original one. Rowntree was writing about a cycle of poverty at the beginning of this century. Where the implications of the 'chaos/complexity' programme matter is in relation to the character and form of public policy. Supply side labour market strategies address the issue of exclusion as if it were a property of individuals – they commit a nominalist fallacy. A systemic understanding of exclusion argues that it is a system property which arises when key social parameters, control parameters, pass crucial values. What is new here is the language, not the understanding. The centrality of full employment to the elimination of exclusion was very well expressed by Beveridge. There is a clear systemic effect here which derives not from some aggregation of the individuals but from system properties expressed by levels of unemployment/labour market flexibility and ranges of inequality. The first is at least in part a product of policy initiatives relating to trade union and/or legally-based employment protection. The second is essentially a product of fiscal policies because it is post-tax incomes and benefit levels which determine the extent of real social inequalities. Of course, tax revenues also are the basis of public sector employment, both in terms of volume and of relative remuneration.

The differences in policy strategies, which can here be equated with the deliberate modification of control parameters for the social system, are what determine the outcome state of the social order. With relatively high levels of redistribution through the maintenance of high levels of public sector employment in 'de-commodified production' and/or high levels of wage substitution benefits, coupled with relatively strong job protection and labour market inflexibility, there will be a strong social market and minimal experience of social exclusion. The absence of job protection and of fiscally-based redistribution creates a polarised and divided social order (see Byrne 1997c, 1997d for a development of this theme).

The macro level of bloc can be examined both by conceptual analogy and by simulation modelling, in the latter process replacing the linear models of traditional economic modelling with non-linear models and iconic procedures. It will be particularly important to include a full range of variables in the specification of the phase states which models are intended to replicate as analogies. At last we might have that combination of economic and social description and, if not prediction, possibilities (the emphasis on the plural is very important) which the social indicators movement of the 1960s (see Booth 1988) hoped to achieve.

Planning and divided places

The meso-level of regional and urban planning is of particular interest as a locale of 'applied social science' based on the 'chaos/complexity' programme. As Chapter 8 shows, planning theorists are already engaged with the ideas and with the use of models based upon them. I want to hurry that process along for two reasons. The first is to do with the nature of demonstration. Macro policies are usually medium term in relation to implementation. When meso-level planning processes are in train, they can have very rapid effects. However, given the way in which the actual material construction processes (all too often absolutely literally) concretise in space, then land use planning can set the basis of the spatial aspects of social life for a long time ahead. Things are built and stay there. Of course, different social contexts can lead to a substantial modification of the use of existing structures, and processes such as gentrification and its opposite of downward filtration can redefine social space, even within an existing constructed cityscape. However, planning does matter and it is really necessary to catch it when it is in motion.

This last point requires some expansion. Simple development control in planning is a continuous process but the development and implementation of large scale strategic planning, even when the strategy takes the form of an assertion of 'non-planning', is an episodic process with the consequences of each round having long term effects. In the UK we are just at the end of the planning regime introduced by the Tories in the early 1980s in which a range of techniques and agencies, principally Urban Development Corporations and Enterprise Zones, were used to allow massive public subsidy to development outwith the democratic control of elected local government. As it happens these things have done much less damage than they might have because in general they got going on the downslope of the property cycle, although individual examples, like Gateshead's Metro Centre, have done very great damage to the retail and transport systems of the city regions in which they are located.

However, we may have a chance to do it differently now, so a bit of thought is worthwhile. The UK planning regime since 1982 has been primarily focused on the achievement of physical development, regardless of its social content or consequences. Given the present government's commitment to the resolution of social exclusion as a social issue we might envisage a planning regime which placed that as central in its objective set. Here the ideas about the use of the data streams of governance itself, raised by Blackman in the material discussed in Chapter 8, become highly relevant. For once a technique adopted from the physical sciences may be useful. We can employ the 'near neighbour' approach to explore the likely trajectory of the specific urban space for which we are planning. That is, we can look at city regions which resemble the one with which we are dealing and see what regresses we can construct for their trajectories. In a very simple way I have attempted to do this in a comparison of the actual impacts of deindustrialisation as it has happened in the UK metropolitan counties of Tyne and Wear and South Yorkshire, in relation to the potential for deindustrialisation in the Katowice Vovoidship in Poland (see Byrne 1997d). Here those who come after may learn something from the experiences of those who have gone before. What planning strategies might create a socially sustainable city as opposed to one characterised by extreme social polarisation?

What is being proposed here is applied and grounded iconographic speculation – the use of the 'macro-scope' of the computer both to identify historical dynamics of particular socio-spatial systems – with models of how such systems might have been different at this point in time – coupled with forward projections using the whole repertoire of 'chaos/complexity' tools. This is a new kind of 'social engineering science', a rational programme not of assertion based on absolute prediction, but of social action based on specification of the multiple but not limitless range of urban options.

The discussion thus far has emphasised the use of quantitative tools, even if these are to be used in an exploratory way and even if the results are often pictorial/graphic/iconic representations rather than exact numerical expressions and totals. It seems appropriate here to speculate about the potential of structured qualitative tools as part of the kit of urban planning as a process. I am thinking here of the use of computer-based qualitative analytical techniques as a way of ordering and interpreting both documentary/oral history and the results of contemporary participative processes – not so much focus groups as mutiplicities of citizens' meetings. The historical process is inherently dynamic and we can achieve regressive histories of its complex trajectories, especially the way in which local social times come to bifurcation points.

However, the convergence of quantitative and qualitative goes beyond this important tool-based common 'macroscopic view'. We have the possibility of qualitative representations of alternative futures. Here the qualitative representation can be both literary and pictorial. Indeed, we might turn to that newish exemplar of popular culture, the graphic novel, in which science fiction is already making use of the ideas of 'chaos/complexity' as a foundation for its ways of representing futures (again the crucial emphasis is on the plural).

Conclusion

So, to conclude the conclusion: this book ends with the proposal of a new complex-based social engineering in which rational knowledge informs social action but cannot determine it because agency, let us hope the collective agency of free citizens – the proper actors of democratic modernity, is the perturbative force which chooses (no need for inverted commas here) the future that will be from the range of possibilities that might be. In this process applied social science matters because it is the foundation of the description of what those possibilities might be, which description is based on an understanding of how things became as they are (processes of regress) and simulation of how they might be in the future. As I write this Iain M. Banks' 'Culture' comes to mind immediately. Well, that is perhaps where complex 'general systems' might take us – a decent sort of utopia after all.

GLOSSARY

Attractors The idea of attractor is introduced in the entry here dealing with 'phase/state/condition space'. In the development of a dynamical system over time we have attractors if the system's trajectory does not move through all the possible parts of an n+1 (the +1 representing time) state space, but instead occupies a restricted part of it. The simplest form of attractor is a point. In some simple physical systems such as the swinging of an unforced pendulum under gravity, the ultimate steady state of the object is still at a point. Everything reaches an equilibrium and stays there. In other systems the condition changing over time does so by passing through a range of values within limits in an exact and ordered way. A frictionless pendulum swinging in a vacuum is an exact example. If we know the starting conditions and the time since starting we know the exact position of the pendulum. The trajectory of such a system constitutes a limit cycle attractor.

Both the above are simple attractors. For systems which have point or limit cycle attractors it is possible to have a linear description and to predict a future state on the basis of the knowledge of the present condition of the system and of this linear description or dynamic. However, there is a development of the idea of limits in which exact prediction of future state is not possible. A domestic central heating system provides a good example. The negative feedback control exercised by the thermostat switches the system on if ambient temperature drops below a set level and off if it rises above it. The condition of the system varies between these upper and lower limits but never crosses beyond them. However, we cannot predict the exact temperature at any point in time other than saying that it will be between these limits. The thermostat does not 'bother' about temperatures within the boundaries set for it. Contingent factors like open windows, numbers of people in a room, the heating effect of a personal computer, can all move the temperature anywhere in between the limits but only cause a feedback regulation if the limit is reached. There is no regular cycle through possible values as was the case for our ideal pendulum. If we map out the trajectory of a system such as this through time we find that when we have lots of measurements (as we might if we measured the temperature of a centrally heated room every minute for a month with external temperature providing a background level and a second dimension, and time a third) the path will look rather like a raggy doughnut. Mathematically this figure is called a torus. This behaviour is characteristic of systems governed by negative feedback. We cannot say exactly where within the boundaries the system will be, but it will be somewhere within those limits. If a point attractor is a mathematical model for an equilibric system, then a torus is a model for a system close to equilibrium in which departures from equilibrium are constrained within limits.

Let us take the example of the temperature of a room further by considering the typical English dwelling equipped with central heating but not air conditioning. For most of a typical English year the temperature of the room will be governed by the actions of the central heating system. However, suppose there is a heatwave – we do have them and may have more if the world climate is changing. Then when the temperature rises above the upper limit for the thermostat, the central heating switches off, but the temperature goes on rising regardless. The limits are broken and another set of temperatures become possible. External heating, in the form of the weather system, renders the central heating irrelevant. There is a kind of budding off from the torus which establishes a new domain for the trajectory. We have a change in character, a phase shift. The pattern of temperatures in the room now is quite different. Here we have two domains of temperature and which one the room is in is affected by a small change. This is a sort of very simple example of a butterfly or Lorenz attractor. We have moved beyond simple to strange attractors.

Bifurcation Systems which have a chaotic dynamic develop through a pattern of bifurcations. Feigenbaum's number describes the scaling ratio, i.e. the ratio of the differences between successive values of a parameter, changes in which determine the pattern of bifurcations. As this pattern progresses mathematically it takes smaller and smaller changes in the parameter to induce a bifurcation. This ratio seems to be a universal mathematical constant. Stewart (1997) provides a very clear discussion of this in mathematical terms. What may be of more immediate interest to social scientists is the actual change in parameters required at the beginning of a cascade of bifurcations. In the equation of a logistic map $x \rightarrow kx(1-x)$ when k is 3 a two cycle occurs, the first bifurcation. At 3.5 the period changes to 4 and so on. If we think of k as the control parameter of a system, then we are likely to be interested in changes in it which will produce bifurcations. Note that at the bifurcation point very small differences in control parameter values determine which path the system will follow.

Catastrophic change/chaotic change/complex change What all these terms have in common is that small changes produce big and non-linear outcomes – the last straw breaks the camel's back. That is a good example of a catastrophic change. A small addition to load changes the whole status of the camel from standing and functional to broken-backed and down. One state is replaced by another through a non-linear transformation which is nonetheless singular. There is only one new state possible. Chaotic transformations are not really about states or steady conditions. Rather they are about trajectories, about the dynamic development of systems. The connection is the idea of *bifurcation* which describes the development of very different system trajectories in consequence of very small variations in the values of initial conditions. The usual form of chaotic attractor which is most described is the *Lorenz* or *butterfly* attractor. Here the system will end up as it were within one or another torus style region but we don't know which. *Complexity* which is not really a mathematical concept at all, in this sense, describes transformations which involve the emergence of new system properties. Complexity is a scientific and inductive idea. It deals with the discovery of the immanent properties of systems as these develop through time. However, there is a mathematical aspect to complexity. The domain of complexity 'between order and chaos' can be considered to be the beginning part of a bifurcation cascade in which large changes in parameter values are required for a bifurcation, and the range of possible states, whilst greater than one, is still limited. Casti (1994) and Stewart (1997) both deal with these topics in a clear way.

Clusters Clusters are the product of numerical taxonomy procedures. They are types, qualitative sets, which 'emerge' from the application of computation to large multi-variate data sets. Of course the clusters we get depend on what we are looking for, what measurements we have made to begin with, and which of these measured variates we use as classificatory principles. I regard the choosing here as essentially a qualitative version of inductive probability. We pick on the basis of pre-existing knowledge. I was very struck by the pictorial resemblance between graphical representations of clusters and graphical representations of strange attractors. Likewise a cluster fusion diagram looks exactly like a bifurcation diagram in appearance. The iconic resemblance seems to me to indicate an ontological similarity. In this text clusters are seen as a possible way to operationalise attractors using quantitative tools for a qualitative purpose.

Control parameter(s) When we examine real dynamical systems we often find that their trajectories are governed by particular variable aspects of them rather than by all aspects of them. Note that we are not necessarily dealing with single variables. Rather we may be dealing with several variables and with the interactions among them. However, we are very likely to be able to describe the actual development of a system's trajectory through state space in terms of the effects of a set smaller than that which is used in constructing the state space. The variable(s) in this set are control parameters. It is likely in systems with a complex determinant form that changes in the values of control parameters will produce non-linear changes in the system's trajectory which may involve either catastrophic or chaotic transformations. One implication of the existence of control parameters is that strange attractors may have dimensions less than that of the state space, and that this dimensionality may be fractal.

Determinist A dynamic is determinist if knowledge of it and of the initial state of a system is all we need to know to predict the future of the system. Note that this is a matter of in principle. In chaotic determinism we cannot know the initial state of the system with sufficient precision to predict its future trajectory.

Dynamic The formal mathematical equation which describes how something changes over time. We are most familiar with Newtonian dynamics which describe the linear changes of position of objects in space over time. Given a description of initial conditions and the dynamic we can predict futures in a linear system. The term is generalisable to all rules for development through time, including non-linear developments in the condition of whole systems as opposed to simple objects. A system whose development through time can be described by a dynamic is a dynamical system. The tent map and logistic map are two quite simple looking equations which are non-linear in that very small changes in the values of parameters describing initial conditions produce qualitatively different outcomes in the dynamical development of systems described by them (see Peak and Frame 1994 for a developed discussion of this topic).

Feedback Feedback describes the consequences of change in a system. Self-governing systems characteristically contain negative feedback. Boundary testing behaviour leads to a damping back. The thermostat in a central heating system is a negative feedback device, as is the weighted governor attached to revolving shafts. In the latter case, as the shaft revolves faster the governor sticks out, exercising a countervailing centrifugal force. Plainly the functionalist account of social orders depends on the existence of negative feedback systems, usually considered to centre on agencies enforcing social norms, which are analogous to the biological negative feedback in an organism. Positive feedback occurs when a change tendency is reinforced rather than damped. Howl in a microphone/speaker system is an example. Here the noise of the speaker is picked up by the microphone, which amplifies it, broadcast through the speaker, amplified again, and so on. The multiplier and accelerator effects in the Keynesian account of economic cycles are good social examples of positive feedback. The significance of positive feedback is that it is not 'boundary defending' but is likely to lead to boundary breaking and transition to a new phase state.

Fractal Fractals are important in chaos theory. Essentially a fractal is an object which has a dimensionality which is not a whole number – it is fractional, hence fractal. This is best understood by thinking about how good something is at filling up a given dimensionality. Clearly a plane completely fills up two dimensions and a line doesn't. A coastline, whose length depends on the scale at which we choose to measure it, is better at filling up two dimensions than a true straight line. There are many interesting aspects to fractals but there are two which matter here. First, strange attractors can have fractal dimensionality within a state space which by definition has a dimensionality which is a whole number. Indeed, looking for this fractional dimensionality is one way of establishing the existence of chaotic determination. Second, fractals tend to be self-similar. In other words they look the same at whatever scale they are examined. Again a coastline illustrates the point. If we look at a portion of it drawn on a 1 to 5 million map, 1 to 50,000 map, 1 to 1, or even scaled up at 50,000 to 1, we find the same sort of wriggly line. Mandelbrot developed the theory of fractals and his Mandelbrot set is one of the best-known examples. Self-similarity is an important property whenever we are dealing with space.

Interaction In strict terms the kind of interaction we are interested in occurs when what physical scientists call superposition breaks down. In other words the effect of two or more variable causes acting together is not simply the sum of their effects taken separately. Instead we find that there are complex emergent properties. The relationship among the variables alters their causal propensities. This gels very well with the theory of complex and contingent causes which is the core of Bhaskar's realism. Interaction in data sets is not a nuisance. It is the mark of the obdurate complexity of the world.

Isomorphism This term applies at the point where ontology and epistemology meet in practice in any scientific description of the world, although it is most usually applied in relation to quantitative description. A description and the world are isomorphic when the elements of the description correspond to entities in the real world and when the rules describing the relationships among elements in the description correspond to the actual relationships among entities in the real world. The quantitative consideration of isomorphism depends on the transformation of uninterpreted into interpreted axiomatic systems. Abstract mathematical systems in which the terms in equations have no meaning outside the mathematical system are 'uninterpreted axiomatic systems'. When the terms in the equations are considered to describe real entities and the relationships among them, then the system is interpreted and is only valid if the abstract mathematics are isomorphic with reality. Usually this sort of discussion is conducted in relation to measurements at the ratio scale level and the generation of law like rules taking the form of equations, but it is equally applicable to simple typology generation and the representation of reality, not through equations, but through geometrical depiction.

Phase space/state space/condition space These three terms are synonyms. Probably the best usage is 'state space' because that conveys the idea of the whole state of the system. We can describe this state in multi-variate terms. That is, we can measure any meaningful set of aspects of the system. Each of these variable aspects can be considered as a dimension in a multi-dimensional space. If there are n variables there will be n dimensions. The state of the system at any instant can then be described by its co-ordinates in this n dimensional space with the measured value for each variable aspect being the co-ordinate for that dimension. If we think about the conventional variable/case rectangular matrix which is the general product of a survey, then we can see the columns which are variables as the dimensions of a state space and the rows which represent variable values for single cases as each being a set of co-ordinates in state space.

In dynamic treatments we introduce the additional dimension of time and we consider changes in the system's co-ordinates as measured through time. The path constituted by successive positions in the multi-dimensional space is the trajectory of the system. A very simple example of state space is provided by considering the relationships between a measure of voting behaviour and income category with the system being the individual voter. We should easily be able to see how this could be represented as a two dimensional table. If we have access to longitudinally-ordered data we can plot this relationship at successive time points, perhaps in the UK at successive general elections. In abstract terms we could expect to find the path of the trajectory moving anywhere within the possible n+1 dimensional state space which is described by the n descriptive variables (here two, voting behaviour and income level) and time. When trajectories don't do this, when instead they occupy only restricted parts of the available condition space, we have 'attractors'. Note that I have deliberately selected two variables which are at best ordinal (voting behaviour ordered from left to right) rather than continuous. Social scientists used to the analysis of contingency tables should be able to visualise the condition space here as a cube of cells with some being quite full and others empty or nearly so. The full cells are the attractor states. It is very important to note that what is involved here is not the use of a contingency table to infer the properties of the world from a sample of it. Instead, we are looking at the contingency table as a graphical representation of the way the world is through time. The example I have suggested is a typical social science one. Whereas the typical example of the physical sciences involves the plotting of many time points for a single case, we are plotting a few time points for many cases. It should be noted that the physical sciences also have the idea of many cases in their use of the term 'ensemble' to describe not one but many systems which belong to the same general group.

Qualitative Ernest Rutherford once said (according to Stewart 1997: 205) 'Qualitative is poor quantitative'. This is very much the same sort of thinking as informed Karl Pearson's idea of tetrachoric correlation in trying to deal with the inheritance of absolute genetic characteristics like blood group. For us, qualitative differences are differences of category. In measurement terms they are differences at the nominal level. Non-linearity and the issue of interaction/failure of superposition means that for much of reality we can tell Rutherford that quantitative is merely qualitative which has not yet become qualitative.

Random   In any system where there is randomness there is an inability to predict, regardless of the degree to which we are able to establish the initial condition of the system. An example of mathematical randomness is the decimal expansion of Pi where knowledge of any run of numbers gives us no basis for predicting any future run of numbers. An example of physical randomness is provided by the direction of an Alpha particle in radioactive decay. In terms of information theory something which is random cannot be described other than by reproducing it in its entirety. We have to be careful to distinguish randomness as a property of a system from randomness with regard to elements contained within the system. The typical discussion of randomness in the social sciences relates to statistical inference. We attach probabilities to statements because they are based on small samples of large universes rather than on the whole universes and are able to do so because the samples were randomly drawn, i.e. drawn in such a way that all samples of the size selected had an equal chance of being selected. Randomness must be distinguished from contingency. The former term is descriptive of indeterminacy. The latter does not imply indeterminacy but rather a specific history of determination among the many possible histories which might have occurred. Gould discusses exactly this point (1991).

Strange attractor   There are two descriptions of strange attractors. One is mathematical. A strange attractor is a domain in a condition space which has a fractal dimensionality, although some self-similar fractals may actually have whole number dimensions (for example the Mandelbrot set has a dimensionality of two). However, for our purposes in science it is more important to concentrate on the way in which strange attractors describe domains of uncertainty. In the case of a torus, which is sometimes described in the literature as a strange attractor and sometimes not so classified, the uncertainty is within a set of boundaries. We can see this as a model of a self-regulating and bounding system. For higher order attractors there is indeterminacy within boundaries, but also more than one possible set of boundaries. The two wings of the 'butterfly attractor' (Lorenz attractor) can be thought of in this way. There is indeterminacy within them. There is also the non-linear transformation in which very small changes in control parameters (including the interactions among them) determine which of the two bounded sets the system will be moving through. The term 'butterfly' is a description of the appearance of the two dimensional graphic representation of the three or higher dimensional form of this attractor.

NOTES

INTRODUCTION

1 It would be absolutely wrong to speak of higher and lower levels here.
2 Brunner's book is complex in form in that it is explicitly modelled on Dos Passos' multi-interwoven strand *USA* – another resonance.

1 UNDERSTANDING THE COMPLEX

1 The use of the term 'chaos' has become unpopular with many mathematicians and 'scientists', largely it seems because the ideas have resonated with a much wider public which is not confined to their own particular part of academia. They tend to prefer the term 'dynamists'. In this book this pomposity will not be indulged. 'Chaos' will be used to describe the scientific ideas, with 'science' here meaning all forms of organised knowledge about reality, and I will follow Hayles (1991) in using the term 'chaotics' for cultural resonances of a non-causal kind.
2 Although we should note Price's pertinent warning to the effect that: 'General systems theory focuses on the totality rather than its constituent parts. Thus, it adheres to holism in the conventional sense of the word. Complexity theory views this type of holism as just as problematic as the reductionism it nominally opposes – the conventional theory holism is reductionism to the whole. Holism typically overlooks the interactions and the organization, whereas complexity theory pays attention to them' (1997: 10).
3 But note Price's warning as quoted above. We are dealing with complex holism, not reduction to the whole.
4 Lovelock, who does accept the holistic implications of his position, is far too polite (1995b: x) about those who dismiss holistic thinkers like himself as 'very stupid people' and cling to the reductionist faith of their kind of science, in the face of reality as it really is. Such accusations should be returned with interest.
5 See Littell *The Visiting Professor* (1993) for an entertaining fictional exposition of the difference between chaos and randomness.
6 The distinction is not absolute in terms of content. Kauffman's approach is rather close to Prigogine's, although the latter gets only the most peripheral of citations in Kauffman's key text (1995).

7 Using the notation conventional in social statistics texts.

8 Correlation is not causation, of course.

9 Which it isn't: see Chapter 3 for some rude remarks about experiments.

10 I would describe it as an intellectual anti-programme. It is intellectual and it leads to inactivity.

11 Oral testimony has informed me that navigators were issued with 5-inch slide rules in order to carry out this job. If they wanted the increased accuracy of a 10-inch slide rule they had to buy their own. Somehow, I believe this.

12 The word 'determine' requires very careful consideration. Williams (1980) considered that it should always be considered in social science as referring to the setting of limits. That resonance booms.

13 The use of the word 'chooses' lays this account open to the charge of 'teleology'. Where conscious human action is involved I have no problem with this, but there is a substantive general issue and the use of 'chooses' here does not imply that some general or divine will is at work.

14 See Gleick (1987) for a good exposition of these ideas.

15 Of course, human activities in promoting global warming may be engendering yet another attractor state, but since the only available model is abiotic Venus, I am relying on Gaia to sort us out before we get to that stage. It should be noted that attempts at planetary engineering designed to reduce global warming, for example the seeding of marine deserts with iron in order to promote algal growth, the capture of carbon dioxide by algae, and hence a reduction in greenhouse gases, may in a chaotic system, have the effect of starting an Ice Age.

16 Hayles is worth quoting here. She remarks: 'Weissart arrives at an insight that I think deserves to be underscored. He points out that a phase space mapping is essentially a spatialization of a system's temporal flow. Thus complex evolutions through time are transformed into complex physical shapes that can be intuitively appreciated. I emphasise the *intuitive* [original emphasis] aspect of this knowledge (as does Weissart) because the forms are so complex that they never resolve into completely ordered structures. No matter how fine the resolution, some chaotic or "fuzzy" areas always remain' (1991: 27).

17 Ruelle (1991: Chapter 10) offers a relatively pain-free mathematical guide to doing this.

18 Simone Weil reminds us that in Greek thought a crucial role of the gods was the setting of limits.

19 Plato's conception of the existence of ideal forms, of which reality is but a shadow, is best illustrated by the myth of the cave in *The Republic*. Thom's (1975, 1983) position is essentially Platonic in form. Turner (1997) in his fascinating discussion of attractors expresses what seems to me a very Platonist view of them.

20 This term is due to Reed and Harvey.

2 THE REALITY OF THE COMPLEX

1 My argument that 'predictive choice' is possible goes considerably beyond the 'soft foundationalism' asserted by Khalil (1996) but is not equivalent to the positivist conception of a covering law. It is something different.

2 The modernist programme in science cannot be reduced to positivism. This is particularly evident in relation to the development of epidemiologically-founded public health, but is central to the core content of evolutionary theory, especially as expressed by Wallace.

3 An Anglicisation of a Gaelic expression meaning 'the cap of death'. In my vernacular it means put a stop to. Another way of making the point would be to suggest that complexity theory will knock postmodernism on the head.

4 His reference to the amateur character of such endeavours in sociology is diversionary. It is very much the task of any group of scientists to sort out the metatheoretical basis of their programme, precisely because this is essentially an inductive process based on a reflexive consideration of the nature of their own practices. The last sort of people to whom this task should be assigned are deductively inclined philosophers.

5 The recent efforts at the development of 'evidence-based medicine' seem to be informed by this perspective, although it is certainly possible to conceive of an evidence-based medicine which is not positivist. Essentially, positivism emerges in a methodological programme centring on the experiment as the valid method. Far from this being true, the non-linear character of reality means that the range of phenomena which can be accessed by experimental approaches is, whilst not trivial, strictly limited. Those limits may be being reached.

6 There is an interesting illustration of this in the experience of the Arab seamen imported into Tyneside as fireman–trimmers. These exceptionally fit and tough young men (just think about the job they were actually doing) had an annual mortality rate of 6 per cent from TB, three times that of people brought up on Tyneside. As was recognised by the medical officer of health in South Shields at the time, the reason for this was that they had not been exposed to TB in their childhood in rural Yemen and were particularly vulnerable to it in young adult life.

7 The present author, who is Tyneside Irish, was exposed to an active case of TB at school in the 1960s. I manifested an extreme reaction on the Heaf test, showing the presence of antibodies to TB in my blood, but had no clinical signs of the disease whatsoever. The chest physician who established this cheerfully commented that as I belonged to a generation fed on steak and chips and living in good housing, and as moreover my parents (both of whom had siblings who died in adult life of TB), had never had the disease, this was not surprising. I had 'been bred for resistance, was housed like a racehorse and was fed like a fighting cock' (a direct quotation which I have not forgotten). That is complex and contingent causation. I would only add that there was a definite contingency to the emergence of TB death rates as empirical. That happened only with the development of systematic social statistics, of which more in the next chapter.

8 It is important to note that the argument is with Gould's emphasis on contingency in this book. In an article published at the same time and cited by Harvey and Reed (1994) he explicitly associates his account of punctuated equilibria with Prigogine's account of bifurcation (Gould 1988) and his enthusiastic endorsement of Kauffman's work is also significant. I am taking issue with the earlier position for purely heuristic reasons because

Gould writes so clearly that he provides a superb basis for constructive argument.

9 I must have used this quotation more than twenty times. The constant repetition is an indication of sincere agreement, even more sincere now that I have complexity theory to validate it as an account of the nature of reality.

10 That said, the nature of the current debate between proponents of the social construction of science and its positivist and reductionist defenders resembles nothing so much as the image of two bald men fighting over a comb, suggested by Borges as a description of the Falklands War.

11 I have taken this example because Graham, for a postmodernist, writes clearly and expresses the ideas coherently. Indeed, her work is substantively interesting and in the example chosen I would agree absolutely with the conclusions she draws about the role of regulation theory in relation to economic development practices, whilst rejecting absolutely the way she takes in arriving at these conclusions.

12 Of course, one of the crucial elements of the postmodernist programme is precisely the rejection of the notion of any progress or development in human history.

13 Price is very good on this issue. He remarks: 'The complexity view is, in its most general articulation, that modern sociology (and all science) is in need of modification. By correcting inadequacies in our scientific paradigm, we may appropriately and fruitfully continue to do "science". Foucault, on the other hand, and typically postmodern in this regard, sees modern science as being in need of problematization. His goal is to show the fundamental, irreparable shortcomings and contingencies in the concept of human science. Complexity offers covering laws; Foucault abhors totalizations. Both views emerge from different historical contexts and domain assumptions' (1997: 4).

14 The gender neutral form of the Latin is appropriate here. There were *dominae* as well as *domini*. The undeniable fact that reductionist science has under specific historical and social conditions generally been practised by men, does not make it inherently masculine.

15 Although it is an excellent description of geography's disciplinary trajectory over the last twenty-odd years. That subject was dominated by a positivist programme founded on a very linear version of quantitative reasoning, became profoundly structuralist (and geographical versions of realism remain pretty structuralist), and has now turned to a postmodernist/poststructuralist account in which the programme of general explanation in causal terms has been essentially abandoned (see Byrne 1995b). It is always as well to remember Weber's dictum that to be adequate, explanations must be adequate at both the level of meaning and the level of cause.

16 I would argue contra a version of modernism, not of modernism in toto. See Chapter 6 below.

17 Archer's recent writings on realism and emergence (1996) gel well with this account, although her dismissal of empiricism in general is not acceptable. See Byrne (1997c) for a discussion.

3 COMPLEXITY AND THE QUANTITATIVE PROGRAMME IN SOCIAL SCIENCE

1 Williams is being far too Platonist here. Statistical theory developed out of the need to handle the quantitative information generated precisely by the measurement movement he describes, and was moreover very much socially constructed. See MacKenzie (1979).

2 Indeed there is another novel aspect to the application of formalised mathematical systems to reality which is central to the development of the chaos/complexity programme. That is the extent to which it derives from a wholly novel experimental mathematics which was made possible by the development of electronic computing. Feigenbaum's series was established exactly in this way through an experimental mathematics using an electronic calculator. Cohen and Stewart (1995) raise the problem of what we might do with such an experimental mathematics in which formalised proof is essentially irrelevant so long as relationships hold in calculable instances. Given the implications of Gödel's work, that might be all we can ever have.

3 In one of the most useful books so far published on the application of chaos/complexity theory to the social sciences.

4 The term 'qualitative' here might be confusing. It does not mean interpretative, directed towards adequacy at the level of meaning. Rather it involves a shift from thinking in terms of the continuous character of measurement into an account which argues for categorical changes in form. The idea is very close to what Marx meant by 'transformation of quantity into quality'.

5 Although the survey method is, rightly, described here as sociological, it is of course the method through which all quantitative data of any significance about the real social world are constructed/collected, and is therefore the basis of any sort of inductive programme in economics and political science.

6 Weber did demand adequacy at this level as well as adequacy at the level of meaning, if any sociological explanation was to be adequate overall.

7 Attempts to get round this by procedures like structural equation modelling seem to me not to resolve this problem at all and to represent merely an even more extreme reification of the decidedly socially generated procedures of factor analysis in which they are founded.

8 The problem of reification is that which stems from the possibility that our concept does not correspond to any aspect of reality but is simply a social construct of our scientific procedures. Examples are provided by many of the terms of psychiatry – is there a disease entity of 'sociopathy' or simply a concept reified by a classificatory procedure? Issues of operationalisation might be considered to arise when the concept does correspond to an aspect of reality and we move towards a set of measurement rules to produce a quantified version of it.

9 Measurement by fiat is measurement which simply assumes the relationship between the measured and the concept of interest.

10 Type II or Beta errors are the representation in inferential reasoning of Popper's assertion that we can only falsify, never prove. They represent the risk of accepting a false null hypothesis – the fallacy of affirming the consequent.

11 The reliance of inference on formal hypothesis testing does mean that its procedures correspond exactly to, and are indeed the type of, the hypothetico-deductive method. This does not mean that they are about causality, although they may be used to test causal models and in such usage form the basis of statistically grounded experimental designs. It should be noted that Baysian methods retain hypothesis testing, although the introduction of conditional probabilities does introduce an intensely subjective element in their approach.

12 Post Reimann we have to accept that there is an infinity of possible algebras, in that any axiomatic system which is not self-contradictory can be the basis of an algebra.

13 Bartlett (1990) uses exactly this model to show how relatively small perturbations can produce chaotic effects, merely by introducing a periodic component representing seasonal effects.

14 This is often written as 'wrest' rather than 'wring' but I find the latter imagery more appropriate.

15 A good example is provided by the contrast between the steady incremental but not dramatic or transformational experimentally-founded in the controlled trial form programme of chemotherapy for neoplasms affecting children and young adults, and the dramatic and transformational effect of antibiotics which were not validated by a programme of clinical trials.

16 This used to be called the Social Science Research Council but the word 'science' was dropped at the insistence of the 'cerebral' Sir Keith Joseph when he was Secretary of State for Education and Science, on the grounds that being without a causal programme the social sciences were not science. One of the minor satisfactions of working through chaos/complexity is the realisation of what rubbish that assertion was.

17 See the discussion of this problem in relation to Mouzelis' arguments in Chapter 2.

18 It should be noted that prediction here is not forward prediction. We cannot establish a general law independent of a specific history. What we can do is retrospectively model in mathematical terms the histories of that set of women who lived through the particular period. This is Gould's history, not the establishment of a prospective predictive rule.

4 ANALYSING SOCIAL COMPLEXITY

1 In particular in the analysis of complex movements in what appear to be the chaotic forms of financial markets, especially the movements in derivatives.

2 One of these, the set of cluster analysis techniques, was developed by biologists, but they developed it in order to handle ecological and other descriptive data which described aspects of reality, not for the handling of experimental results.

3 This was a very crude operationalisation of Pahl's (1985) notion where 'work rich' meant more than one full-time equivalent employed person (part-time counting as half), 'work average' meant exactly one full-time equivalent employed person, and 'work poor' meant less than one full-time equivalent employed person.

4 Age category, work connectedness, and Registrar General's social class could be treated as ordinal but are regarded as categorical here. I would argue that age category of parents is categorical in that it reflects different cohorts of experience.

5 They do not need to be relatively large because of the operation of the law of large numbers.

6 It was terminated with the absurd abolition of the county-wide authority.

7 SPSS is the Statistical Package for the Social Sciences. This is available in a variety of formats but the command examples here derive from the general syntax employed.

8 With the system defined in locality terms. See Chapter 5 for an elaboration of this.

9 The 'New Zone' command is used within SASPAC, the package which handles UK Population Census-derived small area statistics, to construct measures for spaces made up of aggregates of smaller spaces. See SASPAC handbook for details.

10 Type here being determined by common cluster membership as derived from some process of numerical taxonomy.

11 Since I follow the definition of the 1837 Irish Royal Commission on the Poor Law and define true unemployment in terms of the numbers of 'those who have not work and want it', I would usually add the total number of 'permanently sick' of working age to get a more realistic count of the unemployed, and would in any event always use census self-definition-based totals when available instead of vastly over-cooked official counts.

12 NOMIS stands for National On-line Manpower Information Service, located in the University of Durham.

13 Under SPSS hierarchical clustering procedures clusters remain in the cluster to which they were first allocated and cannot be moved to a more appropriate one at a later stage. The method suggested here gets round this problem.

14 Special procedures should be used with frequency or binary as opposed to continuous data, but in practice simple methods remain robust and interesting at differentiating using even just binary data.

15 Morenoff and Tienda (1997) present a cluster analysis-based account of socio-spatial change in Chicago which is a good example of time-ordered classification as a way of describing dynamic change. This will be discussed further in Chapter 5.

16 Gilbert is talking about the way in which sociologists characteristically infer beyond the actual population from which they have sampled. For example in Byrne et al. (1985) the arguments about the relationship between housing conditions and health are considered to be likely to exist in places other than in Gateshead where the study was carried out. However, the force of statistical inference still applies in that the relationships are really considered to exist in Gateshead at least. In other words we still infer to the actual population studied.

17 The ratio of male non-employment levels at these two time points is 1 to more than 3. In other words it is greater than the first Feigenbaum number. Scanning data sets for changes of this sort of order in theoretically and substantively important system descriptor variables is a good way of seeing what might have caused system changes.

18 In a flat file a hierarchical data set is written as one file with all values for higher containing levels attached to the individual cases at the lowest level, which are contained within the higher levels.

19 The term 'icon' is obviously more appropriate for the kind of still representations generated by correspondence analysis than it is for the dynamic movement of chaos computer graphics, but only in a very literal way.

5 COMPLEX SPACES

1 Social boundaries change in space over time. A very good example is provided by the common UK operationalisation of local labour markets in terms of Travel to Work Areas. The boundaries of these are created after each decennial population census to describe the smallest aggregate of local authority areas within which 80 per cent of the residential population who work, do work, and within which 80 per cent of those who work also live. Patterns of industrial change can change these very significantly, but that reflects new social orders in space. The actual ground plan is not what matters. What matters is the social arrangement in space.

2 The general population scale of such regions2 is about 5 million. This makes some smaller nation states, e.g. the Scandinavian ones, regions2 in scale.

3 Gender is not a significant spatial sorter. Sexual orientation as a component of lifestyle may be, but lifestyle sorting, although of extreme interest to those elements of the intelligentsia who would love to be bohemians if only they could find bohemia, is not of much significance in comparison with the enormous importance of class and the considerable importance of ethnicity.

4 This term has acquired connotations over and beyond its apparent positional content. Wilson (1992) now employs the term 'ghetto poor' and I prefer that of dispossessed working class – see Byrne (1995b).

5 We can go back to Bedford Falls here. Capra, an arch modernist in my opinion, was certainly able to imagine what Bedford Falls would have been without the agency of George Bailey – it would have been Pottersville. Note that there was not an infinite possible range of others – just one, the other wing of the bifurcation where George's agency had been the significant perturbation.

6 Warf was quite severely taken to task by the commentators on his paper (see in particular the remarks of Short 1993). I generally agree with those comments.

7 Although even here the operationalisation of Teesside as the former Cleveland County is inexact. There are parts of North Yorkshire which are essentially Teesside's suburbs, notably the Hambleton district in general and Northallerton in particular.

8 The most important democratic level abolished was the conurbation-wide planning and co-ordination level of the Greater London and Metropolitan Councils. Cleveland hung on for a while because of its anomalous position as an urban shire county, but it went in the end.

9 Teesside is here operationalised as Cleveland County.

10 Of course, there are essentially gendered inequalities within households and consumption is not equal for all household members. Nevertheless it is household membership which matters most.

11 For example, detailed accounts of changes in the composition of its housing stock by form, location and tenure.

12 The use of that expression 'catchment area', which suggest an organic link between central urban labour markets and suburban residents, is historically accurate. However, the development of 'edge city' residential *and* employment zones, may mean that the suburbs no longer drain into the city.

13 Fitch sardonically remarks that: 'A focus on the Rockefeller family may annoy academic Marxists for whom the capitalist is only the personification of abstract capital and who believe, austerely, that any discussion of individuals in economic analysis represents a fatal concession to populism and empiricism' (1993: xvii).

6 THE COMPLEX CHARACTER OF HEALTH AND ILLNESS

1 Of course small size was probably a survival advantage under conditions of trench warfare.

2 The two sides of the health transition, which has never been a gradual or incremental process but has rather involved a clear non-linear change, can be considered as distinct attractors. The re-emergence of tuberculosis demonstrates very clearly that if key control parameters are reversed in value – if extensive exclusionary poverty is allowed to re-emerge, then the health transition is a reversible process.

3 The River Wear in Durham was channelled at this time and turned from a stagnant ditch into a fast flowing stream. The result was the elimination of the malaria which the 1842 Health of Towns Committee had reported as a serious problem in the town. The reason was of course that the river was now too fast for mosquito larvae. The actual specific aetiology of malaria was not to be discovered for another sixty years.

4 The very interesting Lancashire study of differential child and maternal mortality in three industrial towns shows the enormous significance of working-class women's collective action in socialist politics. See Lancaster Regionalism Group (1985).

5 The general issue of ecological correlation is well discussed in Bulmer (1986).

6 In the northeast of England the relationship is rather more masked than it might otherwise be, not only by the effects of individual mobility in space, but because former coalfield areas on the fringe of the Tyne Wear Conurbation have become middle-class residential suburbs whilst retaining an elderly population resident before gentrification, many of whose males worked in mining. The premature mortality among that group is very high. Nonetheless the social divide is also a health divide.

7 For example, in his discussion of the use of quantitative methods by British sociologists, Bechhofer (1996) reviewed the journals *Sociology, Work and Employment* and *Sociological Review*, but ignored *The Sociology of Health and*

Illness in which quantitative work of the kind exemplified by Blaxter is strongly represented.

8 Lovelock's conception of Gaia resonates pretty well absolutely with the chaos/complexity account. See Lovelock (1995).

9 In Kuhnian terms we have a normal science here, i.e. 'a' temporally specific normal paradigm, rather than 'the' all embracing all time normal science.

10 Now we have to have healthy cities – an example of social inflation of some importance. Sunderland's elites were delighted when their clapped out industrial dump was designated as a 'city' rather than a town.

11 Interestingly the implications of these limits are clearly understood by fiscal conservatives who seek to limit the resource demands of curative health care systems by a reorientation of public policy towards programmes of prevention, albeit prevention founded on the transformation of individual behaviours rather than on the reduction of social inequalities.

12 It is surprising that there is not an explicit turn towards Baysian methods here. These would allow exactly for the combination of clinical knowledge and statistical reasoning which is endorsed by proponents of evidence-based medicine.

13 Changes in the National Health Service were in the organisational forms of delivery of health care, not in the underlying commitment to health equity.

14 That word is used to signify the strength of the empirical evidence for the following argument, which evidence is typified by the oft cited work of Wilkinson and his co-workers.

7 COMPLEXITY, EDUCATION AND CHANGE

1 The exception to this is the development in association with the programme of visual methods based on graphical interfaces. These have considerable potential in relation to iconographic modelling.

2 Particularly in relation to discussions of the formation of a separate and disadvantaged 'ghetto poor', to use Wilson's preferred terminology (1992), although his earlier term 'the underclass' (see Wilson 1987) has wider currency. Wilson's reasons for rejecting the earlier formulation, given the use made of it by New Right ideologues, are wholly persuasive.

3 This study has been selected because it is clear and coherent. I have a good deal of sympathy with the objectives of the authors but I think they have got the story wrong, in what is substantively an interesting and well done piece of work.

4 GCSEs (General Certificate of Education) are the examination taken by most UK school children in the eleventh year of their schooling, at age 16. They have replaced the former 'academically-oriented' Ordinary Level examination which was designed as a lead into university entry when that was an elite route only.

5 In the UK system the minimum legal school leaving age is 16, after GCSE exams, and there are a variety of post-16 examinations of which A level is the most prestigious. The actual group being examined are not all children but those who have done reasonably well at 16. GCSE performance has far more social salience than A level for most children. Also it seems odd to control for A level score against GCSE score for only half of the entrants when it would be perfectly easy to include a GCSE score as an input figure

for all students. Gray *et al.* (1995) have studied GCSE performance against achievement at age 11.

6 Children generally want to be educated with those they went to primary school with, and there are 'keep them away from those bloody snobs' pressures to consider.

7 Catholic schools are allowed to admit up to 30 per cent of non-Catholic pupils and most do so, given their differential popularity. Many parents rediscover rather obscure Catholic antecedents when seeking schooling for their children.

8 I must record my absolute agreement with the integrationist arguments of these authors based on experience of the outcomes of ethnic (religious rather than racially-founded) separation in schooling in Northern Ireland and integration in schooling in the English city of Leicester. The benign effects in the latter place are evident and outstanding.

8 COMPLEXITY AND POLICY

1 Ignorance of social reality extended to a profound ignorance of physical chemistry as well. The term was meant to imply that the initial dollops of public dosh would start a true market which could then be left to its own devices. Catalysed reactions stop working when the catalyst is removed!

2 Banks plainly uses this term in a deliberate and informed way. He has read his systems theory.

3 Many of whom are perhaps best understood as comprador intelligentsia, in the way in which the comprador bourgeoisie in Maoist class analysis were that section who did not serve the national Chinese system but instead facilitated its looting by imperialism. In the same way these hired hands of globalising capital, many of them, like Blair, lawyers, live from the services, both practical and ideological, which they perform for their paymasters.

9 CONCLUSION

1 Of course, a good deal of the deindustrialisation of the late 1970s and early 1980s in the UK was the product of specific national policies which privileged finance over industrial capital through the maintenance of a very high exchange rate.

2 And universalist to boot but that is another fight and probably another book.

3 These binary pairs, although clearly closely related, are not synonym-based. It is possible to be quantitative in descriptive terms without the causal programme central to nomothetic science.

BIBLIOGRAPHY

Adam, B. (1994a) 'Beyond boundaries: reconceptualizing time in the face of global challenges' *Social Science Information* 33(4): 597–620.

—— (1994b) *Time and Social Theory*, Cambridge: Polity.

—— (1995) *Timewatch*, Cambridge: Polity.

Albert, A. (ed.) (1995) *Chaos and Society*, Amsterdam: IOS Press.

ALCD (1997a) 'Methodology and software for computer-intensive analysis of complex longitudinal data' *ESRC Research Programme into the Analysis of Large and Complex Datasets*, Swindon: Economic and Social Research Council.

—— (1997b) 'Using multi-level models for the analysis of large and complex data sets' *ESRC Research Programme into the Analysis of Large and Complex Datasets*, Swindon: Economic and Social Research Council.

Ambrose, P. (1994) *Urban Process and Power*, London: Routledge.

Amin, A. (ed.) (1994) *Post-Fordism*, Oxford: Blackwell.

Archbishop of Canterbury's Urban Priority Commission (1984) *Faith in the City*, London: Church House Publishing.

Archer, M. (1996) 'Social integration and system integration: developing the distinction' *Sociology* 30(4): 679–99.

Ashton, J. R. (1988) *The New Public Health*, Milton Keynes: Open University Press.

Baker, P. L. (1993) 'Chaos, order and sociological theory' *Sociological Inquiry* 63(4): 406–24.

Bagguley, P., Mark-Lawson, J., Shapiro, D., Urry, J., Walby, S. and Warde, A. (1990) *Restructuring: Place, Class and Gender*, London: Sage.

Bankston, C. and Caldas, S. J. (1996) 'Majority African American schools and social injustice: the influence of de facto segregation on academic achievement' *Social Forces* 75(2): 535–55.

Barnett, C. (1986) *Audit of War*, London: Macmillan.

Barrow, J. D. (1992) *Pi in the Sky*, Harmondsworth: Penguin.

Bartlett, M. S. (1990) 'Chance or chaos?' *Journal of the Royal Statistical Society* 153(3): 321–47.

Bateson, N. (1984) *Data Construction in Social Surveys*, London: Allen and Unwin.

189

Batty, M. (1995) 'Cities and complexity: implications for modelling sustainability' in Brotchie *et al.* (eds) op. cit., 469–86.

Batty, M. and Xie, Y. (1997) 'Possible urban automata' *Environment and Planning B – Planning and Design* 24: 275–92.

Batty, M., Couclelis, H. and Eichen, M. (1997) 'Urban systems as cellular automata' *Environment and Planning B* 24(2): 159–64.

Bechhofer, F. (1996) 'Quantitative research in British sociology' *Sociology* 3(30): 583–92.

Benton, T. (1991) 'Biology and social science: why the return of the repressed should be given a (cautious) welcome' *Sociology* 1(25): 1–29.

Beynon, H., Hudson, R. and Sadler, D. (1994) *A Place Called Teesside*, Edinburgh: Edinburgh University Press.

Bhaskar, R. (1986) *Scientific Realism and Human Emancipation*, London: Verso.

Blackman, T. (1995) *Urban Policy and Practice*, London: Routledge.

Blackman, T., Keenan, P. and Coombes, M. (1994) 'Developing GIS for urban policy and research in local government in the UK', Newcastle City Council: mimeo.

Blane, D., Brunner, E. and Wilkinson, R. (eds) (1996) *Health and Social Organization*, London: Routledge.

Blane, D., White, I. and Morris, J. (1996) 'Education, social circumstances and mortality' in Blane, D. *et al.* (eds) op. cit., 171–87.

Blaxter, M. (1990) *Health and Lifestyles*, London: Routledge.

Blowers, A. (ed.) (1993) *Planning for a Sustainable Environment*, London: Earthscan.

Bookchin, M. (1995) *From Urbanization to Cities*, London: Cassell.

Booth, T. (1988) *Doing Policy Research*, Aldershot: Gower.

Borrie Commission Report on Social Justice (1994) *Social Justice*, London: Vintage.

Bradbury, F. C. S. (1933) *Causal Factors in Tuberculosis*, London: National Association for the Prevention of Tuberculosis.

Brotchie, J., Batty, M., Blakely, E., Hall, P. and Newton, P. (eds) (1995) *Cities in Competition*, Sydney: Longman Australia.

Brown, C. (1995) *Chaos and Catastrophe Theories – Sage Quantitative Applications in the Social Sciences 107*, London: Sage.

Brown, T. A. (1996) 'Measuring chaos using the Lyapunov exponent' in Kiel, L. D. and Elliott, E. (eds) op. cit., 53–66.

Bulmer, M. (ed.) (1986) *Social Science and Social Policy*, London: Allen and Unwin.

—— (1986) 'The ecological fallacy – its implications for social policy analysis' in Bulmer, M. (ed.) op. cit., 207–22.

Byrne, D. S. (1989) *Beyond the Inner City*, Milton Keynes: Open University Press.

—— (1994) *Deindustrialization, Planning and Class Structures*, unpublished PhD thesis, University of Durham.

—— (1995a) 'Deindustrialization and dispossession' *Sociology* 29: 95–116.

—— (1995b) 'Radical geography as "mere political economy" – the local poltics of space' *Capital and Class* 56: 117–38.

—— (1997a) 'Chaotic places or complex places: cities in a post-industrial era' in Westwood, S. and Williams, J. (eds) op. cit., 50–72.

—— (1997b) 'Social exclusion and capitalism' *Critical Social Policy* 17(1): 27–51.

—— (1997c) 'Simulation – a way forward?' *Sociological Research Online* 2 2 http://www.socresonline.org.uk/2/2/contents.html.

—— (1997d) 'Land versus people: the urban process in the reconstruction of industrial cities' paper given at the Annual Conference of the Polish Sociological Association, Katowice.

Byrne, D. S. and Rogers, T. (1996) 'Divided spaces: divided schools' *Sociological Research Online* 1 2 http://www.socresonline.org.uk/socresonline/1/2/3.html.

Byrne, D. S., Williamson, W. and Fletcher, B. (1975) *The Poverty of Education*, London: Martin Robertson.

Byrne, D., McCarthy, P., Harrison, S. and Keithley, J. (1985) *Housing and Health*, Aldershot: Gower.

Capra, F. (1996) *The Web of Life*, London: HarperCollins.

Carstairs, V. and Lowe, M. (1986) 'Small area analysis: creating an area base for environmental monitoring and epidemiological analysis' *Community Medicine* 8: 15(3): 210–14.

Carstairs, V. and Morris, R. (1989) 'Deprivation and mortality: an alternative to social class' *Community Medicine* 11: 210(2): 146–57.

Cartwright, T. J. (1991) 'Planning and chaos theory' *Journal of the American Planning Association* 57: 44–56.

Castells, M. (1977) *The Urban Question*, London: Edward Arnold.

Casti, J. L. (1994) *Complexification*, London: Abacus.

Centre for Environmental Studies (1985) 'Outer estates in Britain: East Middlesbrough case study' *CES Paper No. 26*, London: Centre for Environmental Studies.

Charlton, B. and Kelly, M. P. (1993) 'Health promotion – time for a new philosophy' *British Journal of General Practice* 43(367): 84–5.

Clarke, G. M. (1971) *Statistics and Experimental Design*, London: Edward Arnold.

Cochrane, A. (1987) 'What a difference the place makes: the new politics of locality' *Antipode* 19: 354–63.

Cohen, J. and Stewart, M. (1995) *The Collapse of Chaos*, Harmondsworth: Penguin.

Coleman, J. S. (1966) *Equality of Educational Opportunity*, Washington, DC: US Department of Health, Education and Welfare.

—— (1990) *Foundations of Social Theory*, Cambridge, Mass.: Harvard University Press.

Conté, R. and Gilbert, N. (1995) 'Introduction: computer simulation for social theory' in Gilbert, N. and Conté, R. (eds) op. cit., 1–18.

Crooke, S., Pakulski, J. and Waters, M. (1992) *Postmodernization*, London: Sage.

Crutchfield, J. P. (1992) 'Knowledge and meaning: chaos and complexity' in Lam, L. and Naroditsky, V. (eds) op. cit., 66–101.

Dale, A. and Davies, R. B. (1994) *Analyzing Social and Political Change*, London: Sage.

Dale, A., Arber, S. and Procter, M. (1988) *Doing Secondary Analysis*, London: Unwin Hyman.

D'Arcy Thompson, W. (1942) *On Growth and Form*, Cambridge: Cambridge University Press.

Davies, J. G. (1972) *The Evangelistic Bureaucrat*, London: Tavistock.

Davies, J. K. and Kelly, M. P. (eds) (1993) *Healthy Cities*, London: Routledge.

Davies, R. B. (1994) 'From cross-sectional to longitudinal analysis' in Dale, A. and Davies, R. B. (eds) op. cit., 20–40.

De Greene, K. B. (1994) 'The rocky path to complex system indicators' *Technological Forecasting and Social Change* 47: 171–88.

Dennis, N. (1970) *People and Planning*, London: Faber and Faber.

—— (1972) *Public Participation and Planners' Blight*, London: Faber and Faber.

Dickens, P., Goodwin, M., Gray, F. and Duncan, S. (1985) *Housing, States and Localities*, London: Methuen.

Draper, D. 'Discussion of Goldstein and Spiegelhalter op. cit.' *Journal of the Royal Statistical Society – Series A* 3: 416–18.

Duncan, S. (1986) 'What is locality?' *Urban and Regional Studies Working Paper No. 51*, Brighton: University of Sussex.

Dunleavy, P. (1981) *The Politics of Mass Housing in Britain*, Oxford: Clarendon Press.

Editorial (1997) *Environment and Planning B* 24(3): 317–18.

Esping-Andersen, G. (1990) *The Three Worlds of Welfare Capitalism*, Cambridge: Polity.

Esser, J. and Hirsch, J. (1994) 'The crisis of Fordism and the dimensions of "post-Fordist" regional and urban structure' in Amin, A. (ed.) op. cit., 71–98.

Etzioni, A. (1995) *The Spirit of Community*, London: Fontana.

Eve, R. A., Horsfall, S. and Lee, M. E. (1997) *Chaos, Complexity and Sociology*, London: Sage.

Everitt, B. (1974) *Cluster Analysis*, London: Heinemann.

Everitt, B. and Dunn, G. (1983) *Advanced Methods of Data Exploration and Modelling*, London: Heinemann.

Eversley, D. (1990) 'Inequality at the spatial level – tasks for planners' *The Planner* 76: 12 March.

Fainstein, S., Gordon, I. and Harloe, M. (1992) *Divided Cities*, London: Blackwell.

Featherstone, M., O'Conner, J., Phillips, D. and Wynne, D. (1994) *Lifestyle and Cultural Consumption in the City*, ESRC End of Project Report Ref: R000–23–3075.

Feigenbaum, M. J. (1978) 'Quantitative universality for a class of nonlinear transformations' *Journal of Statistical Physics* 19: 25–52.

Fitch, R (1993) *The Assassination of New York*, London: Verso.

Forrest, R., Murie, A. and Williams, P. (1990) *Home Ownership: Differentiation and Fragmentation*, London: Unwin Hyman.

Fraser, G. M. (1992) *Quartered Safe Out Here*, London: Havill.

Gell-Mann, M. (1994) *The Quark and the Jaguar*, London: Abacus.

Gilbert, N. (1993) *Analysing Tabular Data*, London: UCL Press.

—— (1995) 'Emergence in social simulation' in Gilbert, N. and Conté, R. (eds) op. cit., 144–56.

—— (1997) 'A simulation of the structure of academic science' *Sociological Research Online* http://kennedy.soc.surrey.ac.uk/socresonline/2/2/3/html.

Gilbert, N. and Conté, R. (eds) (1995) *Artificial Societies*, London: UCL Press.

Gilbert, N. and Doran, J. (eds) (1994) *Simulating Societies*, London: UCL Press.

Gleick, J. (1987) *Chaos: Making a New Science*, New York: Viking-Penguin.

Goldstein, H. (1987) *Multilevel Models in Educational and Social Research*, London: Griffin.

Goldstein, H. and Spiegelhalter, D. J. (1996) 'League tables and their limitations' *Journal of the Royal Statistical Society – Series A* 159(3): 385–443.

Gould, S. J. (1988) 'A start on progress and directionality in evolution' *Journal of Palaeontology* 3(62): 319–29.

—— (1991) *Wonderful Life: the Burgess Shale and the Nature of History*, Harmondsworth: Penguin.

—— (1996) *Life's Grandeur*, London: Jonathan Cape.

Graham, G. (1992) 'Postfordism as politics: the political consequences of narrative on the left' *Society and Space* 10: 393–410.

Gray, J., Jesson, D. and Goldstein, H. (1995) *Changes in GCSE Examination Performance using Value Added Analysis over a Five Year Period in One Local Education Authority*, Cambridge: Homerton College.

Gulbenkian Commission (1996) *Open the Social Sciences*, Stanford, CA: Stanford University Press.

Halfpenny, P. (1997) 'Situating simulation in sociology' *Sociological Research Online* http://www.socresonline.org.uk/socresonline/2/3/9.html.

Hall, P. (1992) *Urban and Regional Planning*, London: Routledge.

Harris, B. (1995) 'The nature of sustainable urban development' in Brochie, J. et al. (eds) op. cit., 444–54.

Harvey, D. L. and Reed, M. H. (1994) 'The evolution of dissipative social systems' *Journal of Social and Evolutionary Systems* 17(4): 371–411.

Hayles, N. K. (1990) *Chaos Bound*, Ithaca, NY: Cornell University Press.

—— (1991) *Chaos and Order*, Chicago: University of Chicago Press.

Hegedus, J. and Tosic, I. (1994) 'The poor, the rich and the transformation of urban space' *Urban Studies* 31: 989–93.

Hellevik, O. (1984) *Introduction to Causal Analysis*, London: Allen and Unwin.

Hennessy, P. (1993) *Never Again*, London: Arrow.

Hill, R. L. and Feagin, J. R. (1987) 'Detroit and Houston: two cities in global perspective' in Smith, M. P. and Feagin, J. R. (eds) op. cit., 155–77.

Hirsh, A. (1981) *The French New Left*, Boston: South End Press.

Imrie, R. and Thomas, H. (eds) (1993) *British Urban Policy and the Urban Development Corporations*, London: Paul Chapman.

Irvine, J., Miles, I. and Evans, J. (1979) *Demystifying Social Statistics*, London: Pluto.

Jaditz, T. (1996) 'The prediction test for nonlinear determinism' in Kiel, L. D. and Elliott, E. (eds) op. cit., 67–88.

Johnson, G. (1996) *Fire in the Mind*, London: Viking.

Kauffman, S. (1993) *The Origins of Order*, London: Oxford University Press.

—— (1995) *At Home in the Universe*, London: Viking.

Kelly, M. P., Davies, J. K. and Charlton, B. (1993) 'Healthy cities: a modern problem or a postmodern solution?' in Davies, J. K. and Kelly, M. P. (eds) op. cit., 159–67.

Kempen, E. T. (1994) 'The dual city and the poor: social polarisation, social segregation and life chances' *Urban Studies* 31: 995–1015.

Khalil, E. L. (1996) 'Social theory and naturalism' in Khalil, E. L. and Boulding, K. E. (eds) op. cit., 1–39.

Khalil, E. L. and Boulding, K. E. (eds) (1996) *Evolution, Complexity and Order*, London: Routledge.

Kiel, L. D. and Elliott, E. (eds) (1996) *Chaos Theory in the Social Sciences*, Ann Arbor: University of Michigan Press.

Lam, L. and Naroditsky, V. (eds) (1992) *Modelling Complex Phenomena*, New York: Springer-Verlag, 66–101.

Lancaster Regionalism Group (1985) *Localities, Class and Gender*, London: Pion.

Lash, S. and Urry, J. (1987) *The End of Organized Capitalism*, Cambridge: Polity.

—— (1994) *Economies of Signs and Space*, London: Sage.

Lee, R. (1995) 'Look after the pounds and the people will look after themselves' *Environment and Planning A* 27: 1577–94.

Lemann, N. (1991) *The Promised Land*, London: Macmillan.

Levitas, R. (1996) 'The concept of social exclusion and the new Durkheimian hegemony' *Critical Social Policy* 16(1): 5–20.

Levitas, R. and Guy, W. (1996) *Interpreting Official Statistics*, London: Routledge.

Lewin, R. (1993) *Complexity*, London: Phoenix.

Lewis-Beck, M. (1995) 'Series editor's introduction' to Brown, C. op. cit.

Littell, R. (1993) *The Visiting Professor*, London: Faber and Faber.

Lovelock, J. (1995a) *The Ages of Gaia*, Oxford: Oxford University Press.

—— (1995b) *Gaia*, Oxford: Oxford University Press.

McBurnett, M. (1996) 'Probing the underlying structure in dynamical systems: an introduction to spectral analysis' in Kiel, L. D. and Elliott, E. (eds) op. cit., 31–52.

McIntyre, S., MacIver, S. and Sooma, A. (1993) 'Area, class and health' *Journal of Social Policy* 22(2): 213–34.

McIver, R. M. (1942) *Social Causation*, Boston: Ginn.

MacKenzie, D. (1979) 'Eugenics and the rise of mathematical statistics in Britain' in Irvine, J. *et al.* (eds) op. cit., 39–50.

McKeown, T. (1979) *The Role of Medicine: Dream or Nemesis?*, Oxford: Blackwell.

McNeill, W. H. (1979) *Plagues and Peoples*, Harmondsworth: Penguin.

Marcuse, P. (1989) 'Dual city – a muddled metaphor for a quartered city' *International Journal of Urban and Regional Research* 13: 697–708.

Marsh, C. (1982) *The Survey Method*, London: Allen and Unwin.

Massey, D. (1992) 'Politics and space/time' *New Left Review* 92: 65–84.

Massey, D. S. (1996) 'The age of extremes: concentrated affluence and poverty in the twenty-first century' *Demography* 33(4): 395–412.

Massey, D. S. and Denton, N. A. (1993) *American Apartheid*, Cambridge, Mass.: Harvard University Press.

Michaels, M. (1995) 'Seven fundamentals of complexity for social science research' in Albert, A. (ed.) op. cit., 15–34.

Morenoff, J. D. and Tienda, M. (1997) 'Underclass neighbourhoods in temporal and ecological perspective' *Annals of the American Academy of Political and Social Science* 551: 59–72.

Mouzelis, N. (1995) *Sociological Theory: What Went Wrong?*, London: Routledge.

Newman, D. V. (1996) 'Emergence and strange attractors' *Philosophy of Science* 63: 245–61.

Nicolis, G. (1995) *Introduction to Nonlinear Science*, Cambridge: Cambridge University Press.

Nicolis, G. and Prigogine, I. (1989) *Exploring Complexity*, New York: W. H. Freeman and Co.

O'Connor, J. (1982) 'The meaning of crisis' *International Journal of Urban and Regional Research* 5: 301–28.

OECD (1997) *Societal Cohesion and the Globalizing Economy*, Washington, DC: OECD.

Outhwaite, W. (1987) *New Philosophies of Social Science*, London: Macmillan.

Pahl, R. (1985) 'The restructuring of capital, the local political economy, and household work strategies' in Gregory, D. and Urry, J. (eds) *Social Relations and Spatial Structures*, London: Macmillan, 242–63.

Payne, C., Payne, J. and Heath, A. (1994) 'Modelling trends in multi-way tables' in Davies, R. B. and Dale, A. (eds) op. cit., 41–74.

Peach, C. (1996a) 'Does Britain have ghettoes?' *Transactions of the Institute of British Geographers* NS 21: 216–35.

—— (ed.) (1996b) *Ethnicity in the 1991 Census* Vol. 2, London: HMSO.

Peak, D. and Frame, M. (1994) *Chaos Under Control*, New York: W. H. Freeman.

Phillips, D. (1995) 'Correspondence analysis' *Social Research Update* 7 http://www.soc.surrey.ac.uk/stu/SRU7.html.

Plewis, I. (1994) 'Longitudinal multilevel models' in Davies, R. B. and Dale, A. (eds) op. cit., 118–35.

Portugali, J., Benenson, I. and Owen J. J. (1997) 'Spatial cognitive dissonance and sociospatial emergence in a self-organizing city' *Environment and Planning B* 24: 263–85.

Porush, D. (1991) 'Fictions as dissipative structures' in Hayles, N. K. (ed.) op. cit., 54–84.

Price, B. (1997) 'The myth of postmodern science' in Eve, R. A. *et al.* (eds) op. cit., 3–14.

Prigogine, I. and Stengers, I. (1984) *Order out of Chaos*, New York: Bantam.

Ratcliffe, E. (ed.) (1996) *Ethnicity in the 1991 Census* Vol. 3, London: HMSO.

Raudenbush, S. W. and Willms, J. D. (1995) 'The estimation of school effects' *Journal of Educational and Behavioural Statistics.*

Reed, M. and Harvey, D. L. (1992) 'The new science and the old: complexity and realism in the social sciences' *Journal for the Theory of Social Behaviour* 22: 356–79.

Reed, M. and Harvey, D. L. (1996) 'Social science as the study of complex systems' in Kiel, L. D. and Elliott, E. (eds) *Chaos Theory in the Social Sciences*, Ann Arbor: University of Michigan Press, 295–324.

Rivlin, A. (1971) *Systematic Thinking for Social Action*, Washington, DC: The Brookings Institution.

Room, G. (ed.) (1995) *Beyond the Threshold*, Bristol: The Policy Press.

Rose, N. (1996) 'The death of the social? Refiguring the territory of government' *Economy and Society* 25: 327–56.

Ruelle, D. (1991) *Chance and Chaos*, Harmondsworth: Penguin.

Sackett, D. L. (1995) 'On the need for evidence based medicine' *Health Economics* 4(4): 249–54.

Sackett, D. L. and Rosenberg, W. M. C. (1995) 'On the need for evidence based medicine' *Journal of Public Health Medicine* 17(3): 330–4.

Sayer, A. (1992) *Method in Social Science*, London: Routledge.

Séror, A. C. (1994) 'Simulation of complex organizational processes: a review of methods and their epistemological foundations' in Gilbert, N. and Doran, J. (eds) op. cit., 19–40.

Short, J. R. (1993) 'The myth of postmodernism' *Tijdschrift voor Economishce en Sociale Geografie* 3(84): 169–70.

Skinner, C. (1997) 'Complex datasets as departures from ideal data sets' paper given at the ALCD ESRC Conference, Warwick.

Sloggett, A. and Joshi, H. (1994) 'Higher mortality in deprived areas' *British Medical Journal* 309(6967): 1470–4.

Smith, N. (1996) *The New Urban Frontier*, London: Routledge.

Steedman, J. (1980) *Progress in Secondary Schools*, London: National Children's Bureau.

Susser, I. (1973) *Causal Thinking in the Health Sciences*, Oxford: Oxford University Press.

Tarlov, A. R. (1996) 'Social determinants of health: the sociobiological transformation' in Blane, D. *et al.* (eds) op. cit., 71–93.

Therborn, G. (1985) *Why Some Peoples are More Unemployed than Others*, London: Verso.

Thom, R. (1975) *Structural Stability and Morphogenesis*, Reading, MA: W. A. Benjamin.

—— (1983) 'By way of a conclusion' *Substance* 40: 78–83.

Thompson, E. P. (1978) *The Poverty of Theory*, London: Merlin.

Townsend, P., Phillimore, P. and Beattie, A. (1988) *Health and Deprivation*, London: Croom Helm.

Trisoglio, A. (1995) 'Complexity: the challenges' Paper presented at workshop *Risk, Policy and Complexity*, IIASA Laxenburg.

Tukey, J. W. (1977) *Exploratory Data Analysis*, Reading, Mass.: Addison-Wesley.

Turner, F. (1997) 'Foreword: chaos and social science' in Eve, R. A., Horsfall, S. and Lee, M. E. *Chaos, Complexity and Sociology*, London: Sage.

Urry, J. (1988) 'Society, space and locality' *Environment and Planning D: Society and Space* 5: 435–44.

Young, T. R. and Kiel, L. D. (1994) 'Chaos and management science: control, prediction and nonlinear dynamics' by Internet.

Waldrop, M. M. (1992) *Complexity*, London: Viking.

Wallace, D. (1994) 'The resurgence of tuberculosis in New York City – a mixed hierarchically and spatially diffused epidemic' *American Journal of Public Health* 84(6): 1000–2.

Wallace, R., Wallace, D., Andrews, H., Fullilove, R. and Fullilove, M. T. (1995) 'AIDS and TB in New York Metropolitan Region for a sociogeographic perspective' *Environment and Planning A* 7(27): 1085–108.

Warf, B. (1993) 'Postmodernism and the localities debate: ontological questions and epistemological implications' *Tijdschraft voor Economische en Sociale Geografie* 84(3): 162–8.

Westwood, S. and Williams, J. (eds) (1997) *Imagining Cities*, London: Routledge.

Wilkinson, R. (1996) *Unhealthy Societies*, London: Routledge.

Williams, M. and May, T. (1996) *Introduction to the Philosophy of Social Research*, London: UCL Press.

Williams, R. (1979) *Politics and Letters*, London: Verso.

—— (1980) *Problems in Materialism and Culture*, London: Verso.

Wilson, W. J. (1987) *The Truly Disadvantaged*, Chicago: University of Chicago Press.

—— (1992) 'Another look at "The Truly Disadvantaged"' *Political Science Quarterly* 106: 639–56.

Wing, J. K. (1978) *Reasoning about Madness*, Oxford: Oxford University Press.

Wyatt, R. (1996) 'Guest editorial' *Environment and Planning B – Planning and Design* 23: 639–54.

INDEX

Printed in the United Kingdom
by Lightning Source UK Ltd.
113273UKS00001B/59